How

BOEING

Defied the

AIRBUS

Challenge

An Insider's Account

Mohan R. Pandey

Cover: Boeing 777-200LR (Longer Range) Passenger Airplane in Flight [k63081.tif] © The Boeing Company

ISBN: 1450501133
ISBN-13: 9781450501132

Library of Congress Control Number: 2010900168

Printed in the United States of America

To my parents who are in the heavens. I miss them greatly.

CONTENTS

Introduction

Boeing and Airbus are the two global aviation giants and fierce competitors. They make the finest airliners in the world. They have some of the best engineering talent that money can buy. Boeing and Airbus spend billions of dollars to try to outdo each other by introducing newer, advanced models of airplanes that are relatively superior to the competitor's airplane. They are always looking for an edge over the competition. They normally risk tens of billions of dollars on the launch of a new airplane with no guarantee of success in the marketplace. Their new airplanes often push the technological boundaries.

Boeing, founded in 1916, is known around the world as the builder of some of the greatest airplanes in the history of aviation. Airbus, founded in 1970, is a relative newcomer and a glittering symbol of European pride and prestige. Airbus showed great vision by bringing out a big two-engine airplane (twin), the A300, in the early 1970s before any of the established aviation behemoths had the foresight to do it. It popularized the fly-by-wire technology by launching a modern twin, the A320, in the 1980s. Despite all odds, Airbus succeeded in bringing the fractious Europeans with a penchant for internecine battles into one powerful aviation conglomerate ready to mount a formidable challenge to the best of the best in aviation.

In the 1980s, Boeing dominated commercial aviation. For instance, in 1985, McDonnell Douglas with 19% of the market share trailed Boeing, which controlled 58% of the market, and Airbus was a distant third with 11%. With European financial backing, Airbus pursued a strategy to cripple the Americans to such a degree that Europe could permanently wrest from the United States its traditional global dominance of commercial aviation.

Airbus planned to go after McDonnell Douglas first and increase its market share from 11% to 30% by the early 1990s. Boeing would be next.

The first salvo was the launch of the A330 and the A340 in June 1987. The A330 was a twin, and the A340 was a four-engine airplane (quad). The A330 was launched to end the supremacy of the 767—a Boeing twin that had been in operation for nearly a decade and dominated the traffic over the North Atlantic.

The A340 competed directly with the McDonnell Douglas newly launched MD-11. With the inherent pricing advantage, the A340 vanquished the MD-11.

Challenging Boeing would be a bit more difficult. Unlike McDonnell Douglas, Boeing had a family of airplanes and the venerable 747.

The four-engine 747, commonly known around the world as the "jumbo jet," had become the symbol and pride of The Boeing Company and that of the United States. It was a "must-have" airplane for the prestigious airlines of the world. With no real competition for the jumbo jet, Boeing could command top dollar for the airplane. According to reports in the media, the 747 alone contributed to more than 30% of Boeing profits in the 1990s.

Airbus regarded the 747 as the "cash cow" for Boeing. Airbus felt that the 747 allowed Boeing to compete aggressively on pricing on its other airplanes with the competing models from Airbus. For Airbus to overtake Boeing, it had to depose the 747 and thereby weaken Boeing's financial position. Airbus concluded that without the handsome profits from the 747, Boeing would "start to bleed."

In the late 1980s, Airbus was not in a position to challenge the venerable 747 head on. Nevertheless, it had a spirited plan.

The next salvo in the Airbus efforts to overtake the US dominance in commercial aviation was the launch of the "pincer strategy," which was a strategy to squeeze the 747 out of the airline market between the A340 and the yet to be launched super-jumbo, the A3XX. The A3XX was an airplane that would be even bigger than the Boeing jumbo jet, the 747. (The A3XX later became the A380 after the formal launch in December 2000.)

In response to the A330 and the A340, three years later on October 29, 1990, Boeing launched the 777—a twin. Rather than launching a warmed-over 767 as a response to the A330, Boeing showed breathtaking vision and brought out the all-new 777 twinjet.

Since Boeing could not compete with Airbus on pricing, it opted to launch a technologically superior airplane with a nearly double-digit advantage in operating costs over the A340. Only a twin could offer such operating efficiencies over a quad.

The 777 was a large twin for medium-range to long-range operations. It was more fuel efficient and had a lower operating cost than the A340. Airlines felt they could make money operating these large twins over the North Atlantic and other international routes from day one.

The launch of the large twin was a bold and risky move for Boeing. It faced many challenges.

The 777s would require engines capable of generating very high thrust levels—50% more than the engines on the 747s. Such engines were not readily available at the time.

Being a twin, the 777 also had to comply with the regulatory requirement called "extended-range operation with two-engine airplanes (ETOPS)." Under the existing ETOPS rules, Boeing could not certify a twin for direct North Atlantic–type operations from day one nor could the airlines optimally conduct such operations with a twin from the first day of revenue operations. If Boeing were not able to change the ETOPS rules, the demand for the 777 would evaporate overnight.

To Airbus, the "upstart" 777 was in direct competition not only with the A330 but also with the A340. If the "pincer movement" were to succeed, Airbus had to ensure that the A340 prevailed over the 777 on long-range routes.

Airbus saw ETOPS as the 777's Achilles heel. If Airbus could convince the regulators to maintain the status quo—stop Boeing from changing the ETOPS rules—the 777 would flounder. With a tottering 777, the 767 trounced by the A330, and the 747 suffocated by the A340-A380 pincer, Boeing would falter and Airbus would rule.

Airbus upped the ante by launching a highly charged media campaign questioning the safety of the twins—especially the 777—on long-range operations.

Airbus waged the battle for aviation industry dominance in the arcane battlefield of ETOPS. The unprecedented strategic challenge involved tens of billions of dollars in potential airplane orders.

Airbus was a formidable competitor. For the first time since WWII, a European airplane manufacturer, Airbus, not only succeeded in challenging Boeing, the storied American aviation titan, but also nearly crippled the giant—a fate fully realized by McDonnell Douglas, a previous American icon.

By early 2000, nearly 20 years after the inception of the pincer strategy, Boeing had turned the tables. ETOPS never became the 777's Achilles heel. The A340, far from being Europe's flagship and half of Airbus' strategic pincer, lost out to the 777. With the A340 program in tatters and a collapsed pincer, Airbus emulated its archrival Boeing by launching its own long-range twin—the A350XWB (Extra Wide Body).

Boeing, by launching the 777, a highly capable, fuel-efficient, long-range ETOPS twin, turned out to be smarter, more agile, and more visionary than Airbus (and perhaps Boeing itself) expected. The astounding success of ETOPS made literally billions of dollars of difference to Boeing and the world's airlines.

This book chronicles an insider's account of more than two decades of how Boeing fought back in the extremely fierce, high-stakes, and highly political quest for global aviation supremacy, and in the process helped change the direction of aviation forever.

1

THE HISTORY

Boeing and Airbus
A history of big money, risks, and national pride

Even though the Europeans were the early pioneers of flight, Americans began to dominate aviation in the twentieth century. The British Royal Aeronautical Society credits Emanuel Swedenborg of Sweden for his 1717 design as the earliest "rational design" of a flying machine.[1] That was before America, as a nation, even existed; it was actually 15 years before the birth of America's first president, George Washington.

However, it took more than 130 years to build a machine that flew. In 1848, John Stringfellow, an Englishman, made a short flight inside an unused factory, which is regarded by some as the first flight of a heavier-than-air–powered machine. In 1849, an English baronet, George Cayley, who had been working on many principles of aircraft design, built the first full-sized glider that carried a 10-year-old boy and flew several feet (meters) when towed by a rope, confirming the theory of lift. In 1890, Clement Ader, a Frenchman, achieved short hops with his airplane *Eole*.

Orville Wright's 12-second flight at 12 feet (3.7 meters) above the ground for about 120 feet (37 meters) on December 17, 1903, at Kitty Hawk, North Carolina, USA, is universally accepted as the first controlled, sustained heavier-than-air–powered airplane flight. The Wright brothers flew three more flights on the same day, and covered as much as 852 feet (260 meters).

Wilbur and Orville Wright, both school dropouts, had honed their mechanical skills from repairing and manufacturing bicycles of their own design. Their analytical ability, understanding of aeronautical forces, and their fascination with flying contributed to building their airplane, the *Flyer*, with a 12-hp engine. The two American brothers (who remained bachelors because, as Orville said jokingly, they did not have the means to "support a wife as well as an airplane") dominated aviation until 1908.

It did not take long for the founders of Boeing, Douglas, McDonnell, and Lockheed to catch the aviation bug.

In 1915, Bill Boeing, a wealthy 34-year-old Seattle lumberman, enrolled in Martin's flying school, run by one of the founders of Lockheed Martin. The Seattle lumberman felt he could build a better airplane—obviously from his lumber. On July 15, 1916, he formed a company, Pacific Aero Products, which later became the Boeing Airplane Company.

America is all about competition, with a "can-do" entrepreneurial culture and a relentless drive to design a proverbial "better mousetrap." These intrinsic qualities made it possible, on July 20, 1969, for man to walk on the moon—a mere 66 years after the Wright brothers' flight.

Competition creates constant pressure to innovate. It is the survival of the fittest. Shortly after WWI, in 1919, Boeing nearly went under but managed to survive. America's commercial aviation got a big boost when in 1927 the US Congress passed a bill requiring the Post Office to pay private companies to fly mail between distant cities. Boeing won the contract to carry mail between Chicago and San Francisco. Boeing Airplane Company created an airline—Boeing Air Transport (BAT). Having the airline carry a few paying passengers in addition to the mail would be pure profit. BAT purchased Boeing's Model 40A, which carried four passengers in addition to 500 pounds of mail.

Passengers sat inside a dry enclosed cabin while the pilot, like the images made famous by Hollywood, sat in an open cockpit with his leather cap, silk scarf, and aviator goggles. In 1928, BAT introduced Boeing's latest Model 80. At that time, it was considered a luxurious airplane. It had leather seats, hot and cold running water, reading lamps, and a female flight attendant to provide the utmost care and comfort during the 23-hour flight between San Francisco and Chicago.

Boeing merged with Pratt & Whitney. Besides manufacturing airframes, it also started to build engines. BAT merged its air services with other carriers to form United Air Lines, a forerunner of the current United Airlines, offering coast-to-coast passenger and mail service.

In 1933, Boeing's Model 247—a two-engine 10-passenger airplane with all-metal wings—was the fastest airplane of the time. It flew 70 miles per hour (113 km/hr) faster than its competitor, which allowed

United Air Lines to offer 10 daily round trips between New York and Chicago. United was out to corner the US domestic market with a radically new aircraft. As one of the subsidiaries, United was obligated to buy the airplane from Boeing, and the airline would get first priority in delivery positions.

The Model 247 was in big demand from the airlines, but Boeing refrained from selling the airplane to other carriers until United had the 60 airplanes it had ordered. That would take a year. One of the airlines that wanted the airplane was Transcontinental & Western Air, commonly known as TWA. After being rebuffed by Boeing, TWA decided to issue a specification for a new three-engine airliner and invited five companies to submit designs. Douglas submitted instead a design for a two-engine airplane, which it claimed would be more advanced than Boeing's 247.

The Douglas DC-1 was born. TWA liked the airplane. It was a prototype of the production model, the DC-2, which carried four more passengers than the Model 247. Douglas trumped Boeing. It followed the DC-2 with the most famous DC-3, which had its first flight on December 17, 1935—the 32nd anniversary of the Wright brothers' first flight on the windy shores of Kitty Hawk.

By not selling the Model 247 to TWA in an effort to protect the sole-source arrangement with its subsidiary United, Boeing, in effect, forfeited its leadership on the commercial airplane side to Douglas for the next quarter of a century. Boeing's fortunes changed quickly.

Even the Boeing merger of 1929 was short lived. In 1934, the US Government broke off the conglomerate. Pratt and United became two separate companies. Boeing was back to building airplanes.

Boeing had a business downturn in 1934. Payroll dropped from nearly 1,700 to under 700.

The ubiquitous DC-3 made Douglas the commercial airplane manufacturer of choice. By 1939, the DC-3 carried more than 90% of the world traffic. With a total production in its lifetime of 10,300 airplanes, the DC-3 is undoubtedly the world's most popular commercial airplane ever built.

Boeing built only 75 Model 247s. After the breakup, even United bought the DC-3s.

The DC-3 generated enough cash flow for Douglas to update the model frequently. It was offering the DC-7 by the 1950s.

WWII changed American aviation forever. The American manufacturers could not build airplanes fast enough to support the war efforts. However, the end of WWII was a surprise for Boeing. Its employment decreased from nearly 45,000 to around 15,000. The unpredictable nature of military contracts was a wakeup call for Boeing. It no longer wanted to rely purely on the Pentagon for its survival. In early 1952, Boeing gambled the net worth of the company to enter the commercial airplane business by developing the Dash 80, a prototype of the 707 with jet engines.

* * *

The British and the Germans pioneered the jet engines. The Germans were the first to fly a turbojet-powered airplane, which occurred a week before the start of WWII.

The concept of the jet engine is simple—a compressor in the front of the engine compresses the air and pushes it aft. The compressed air is mixed with fuel and ignited in the combustion chamber. The expanding gases exit the engine with high velocity. Just like a balloon that goes flying when its neck is untied and the air inside is released, the airplane moves forward in equal and opposite reaction to the high-speed exhaust. Before exiting, the high-speed exhausts pass at an angle over a set of turbine blades, making the turbine spin fast, similar to a waterwheel. A shaft connects the turbine with the compressor in the front, which compresses the air. The cycle repeats itself. These engines are called turbojets because they are jet engines with turbines.

Turbojets proved to be more reliable than their predecessors, the piston engines, which had too many moving parts and were prone to overheating and failure. In addition, to generate the same level of power, the turbojets were much lighter than the piston engines.

Because the hot air exited the engines at a very high speed, it created a lot of noise. The turbojets were slow to accelerate at takeoff. The turbo fanjet solved the problem.

The turbo fanjets include a big fan in the front of the turbojet. The fan directs air through the compressor just as in the turbojet to the core of the engine, but sends a big volume of air outside the core of the engine. The cooler air creates a shroud around the hot speeding exhaust, thus lowering the noise. The big mass of air pushed back by the fan helps the airplane accelerate quicker at takeoff.

Since the 1960s, most of the engines used are some version of the turbo fanjet or are simply called turbofans.

* * *

Being one of the pioneers of the jet engine technology, the British were eager to exploit its advantages over piston engines of the time. With financial assistance from the British Government, de Havilland—the forerunner of the current British Aerospace (BAE)—came out with the Comet 1. It was an airplane with a pressurized cabin that could be operated above the altitudes where most of the turbulent weather was encountered, allowing a smooth flight for the passengers.

Metal fatigue that led to structural failures doomed the Comet 1. By the time the British solved the problem and introduced the Comet 4 in 1957, Boeing had far exceeded the Comet's capabilities. The Americans exploited the jet engine technology and took the lead. British airplanes such as the Vickers Viscount, Hawker Siddeley Trident, and French Caravelle fared well but the Europeans in general were left far behind. By 1970, the Americans had captured nearly 90% of the "free world's" commercial aircraft market. The free world excluded the Soviet Union and the Eastern European countries behind the so-called "Iron Curtain."

The 707 spurred the American domination.

The prototype of the Boeing 367-80, commonly referred to as the Dash 80, was designed with a dual purpose—as a jet tanker for the Air Force and as a civilian airplane. In 1955, Pan Am became the first airline to order the civilian version, the 707 passenger jet.

Long-range flight at the time meant multi-stop service from Europe to Africa and Asia, and one- or two-stop service between London or Paris and New York.

Douglas was resting on its laurels. It had just introduced the four-engine, piston-powered, propeller- driven DC-7 in the market and did not fully appreciate the potential threat from the Boeing 707 with jet engines.

After all, Boeing did not have much of a reputation on the commercial side of the airplane business. Reportedly, Douglas was told by airlines such as United and American Airlines that the market was not ready for the jet engines. In addition, they did not believe anyone who was important enough would buy a commercial airplane from Boeing.

From 1933 to 1955, Boeing had sold only 147 commercial airplanes in four models. It was a dismal record by any standard.

The Air Force got its first Dash 80 in 1954. It liked the airplane so much that by 1965, it had bought 761 of them.

Pan Am took delivery of the first 707 on August 15, 1958, and inaugurated the daily New York–Paris transatlantic jet service on October 26, 1958. Even though British Overseas Airways Corporation, a predecessor to the current British Airways, had started the weekly transatlantic service on October 4, 1958, with the new Comet 4, it did not get the same media attention as Pan Am's 707—aptly called *Clipper America*.

Boeing had helped create the 707 publicity with a joint advertising campaign with Pan Am. The newspapers were flooded with the advertisements, which said, "Only seven hours to brush up on your French," and highlighted the comfort, speed, and safety of jet flight. The flights with the piston-engine airplanes took nearly 12 hours and had a higher level of cabin noise.

Pan Am competitors who were operating piston-engine–powered propeller airplanes expected to hold on to their operations as they anticipated Pan Am would raise fares for the jet operations. Pan Am disappointed its competitors by keeping the 707 fares at the same level as the piston-engine airplanes, $505 for first class and $272 for economy class.

The Pan Am fare policy hastened the introduction of the jet age. With the 707s, Pan Am dominated the transatlantic market and for a period enjoyed unrivaled success in international operations.

Although the 707 cost twice as much as the piston-engine airplanes it replaced, it earned three times the revenue. Pan Am enjoyed a load factor of nearly 91%. Passengers scrambled to get a seat on the 707.

The 707 changed the way people travelled. People preferred jet-engine airplanes to the piston-powered ones. On January 25, 1959, American Airlines became the first airline to fly the first US transcontinental commercial jet flight (Los Angeles–New York), also a 707. Other airlines desperately wanted to get their hands on jet-engine airplanes. Not having a jet-engine airplane in the fleet, United even canceled its nonstop, transcontinental, piston-powered DC-7 scheduled operations until it received its first jet-engine DC-8.

Jet-engine airplanes revolutionized air travel. In 1960, for the first time in the history of transatlantic travel, more passengers crossed the North Atlantic by airplanes than by ocean liners. Even the US President's airplane, *Air Force One*, was a 707. Ever since the 707, all *Air Force One* airplanes have been Boeing airplanes.

* * *

With cash flow ensured by military contracts, Boeing modified its early 707 design to improve its passenger comfort and its economics when Douglas challenged the 707 with a DC-8. Boeing's upgrade to the 707 allowed it to fly with more passengers nonstop across the Atlantic. Boeing went on to develop a family of airplanes, starting with the very successful three-engine 727. It had a unique wing flap design, which allowed the airplane to take off with maximum payload even from shorter airfields. The sturdy 727 became a workhorse around the world and one of Boeing's best sellers.

The 727 was followed by the 737, which was a smaller twin designed for the short-range domestic market.

Boeing took the leadership in commercial airplanes and never looked back. Douglas lost its dominance forever. By January 1967, Douglas was on the verge of bankruptcy and merged with McDonnell Corporation, which was a military aircraft manufacturer. In the high-stakes game of airplane manufacturing, the competition is cutthroat. Fortunes can change quickly.

The double-decker jumbo jet, the 747, followed the 737. The 747 became the symbol of American aviation prowess around the world and was used in many Hollywood movies. But the timing of the 747 project was not particularly good.

The recession of 1969 led to the cancellation of orders and options, and future orders dried up quickly. Yet again, just like in 1919, 1934, and 1945, The Boeing Company began to question its prospects for survival. It was in the middle of one of the biggest projects in aviation. It had too many unfinished 747s and too much inventory. Employment dwindled from nearly 101,000 in 1968 to around 37,000 three years later, which led to the famous billboard that a Seattle real estate man erected near the heavily traveled Interstate 5. The billboard included a picture of a single light bulb and the caption, "Will the last person leaving Seattle please put out the lights."

Thanks to the immensely popular 727, the Minuteman Missile program on the military side, and its own draconian cost reductions, Boeing survived to become an even stronger player.

The 747 went on to become the "must-have" airplane for airlines around the world. It became a symbol of prestige for the airlines. The airplane dramatically reduced the cost of flying per passenger. For example, over the Atlantic the cost went down by around 30%.

In an industry in which single-digit numbers are often considered big breakthroughs, 30% is enormous. Until the advent of the 747, air travel was for the rich who wore suits and furs, and carried matching luggage. The 747 dramatically changed the economics of flying. Even the so-called hippies—"the flower children"—with long hair and psychedelic T-shirts with luggage matching the T-shirt could be in the same airplane with the caviar and the champagne crowd.

"Since 1969, Boeing has had the market for large aircraft to itself. Airlines wanting a plane capable of carrying more than 350 passengers have had only one choice, the Seattle-made 747, nicknamed the jumbo jet. It became the ubiquitous symbol of mass international travel, and a big earner for its manufacturer. Executives at Airbus reckoned that in some periods Boeing made $40m [million] (£20m) on every 747 sold, a margin that was used to prop up the sales of its other aircraft. Tackling the 747's dominance has been a strategic priority for the European plane maker almost since it was set up in the early 1970s. Its leaders believed that Airbus could not compete on an equal footing unless it had a complete family of products, from small short-haul planes right up to jumbos."[2]

Airbus dreamed of its own jumbo jet. It is difficult to blame Airbus for coveting the 747. In the 1980s and the 1990s, while flying into Tokyo, one could not miss the 747s parked at almost every departure gate at the Tokyo Narita airport, a sight that must have given severe indigestion to the Airbus executives!

The McDonnell Douglas DC10-30, which entered service in December 1972, and the Lockheed L1011-500, introduced in May 1974, were nowhere close to challenging the supremacy of the 747.

Europe showed its technical brilliance with the Concorde—a supersonic airplane capable of cruising at twice the speed of sound—a marvel for aviation enthusiasts. Its first flight was in 1969. As a student studying Aeronautical Engineering in England at the time, I felt very fortunate to witness the Concorde fly over the 1972 Farnborough Airshow. Unfortunately, a technical marvel became a commercial disaster.

"In March 2006, the Concorde was announced the winner of the Great British Design Quest, organized by the British Broadcasting Corporation (BBC) and the Design Museum."[3] An airplane that had the potential to be declared a winner by commercial airlines around the world went on to be declared a winner by a museum!

The 747 also became the first airplane to offer a choice of engines to power the jumbo. The 747 became a big moneymaker for Boeing and helped fund the 757/767 programs and later the entire 777 family.

At the Paris Air Show in June 1991, Airbus announced that it would study the development of its own jumbo jet—the A3XX. In January 1993, Airbus and Boeing agreed to jointly explore the feasibility. In April 1995, Boeing pulled out after concluding that the airplane would have a limited market and the undertaking would be expensive and risky.

Airbus did not agree with the Boeing conclusions. Airbus thought it would be risky not to proceed with the project. Louis Gallois, chief executive of European Aeronautic Defence and Space Company (EADS), the parent of Airbus, who at the time was the chairman of Aerospatiale, commented that Boeing had a monopoly on the market with the 747, which was a fantastic advantage for Boeing. His words were, "They have a product; we have none." After blaming Boeing for delaying the project by a couple of years, Airbus continued with the project.

* * *

By the 1990s, Airbus had become a formidable competitor in the commercial airplane market. It marginalized McDonnell Douglas. Lockheed had neared bankruptcy and had already exited the commercial airplane business for good.

East-West military tensions eased after the end of the Cold War in 1991. Defense budgets were slashed. The "peace dividend" prompted so-called "rationalization" of the defense industry, which led to mergers and acquisitions.

Boeing saw this as an opportunity to stabilize its fortunes from the cyclical commercial airplane business; it wanted a bigger share of the defense industry. At its 80th anniversary in 1996, Boeing launched its new 20-year vision to be a fully integrated aerospace company.

In 1996, Boeing purchased Rockwell International's military and space divisions for approximately $3.1 billion. A year later, McDonnell Douglas merged with Boeing in a $13 billion stock swap.

However, at the 1997 Paris Air Show, Managing Director and Chief Executive Officer of the Airbus Industrie Jean Pierson accused McDonnell Douglas of deliberately losing a US defense contract to facilitate its takeover by Boeing.

Even though the merger took place between two US companies, supposedly at the behest of Airbus, Europeans denounced the deal. They argued that the merger had to pass European muster because their jurisdiction extended to all companies conducting business in Europe. Otherwise, Europe would impose a sanction on Boeing and threaten a trade war with the United States. This was an excellent opportunity for Airbus to get the European Commission to extract the proverbial "pounds of flesh" from Boeing. The media characterized Airbus as a well-oiled political and industrial machine.

On July 23, 1997, the Europeans approved the Boeing-McDonnell Douglas merger. They forced Boeing to cancel its exclusive sales agreements with American Airlines, Delta, and Continental, even though most experts believed this issue had nothing to do with the merger. According to the keen aviation watchers, it looked like the European Commission forced Boeing to accept virtually everything that Airbus wanted.

Boeing continued its buying spree; in October 2000, Boeing acquired the satellite manufacturing operations of Hughes Space and Communications, a subsidiary of General Motors Corporation, for $3.75 billion. Besides these major multi-billion-dollar acquisitions, Boeing purchased several other complementary aviation-related businesses.

Phil Condit, Boeing president and chief executive officer, said, "The assets and capabilities we are acquiring are an extremely good strategic fit with our long-term objective of creating shareholder value. This merger accelerates us on our way to achieving our 20-year vision, which calls for Boeing to be a fully integrated aerospace company designing, producing and supporting commercial airplanes, defense systems, and defense and civil space systems."

However, industry observers felt that such eagerness led to Boeing paying premiums for most of these acquisitions and mergers. Many Boeing long-timers felt that McDonnell Douglas got a better deal from the merger; the common saying around Seattle, Boeing's hometown, was "McDonnell Douglas bought Boeing with Boeing's money."

* * *

In the mid-1990s, Boeing tried to emulate Airbus by aggressively pursuing the market share. In response to higher sales, Boeing decided to increase the airplane production rate on some models. At the same time, to extract efficiencies Boeing had embarked on streamlining design and production by introducing a new system called Define and Control Airplane Configuration/Manufacturing Resource Management. Some described this initiative as trying to change the tires while driving down the road at highway speed.

The attempt to increase the production rate in the midst of switching to a new system failed. In September 1997, Boeing halted the 747 production lines for 20 days and suspended the 737 production lines. This had never happened in Boeing's history. It was a shocker.

The president of Commercial Airplanes and a few senior leaders lost their jobs. Boeing went through another round of layoffs. Boeing ended 1997 by posting its first operating loss in a half-century.

September 11, 2001, commonly known as 9/11, had a great impact on Boeing. The employment at Commercial Airplanes was cut in half. More than 9/11, what really hurt Boeing were the events that led to the firing of the chief financial officer, who was being groomed to be the chairman and chief executive officer of Boeing. In November 2003, Mike Sears was fired for ethics violations in connection with the Air Force's order for 100 refueling tankers. The US Government charged him with a crime. Fifteen months later, the Court convicted Sears of recruiting the procurement official in the Air Force while she was handling military contracts that Boeing was bidding on. Sears received four months of jail time and a $250,000 fine.

The US Justice Department also launched a criminal probe and civil claims against Boeing.

Boeing instituted a code of conduct to combat the fallout from Sears' ethical lapse. Phil Condit, chairman of Boeing—an aviation enthusiast who had joined the company in 1965 and risen through the Boeing engineering ranks, a down-to-earth, friendly person with rugged features—resigned. Harry Stonecipher, the gruff-looking head of McDonnell Douglas at the time of the merger with Boeing, assumed leadership in the interim until a new leader could be selected.

On March 2005, Stonecipher also left Boeing for failing to uphold the intent of the Boeing Code of Conduct that he instituted. Stonecipher had an inappropriate relationship with a lower level female executive.

In 2006, Boeing reached an agreement with the US Justice Department on the criminal probe and civil claims related to the Air Force procurement of refueling tankers. Having accepted responsibility for the actions of its employees, Boeing agreed to pay $615 million in fines, but avoided any criminal charges.

Boeing lost credibility on Capitol Hill, the US legislative body. A reputation built over decades was ruined overnight. These were possibly Boeing's darkest days.

It took the collective Boeing psyche some time to get over the so-called "Sears fiasco" and "Harry's affair." Even though it was purely coincidental that Boeing inherited these executives from the McDonnell Douglas merger, some Boeing old-timers blamed McDonnell Douglas for desecrating Boeing's cherished reputation built over decades by legendary leaders such as Bill Allen and "T" Wilson, and besmirching the standard of integrity that William E. Boeing had imposed on the company bearing his name.

Although the moral lapses of some of these senior leaders sullied the Boeing image, they did not adversely affect Boeing's introduction of the 777 family's newer members in the marketplace. Boeing Commercial Airplanes products have gone on to capture the lion's share of the long-range market. With the passage of time, "I work for Boeing" again became a declaration of pride.[4]

In 2009, besides commercial airliners, Boeing made and/or supported military airplanes, fighters, helicopters, rockets, satellites, the International Space Station, and the space shuttle, among others. Boeing's yearly sales were on the order of $60 billion, nearly evenly split between the commercial airplanes business and defense systems.

After a failed attempt with the Sonic Cruiser, a twin that would fly close to the speed of sound, in April 2004, Boeing launched its newest airplane, the 787. Fuel costs defeated the Sonic Cruiser, but its technology lived on in the 787. After several false starts related to how it would update the venerable 747, Boeing also launched the latest member of the 747 family, the 747-8, in November 2005. With orders of 910—later reduced to 876 as of February 2010—the 787 had become the most successful launch of a new airplane in the history of commercial aviation.

* * *

Airbus came into existence nearly half a century after Boeing.

"French President Charles de Gaulle once raised doubts about the French being able to work together. A nation that made 265 kinds of cheese could not be united without a threat of danger, he said. But officials at Airbus have done even better, uniting a consortium of French, German, Spanish and British manufacturers. The result is an effective and growing challenge to The Boeing Co."[5]

The British were the world leaders in the aircraft industry before WWII but were unable to re-establish their preeminent position after the war. Despite being bankrolled by the government, the Comet and the Concorde were commercial disasters. The government's financial support reduced the overall cost and helped the pricing situation, but it could not turn them into commercial successes.

The name "Airbus" started in 1965 when the Germans formed a group called Studiengruppe Airbus. The group's first task was to find a product niche in the US market to compete with the American behemoths—Boeing, McDonnell Douglas, and Lockheed.

In the 1960s, the Civil Aeronautics Board (CAB) tightly controlled aviation in the United States. The CAB set the fares and dictated where the airlines could fly. But the airlines could decide on the number of flights in a sector, which led to a very high frequency of flights between popular city pairs.

Frank Kolk, senior vice president of engineering at American Airlines, was mesmerized by the cross section of the 747 cabin. He believed the airlines could benefit if they could operate a widebody, twin-aisle airplane like the 747 but with only two engines in these high-frequency domestic sectors.

However, "Kolk's vision died finally at the hands of his boss, C.R. Smith, who had done so much to bring the DC-3 into being. Smith said that it was too soon in the development of the big fans (turbofans) to

risk the safety of a large airplane on only two engines—a strangely irra-
tional and untypically reactionary view for Smith to take, since the twin-
engine DC-3 had rendered the old trimotors into dodos."[6] Besides, the
American manufacturers were not in a hurry to jump at Kolk's idea right
away.

Airbus liked Frank Kolk's idea, and concluded that if such an airplane were built with about a 300-passenger capacity it had the potential
to offer seat-mile costs as much as 30% lower than the most popular
airplane of the time—the 100- to 150-seater Boeing 727.

Airbus found the product niche it was looking for in the US
market.

After several meetings, on September 25, 1967, Britain, France, and
West Germany signed the Lancaster House agreement, setting the Airbus
project in motion. France's Sud-Aviation would take the lead role on the
airframe side while Britain's Rolls-Royce would supply the engines. The
governments fully bankrolled the projects. It was the first time since
WWII that the Germans were included in a European aviation project.
The Concorde was confined to the French and the British.

The group's focus was on filling the perceived product niche and
capturing the American market. The French preferred a US-built
engine, which they hoped would help them get their proverbial "nose"
inside the "American tent." General Electric (GE), because of its willingness to give Snecma—a French engine manufacturer—a big piece of
the work, was the final choice for the engine. The news was a shocker
to Rolls-Royce. On March 17, 1969, the British withdrew from the
project.

The British pullout created another challenge. Germany, with a
small aerospace industry after WWII, risked being overwhelmed by
the French. The Germans preferred the wings built by the British firm
Hawker Siddeley rather than those built by the French. Without the
government funds, Hawker Siddeley was in no position to take such a
risk and, with the British pullout from the project, any hope of British
money evaporated. The upshot was that the Germans found it in their
best interest to finance Hawker Siddeley's continuing participation in
the wing production.

Airbus launched its first aircraft, the A300, at the 1969 Paris Air
Show. On December 18, 1970, Airbus Industrie came into existence. Air
France was the first customer. The saying at the time was that the only

way the government-owned Air France could have avoided buying the A300 with 250 seats would be if the airplane flew backward. Sections and subsections were built at different locations and flown to Toulouse for final assembly in the Super Guppy, a modified Boeing Model 377. Airbus initially started its life in the belly of a Boeing airplane!

Air France started service on May 23, 1974. Sales of the airplane were alarmingly low. Unlike in the United States, French employment policy strongly discouraged laying off workers. Airbus had to produce airplanes even when it had no customers. At one point Airbus had 16 A300s lined up on the tarmac in Toulouse. Similar to the 1971 billboard caption in Seattle "Will the last person leaving Seattle please put out the lights," in 1977 Airbus employees were saying "Don't miss the last train out of Toulouse."

Notwithstanding the dire situation with the A300, in 1978 Airbus had no choice but to launch a $1 billion development program for a derivative of the A300—the A310. If Airbus wanted to stay in the aviation business, it needed an airplane to compete with the recently launched Boeing 767. It was a blessing that the European governments were financing the programs.

Britain announced that it would rejoin the Airbus family on January 1, 1979. Eventually the Airbus Industrie consortium included France's Aerospatiale and Germany's Daimler-Benz Aerospace, each with a 37.9% share while BAE had 20% and Spain's Construcciones Aeronauticas had 4.2%.

The 767 was an entirely new aircraft that closed the gap between the 727 and the A300 and incorporated a widebody, twin-aisle fuselage, a new wing, a new tail plane, and the use of high bypass engines. The Boeing 767 entered service in 1982, one year ahead of the Airbus A310. The next airplane Airbus launched was the A320, a smaller airplane for the short-range domestic market. It was designed to compete against the Boeing 737 family.

Airbus launched the A320 in 1984 for entry into service in 1988. It promoted the A320 as a new- technology airplane with "fly by wire" rather than one with mechanical cables and pulleys to move the control surfaces, and a highly computerized airplane that was immune to "pilot error." But after an A320 crashed on June 26, 1988, at an air show in Habsheim, near Mulhouse in eastern France, Airbus management had to backtrack and blame the accident on "pilot error."

By installing small television screens that opened and closed over the passenger seats rather than one big screen mounted above the aisle, Airbus created an aura of modernity in the A320. Many reputable airlines added the A320 to their fleet, which forced Boeing to revamp its 737 family. The A320 went on to become a best seller for Airbus.

* * *

The American manufacturers, who had previously ignored the scrappy European conglomerate with a couple of airplane models, the A300 and A310 that did not sell well, finally woke up to the challenges lurking across the ocean.

Boeing could no longer afford to ignore Airbus. The A320 proved that Airbus was capable of building airplanes that could challenge the best in the business. After all, it used the same suppliers as Boeing and McDonnell Douglas. The financial backing from the European governments gave Airbus a great cost advantage.

Had it not been for the subsidy, Airbus could have never gotten established in the highly capital-intensive cutthroat business of airplane manufacturing dominated by the Americans. Industry observers considered it only fair that Airbus was heavily subsidized in its early years.

Americans were no longer happy with the continuation of the subsidies beyond the early years. They feared the subsidy allowed Airbus to launch new airplanes just to snatch the market from the Americans, with no regard for profit or loss. Americans believed that Airbus did not need to make a profit because it already had its hands deep inside the European taxpayers' pockets.

Americans charged that, in 1987, at the time of the A330/340 launch, Airbus came to search the taxpayers' pockets for obviously a "loan" that may or may not be paid, and they pulled over $3.5 billion. Some industry experts contend that the "European governments loaned $5.7 billion to Airbus to develop the A330."[7] While the Europeans euphemistically called it a "loan," the Americans preferred to call it a "subsidy."

"The European consortium, meanwhile, strongly denies ever receiving subsidies. There are no subsidies, there never were, an Airbus spokesman said. There were loans, and they are repaid."[8] Invariably, the European Union (EU) also chimed in with a similar message: "the launch aid only amounts to government loans for helping develop new planes. ... the money is legal because it is repaid as Airbus sells aircraft."[9]

According to Airbus' Jean Pierson, "Airbus owners receive loans, not grants, from their respective governments for financing research and development work only of aircraft programs. These loans are repayable and are being paid. Let me inform you that last year (1991) we repaid some $600 million. The figure will be $700 million this year (1992). $1 billion will be repaid each year from 1993 through '96 and $600 million each year thereafter through 2006. More than that, after full repayment of the total initial launch aid a royalty fee per aircraft will continue to be paid by Airbus Industrie until the end of each aircraft program."[10]

Airbus paid the loan as it sold aircraft; the loan would be fully paid off if the sales reached a pre-agreed "set point." Airbus would pay a royalty or success payments if the sales exceeded the set point. So far, it appears that the A320 family of airplanes, having exceeded the set point, is the only airplane that is paying royalty to the European governments.

However, if the sales never reach the set point, there would be no need to pay off the remaining loan. Airbus could consider it a Christmas present! Hence, it would be in best interest of Airbus to have the set point as high as possible.

Airbus and the governments do not publicly disclose the set point used for the loan. It was supposedly set at 1,500 for the A380. Counting all the versions of the 747, including the recently launched 747-8, it took Boeing more than 37 years to sell 1,500 airplanes. McDonnell Douglas sold only 646 DC-10s and MD-11s combined, and Lockheed folded its commercial airplane business after selling 250 L1011s.

According to Airbus, as of February 2010, the total orders for the entire Airbus 340 family were only 378, and 202 for the A380 family.[11] If the number for the A340 or the A380 was also set at 1,500 airplanes, it might be a long time before the European taxpayers see the A340 and the A380 "loans" paid off.

Whether it was called a subsidy or a loan, industry watchers believed the government money allowed Airbus to introduce a new family of airplanes regardless of its cash flow situation. Many analysts believed the "subsidy" or the "loan" helped Airbus become a formidable competitor against the American manufacturers.

* * *

The government support became an issue of great contention on both sides of the Atlantic. In 1990, the US Commerce Department released a study that said, "Airbus programs are 'likely' to accumulate more than $30 billion in government aid by the year 2008 on aircraft programs that are 'not commercially viable.'"[12]

As anticipated, Pierson blasted the United States for a "formidably organized campaign of aggression" and launching a "campaign of denigration" against Airbus and the European aircraft industry. Not to be outdone, he accused Boeing of getting close to $23 billion in indirect subsidy.

Since Airbus could not point to any direct subsidy, it accused Boeing of getting indirect subsidy from the US Government. Because it is difficult to prove or disprove indirect subsidies, some considered it a brilliant stroke from Airbus to thwart the American charge.

Airbus alleged that Boeing indirectly benefited from the research and development (R&D) spending by the defense establishments and National Aeronautics and Space Administration (NASA) research contracts.

Airbus declared, "We will not turn off the tap of government funding while the US faucet is still running."[13]

"Brussels [European Union] accuses Washington of providing vast amounts of hidden support to Boeing through military contracts."[14] The EU and Airbus recognized that EADS also had European military contracts that were comparable to the Pentagon's military contracts with Boeing. But Airbus saw a difference between the two military contracts. "EADS has large military contracts in Europe, but Mr. Bischoff [EADS chairman] says the rate of return is lower than in the United States."[15]

Besides the rate of return, Airbus questioned the quality of the military contracts. Some well-known American aviation writers also shared the Airbus sentiments: "Over the past twenty years, Airbus invested far more heavily in research and development than Boeing. Taking some recent years, 2000 through 2004, Airbus spent more than $8 billion on R&D. Boeing spent less than half that. Yet Boeing is marketing the most technologically advanced of airliners, thanks in part to the smart defense programs it worked on."[16]

Obviously, the aviation writer assumed that the intellectual return was directly proportional to the R&D investment.

According to reports in the media, some European governments were also providing additional subsidies to protect their manufacturers from foreign exchange fluctuations.

In the subsidy saga, the parties were engaged in a one-upmanship game and media spin.

Regardless of the public announcements for preference for negotiated settlement from both sides, the conflict reached the World Trade Organization (WTO). Americans feared the Europeans were trying to stall the process in order to subsidize the A350.

On March 23, 2010, the WTO rendered its final decision on the charges brought about by the United States against the EU. The WTO ruled in favor of the United States and has ruled that subsidies given to Airbus, by European governments, were illegal.[17] The ruling on the case brought about by the EU against the United States is expected in mid-2010.

Boeing had hoped the US actions in the WTO would stop the A350 subsidy. Any subsidy to Airbus' newly launched A350 could adversely affect the market potential of the Boeing 787.

However, regardless of the proceedings at the WTO, it appears the European governments have decided to give Airbus nearly $5 billion in launch subsidy. France is offering €1.4 billion, Germany, €1.1 billion, the United Kingdom €396 million (£340 million), and Spain is expected to loan around €400 million. The UK government even characterized it as an "investment" on the A350 rather than a loan, bailout, or a subsidy.[18] According to the media, Airbus will fully pay the loan only after it sells 1,500 A350s.[19]

* * *

Despite the objections of US trade officials to the European governments' financial assistance to Airbus and their complaint to WTO, in 2008 the US Government saw no problem in benefiting from the European subsidy and taking advantage of the lower Airbus airplane price.

The Air Force requested bids for the first phase of a contract worth more than $100 billion to replace hundreds of aging refueling airplanes. Boeing offered a tanker based on its 767, and Airbus allied with Boeing's American competitor, Northrop Grumman Corporation, and offered a tanker based on the A330.

Apparently, the Airbus airplane was bigger than what the Air Force wanted. However, according to the media, under pressure from an influential US senator, the Air Force revised the language so that the Northrop-Airbus team could enter the competition.

"Northrop Grumman ... fought for contract modifications ... The Air Force said it did not change key contract details, but rather that it made minor adjustments in an attempt to address concerns raised by various companies."[20]

"The most vocal ... proponent of competition has been Sen. John McCain (R-Ariz.), the ranking member of the Armed Services Committee." The media added, "'... if the Air Force runs another single-source competition with Boeing, McCain is going to go berserk,' says the Air Force officer."[21] At the time, Senator McCain was considering a presidential bid.

The media reported that the potential for unwanted scrutiny from Congress might have given Air Force officials incentive to try to satisfy the Northrop-Airbus concerns. The listed price for the A330 was nearly 33% higher than 767's $120 million.

"Northrop officials say they also plan to deeply discount its price. The company could have a competitive advantage there, partly because European governments subsidize the development of new Airbus aircraft. The result is a lower cost of production than Boeing's, giving Airbus the ability to drop the price and still make money. ... Boeing also typically has less price flexibility than Airbus. Says a senior official for Northrop and EADS: 'We think we can win, and price is going to be part of the battleground here.'"[22]

On February 29, 2008, the Pentagon proved the senior official from Northrop and EADS right when it granted the tanker contract potentially worth $100 billion to the Northrop-EADS team. "Air Force Secretary Michael Wynne ... told lawmakers at the Senate Armed Services Committee that EADS, the parent company of the French aircraft manufacturer Airbus, was selected over Chicago-based Boeing Co. because it had a 'less expensive' bid and would produce a 'less risky' plane."[23] The Pentagon confirmed that the Boeing bid was 25% higher than the Airbus bid.[24]

According to the media, influential US Senator John McCain, who went on to win the Republican Party's nomination for the 2008 US presidential election, "... pressed the Air Force to ignore the issue of government subsidies to Airbus when the service solicited bids for the new tanker, contending that competition between Airbus and Boeing was more important than the issue of subsidies."[25] Analysts believed that the senator's intervention stacked the deck against Boeing.

A statement made by the senator a year later indicated that his views on the subsidies were more aligned with Airbus. "In terms of his stance on whether the EU aid should be factored into the competition, McCain said: 'First of all, I'd have to know how those subsidies are. The fact is that we subsidize Boeing because they take the profits from defense contracts and invest those profits into their product. And so we'll have to have an evaluation ... of the whole thing.'"[26]

Interestingly, Senator McCain's presidential campaign slogan was "Country First."

By mere coincidence, Senator McCain was in the Elysee Palace in Paris, France, meeting with French President Sarkozy three weeks after the Pentagon declared Northrop-EADS the winner. The media disclosed that Senator McCain's inner circle in his presidential campaign included EADS lobbyists.

The Pentagon announcement shocked Boeing and set off a firestorm on Capitol Hill—US senators and congressmen were taking sides.

The Democratic presidential candidates also got into the fray. "[Democratic Presidential candidate, Senator] Obama said it was hard for him to believe 'that having an American company that has been a traditional source of aeronautical excellence would not have done this job.'"[27]

The Democratic Party's other presidential candidate, Senator Hillary Clinton, captured the sentiments of the Boeing supporters succinctly in her statement to the media. She said, "I am deeply concerned about the Bush administration's decision to outsource the production of refueling tankers for the American military. It is troubling that the Bush administration would award the second-largest Pentagon contract in our nation's history to a team that includes a European firm that our government is simultaneously suing at the World Trade Organization for receiving illegal subsidies."[28]

With a promise of airplane assembly jobs, EADS also got the state of Alabama's political machinery and its US senators and congressmen to side with the European airplane manufacturer in the competition against Boeing. Senators, congressmen and governors from the states where Boeing planned to build its tankers supported Boeing. Sometimes, it appeared as if most of the Republicans led by Senator McCain supported EADS, while most of the Democrats rooted for Boeing.

* * *

Boeing protested the Pentagon decision. It argued that the Air Force decision-making process was flawed; its 767 was more versatile. Boeing contended that its tanker would cost less over the life of the airplane than the Airbus-Northrop tanker.

On June 19, 2008, the Government Accountability Office (GAO), the investigative arm of the US Congress, backed Boeing's protest by saying the Air Force made errors during the process. The GAO recommended the Air Force reopen the bidding and obtain revised proposals. The Pentagon canceled the contract and agreed to reopen the bidding.

Shortly after the release of the GAO report, the media reported that the European leaders, on various occasions, personally lobbied President Bush to favor Airbus over Boeing in the fierce competition for the aerial refueling tanker contract. Apparently, the European leaders also expressed their concern with the US president over the Pentagon's decision to reopen the tanker competition, as it could jeopardize Airbus jobs in Europe.[29]

Many Boeing sympathizers were astounded by the audacity of the European leaders to lobby the president of the United States of America against an American icon and one of America's biggest exporters, The Boeing Company.

The media reported, "U.S. relations with France and Germany have improved in recent months. In [2008] March, weeks after the Northrop-EADS team won the initial contract, [French President] Sarkozy said he would send 700 additional French troops to Afghanistan as Bush was pushing NATO members to become more involved. In June, Germany pledged $653 million in aid to rebuild Afghanistan. Germany, France and Britain also have been increasingly supportive of other Bush administration foreign policy initiatives."[30]

However, there was no evidence of any quid pro quo arrangement between the aerial refueling tanker contract and the reinvigorated European support for the foreign policy initiatives of President Bush.

On February 24, 2010, the Air Force reopened the bidding.

* * *

Notwithstanding Airbus' desire to rely on the governments for its launch expenses, European governments also preferred to see the mature Airbus slowly weaned out. The government funding had slowly declined with every new airplane launch. For example, the A300/A310 programs, launched in the late '60s and the '70s, had been bankrolled entirely by the European governments. The governments funded only 65% of the A330/340 program.[31]

In July 1992, after several years of negotiations, Europe agreed to limit the "direct" launch aid at 33% of development costs. Jean Pierson, managing director and chief executive officer of Airbus Industrie, called the agreement "balanced and fair to all."[32]

The Americans took it for granted that Airbus automatically expected the European taxpayers to grant the "loans" to fund its programs. In December 2000, the media reported, "The chief executive of Airbus, Noel Forgeard, said the consortium would contribute about $6 billion to the A380 project from its own resources. Subcontractors would fund $2.8 billion on a risk-sharing basis, and the rest would come from repayable state loans. Airbus is not a corporation, and therefore cannot raise money on global capital markets, which has always meant that it has had to fall back on governments as a lending source of last resort. Airbus is a grouping of economic interests, responsible for the final assembly, sales and after sales service of the planes."[33] The media reported that the A380 program cost Airbus approximately $18 billion to $20 billion.

After July 12, 2001, Airbus became a part of a public company whose stocks were publicly traded in the open market. It became a part of EADS, which was formed by the merger on July 10, 2000, of Aérospatiale-Matra of France, Construcciones Aeronáuticas SA (CASA) of Spain, and DaimlerChrysler Aerospace AG (DASA) of Germany.

Even though the EU used the Boeing-McDonnell Douglas merger to extract a few concessions, neither the US Government nor Boeing challenged the formation of EADS or the merger of Airbus into it. Boeing welcomed the potential prospect of Airbus conducting itself as a profit-making publicly traded international business enterprise.

* * *

Before July 12, 2001, Airbus was not a corporation. It was created under a unique arrangement under French law, a "Groupement d'intérêt Economique" (GIE), which was a "grouping of Mutual Economic Interest." It was a form of consortium officially created at the end of 1970 to establish a formal cooperation among the wine producers. GIE was not a company; it did not have to publish accounts nor did it have to pay taxes, unless it chose to do so. Apparently, Airbus never chose to do so.

The GIE arrangement made it almost impossible to trace subsidies, profits, or losses. The governments replaced the bankers and assumed all the risks. The books were totally closed, with impenetrable financial records.

GIE allowed the four Airbus partners to act like subcontractors in developing and manufacturing aircraft subassemblies. Depending on the airplane model, the airplanes were assembled by the French in Toulouse or by the Germans in Hamburg. The partners were paid in proportion to their share of the project after the airplanes were sold. The partners vigorously competed for the share of the work.

Airbus was responsible for the marketing and sales. It also was responsible for coordinating the design and development, managing outside partners or suppliers, and supporting the customers.

GIE accounting was so impenetrable that Airbus itself could not establish the real cost of its airplanes. Even one of the most powerful and domineering managing directors of Airbus had no idea. According to Pierson, "Its [GIE's] principal drawback is that Airbus managers have no idea of the consortium's manufacturing costs."[34]

The partners kept all the financial information close to their vest. Each partner was free to extract as much profit as it could from its share of the work by any method it thought appropriate. "Although none of the partners disclose separate profit and loss figures for their Airbus activities, analysts generally assume that only British Aerospace, which has undergone aggressive cost cutting in recent years, is profitable in any significant way."[35]

Even though Airbus management complained to its partners about not knowing the cost of the airplanes it was selling, it was a moot point. The governments were footing the bill, and Airbus was a new kid on the block; it had to gain acceptance in the marketplace. Market share became the driver. The United States was the prized market. Placing the airplanes in the livery of US carriers provided instant credibility around the world. It did not matter what Airbus had to pay to get there.

* * *

Reportedly, Airbus practically gave away the A300s to Eastern Airlines. It let the airline fly for months before it bought the airplane. "The customer (Eastern) needed the planes and the money to pay for them. Airbus could supply the planes. If it could supply the money as well, the loop could be closed and a deal struck." Airbus not only arranged for loans with generous interest from the banks, but it also loaned millions from its own coffers. When Eastern complained that the airplane was too big and that it would not be able to fill the airplane, Airbus asked Eastern to pay only for the seats it actually used. The chairman of Eastern, Frank Borman, was so ecstatic with the deal that in 1977 he told his staff, "If you don't kiss the French flag every time you see it, at least salute it. The export financing on our Airbus deal subsidized this airline by more than $100 million."[36] This was the price Airbus was prepared to pay to enter the American market.

Airbus entered into a similar deal with American Airlines. It signed a "walk-away lease"; the airline could walk away from the lease with a 30-day notice.

In 1984, Airbus made special arrangements to get Pan Am to add the A300s to its fleet. At the time, Pan Am was in a precarious financial situation. Its balance sheet showed four times debt against its equity.

Even though the Airbus board of directors was used to giving the Airbus airplanes away to gain the market share, reportedly even they could not stomach the special deal with Pan Am. Bernard Lathier, the Airbus managing director, was let go. Pierson became the new man in charge.

Some in the media described Pierson as a hard-nosed executive. "Pierson brought a rougher, more abrasive style to the consortium. He is known in the organization as the Pyrenees Bear, and indeed, he has many bearlike qualities. He is hugely fat, chain smokes, and regularly loses his temper, rowing with allies and enemies with equal enthusiasm. ... Pierson is a ruthless and remorseless executive."[37]

However, others had a very different perspective on Pierson. "The industry has produced few more interesting figures than Pierson. He is a legend. … He had the requisite vision, guts, common sense, and the personal force to persuade colleagues at Airbus to do things his way and to persuade customers—including wary, skeptical American Carriers—to buy his airplanes instead of Boeing's."[38]

Pierson pursued the market share even more aggressively. He also went on to develop a family of airplanes. "In the original methods of financing, Airbus struck a rich seam, and one that it was to exploit ruthlessly. It had made a breakthrough, and sold planes in places that no European manufacturer had previously penetrated. The costs were high and it was far from clear how Airbus would earn a profit from its leasing arrangements. And there was a political cost, a sharp foretaste of the determination of the consortium to bludgeon its way into the market using whatever means necessary."[39]

The media automatically assumed that Airbus was practically giving the airplane away for the market share. Some of the airlines, such as Lufthansa, went out of their way to refute it. "Paris [Air Show] provided the showcase opportunity for Lufthansa to sign a deal reconfirming its original A340-200 purchase commitment. The deal … was reportedly worth some $2.5 billion for all 30 aircraft, and the airline chairman, Reinhardt Abraham, stressed it was not getting the A340 at a 'give away price.'" [40]

With the market share barely in the teens in the late 1980s, Airbus could not compete with Boeing. As the symbol of European pride, it could not quit the business either. Making a profit was out of the question; Airbus could not even break even. It had to do what it needed to increase its market share even if it meant selling the airplanes at the "give away price." Pierson summed up the situation succinctly when he said, "You can't win, you can't break even, and you can't quit."[41]

* * *

Even though Airbus had previously sold its airplanes to Eastern, Pan Am, American and Northwest, the sale of 50 A320s with an option for an additional 50 to United Airlines in July 1992 finally confirmed that Airbus had realized its dream of fully penetrating the US market. United had been one of the biggest customers of The Boeing Company. To facilitate the sale, Airbus even offered several A320s on a walk-away lease, which could be returned to Airbus without penalty after as little as three years. It was a momentous strategic move for Airbus. Besides gaining a prized foothold at one of the biggest airlines in the US, Airbus had trounced the 737s with its A320s.

The A320 sales to United sent shock waves throughout Boeing. It forced Boeing to take a fresh look at its 737 product line.

Under the GIE structure, Airbus had no idea of what its airplanes cost, so the price of the airplane was whatever it took to beat the competition, namely Boeing and McDonnell Douglas, and gain the market share. "For 13 years, legendary super-salesman Jean Pierson pounded tables and twisted arms to build up market share for Airbus Industrie."[42]

In 1998, the newly appointed head of Airbus, Noel Forgeard, announced a change in strategy. "'Market share for me is not itself sufficient to define the way anyone should want to drive a business,' Mr. Forgeard said in an interview as the Farnborough Air Show got under way here, 'and if I have to choose between 55% market share with poor profitability and 45% with good profitability, I would choose the latter ... I'm basically a person dedicated to the bottom line and building shareholder value, ... and I've been appointed to build a single company whose business philosophy will be return on investment and shareholder value.'"[43]

Forgeard, who looked more like a stereotypical accountant than a high-powered executive, came from the private sector—France's entrepreneurial Lagardère Group. He was once an aide to President Jacques Chirac, when Chirac was the French prime minister in the 1980s.

However, when Forgeard announced the sale of as many as 188 A320 family of airplanes to British Airways in 1998, the analysts were not sure if Forgeard practiced what he preached publicly. Boeing suspected that Airbus sold the airplanes at rock-bottom prices to beat the 737s.

"Ayling [Chairman and Managing Director, British Airways] acknowledged as much when he said, 'at the end of the day, it all came down to cost.'"[44]

"Boeing's suspicion that the planes [A320s] were sold at a rock-bottom prices was, for BA's [British Aerospace] Mike Turner (represented British Aerospace at the Airbus supervisory board), uncomfortably close to the mark, 'The marketeers who came to the supervisory board weren't in it for the price,' he says. 'They were in it for volume. The French were driving this volume. And probably in the early years of Airbus, we needed this volume. We needed market share. It wasn't a strategy they would admit to, but we tolerated it. After we did the British Airways deal, I said at the supervisory board, "that's the last time anybody mentions strategy." We need a pricing grid and minimum prices for every aircraft size."[45]

Even after 2001, when Airbus became a part of the publicly traded company EADS, reports indicated that lower pricing continued to be the centerpiece of the Airbus sales strategy. Regarding the sale of A319s to EasyJet in 2002, a retired Airbus executive said, in the end "it was none-theless about price, Airbus did whatever it took to make certain that its price would be lower than Boeing's."[46] The Associated Press reported in 2007, "Aer Lingus will buy 12 Airbus jets, including the new A350 XWB, Chief Executive said the airline negotiated with the Boeing Co., Airbus' U.S. rival, for the possible purchase of its new 787 long-haul jet. But he said Airbus offered 'an exceptional price.'"[47]

* * *

Lower pricing does not always guarantee a sale. The airlines consider many factors during the purchase of airplanes.

In 1991 Airbus was not able to persuade British Airways to buy its airplane. Reportedly, Airbus had made a very attractive offer. When British Airways did not select the newly launched A330 and instead opted for the 777, Pierson did something that was rare in the industry. He declared that he would ask the European Commission to launch an inquiry into the purchasing policies of British Airways.

Airbus also barred its employees from flying on British Airways flights. Airbus announced that it was the consortium's policy to support only customer flights.

Many considered the gesture to be more of a public relations stunt. In the early 1990s, with a limited number of Airbus customers around the world, if Airbus were to literally enforce such a policy, flying would not have been the mode of transportation for Airbus employees on sales missions around the globe.

However, despite the rhetoric and the vociferous public campaign, Airbus never filed a formal complaint with the European Commission charging British Airways with anticompetitive behavior in its purchases of Boeing airplanes.

It is rather unusual for a world-class manufacturer to publicly criticize its customer on the loss of a sale. Even though many in aviation circles considered Pierson's actions to be undignified, they could understand his frustration. With a barely double-digit market share in the 1990s and having to fight for every scrap, it was probably difficult for Airbus to take the loss gracefully.

However, even after becoming a dominant player in airplane manufacturing, Airbus appeared to have resorted to some of the same techniques on a couple of sales campaigns.

"In 2003, Airbus competed against Boeing for the sale of single-aisle aircraft to All Nippon Airways (ANA). Although ANA's selection of Boeing's 737's over Airbus A320's was predictable, Airbus complained that political pressure had steered the decision away from ANA's preference for the A320's. This move by Airbus angered various interested parties in Japan, not least ANA's management, further weakened Airbus's position. Its CEO (Chief Executive Officer), Noel Forgeard, felt obliged to visit Japan and issue an apology to Joji Ohashi, president and CEO of ANA. Not long afterwards, ANA decided to replace its entire fleet of Airbus airplanes-A320's and A321's-with Boeing aircraft. 'We haven't helped ourselves by the way we have dealt with the Japanese,' said Christian Scherer, a highly regarded Vice-President of Airbus."[48]

Airbus made similar remarks when it lost the Air India campaign in 2005. The media reported, "Airbus Industrie, a European consortium, has protested against the decision by Air India to buy 50 aircraft from Boeing of the U.S. Airbus asked for a re-bid after the Indian carrier placed the order valued at Rs. 30bn[billion] (U.S.$690.9m) with Boeing. Airbus claimed the board of Air India had chosen to buy 787 aeroplanes, which do not conform to the internationally accepted norm of eight seats abreast. The European manufacturer has asked that all documents relating to the tendering process be sent to the Central Vigilance Commission (an agency to investigate corruption) and fresh tenders be called for the deal in an effort to ensure fair competition. ... Air India has refuted Airbus charges, saying Airbus was given an equal opportunity to make a presentation for the new aircraft. Air India has categorically maintained that no changes in tender norms were made."[49] Even the French ambassador to India publicly sided with Airbus in the accusation.

Notwithstanding these isolated events, those close to the negotiations often described Airbus sales campaigns as a "colorful mixture of elaborate statecraft, crafty financing, mean street-fighting and boundless cheek."[50] On one occasion, it even included the colorful head of Airbus dropping his pants (trousers for the British or pantaloons for the French) to show the chairman of a US airline that he had nothing more to offer.[51] Apparently, Pierson had been on a diet for several months and looked very shriveled.

* * *

Politics plays a big part in airplane sales. Naturally, every manufacturer tries its best to garner all the political support it can muster. According to the media, European political influence has been a big asset for Airbus. "I am its number one salesman," President Mitterrand once said of Airbus. Media described President Mitterrand as one of the most cunning of European statesmen, a person who had cajoled many world leaders into buying Airbus airplanes.[52]

Normally it is rare for the leader of the world's superpower, the US president, to be peddling Boeing airplanes to foreign heads of state but it does happen, although not at the same frequency as with the European heads of state. Besides being a major source of export revenue and a valuable source of employment, airplanes are often seen as a symbol of national pride.

Sometimes airplane deals are connected to other fringe benefits. Observers have noted that, shortly after making a major deal with Airbus, foreign airlines have received better access to European capitals, more landing slots, or airports with better connections. Shortly after purchasing the A340s in 1994, Air Mauritius was granted landing rights to Paris Charles de Gaulle International Airport, which the airline had been seeking for a long time.

Politicians look for the hot-button issues to exploit, such as Turkey's admission to the EU or the Palestinian cause in the Middle East. Joining the EU has been Turkey's cherished dream, and dangling the membership led to many Airbus airplane sales.

According to media reports, every time there was a Boeing and an Airbus sales campaign in the Middle East, EU leaders paid homage to the Arab leaders and stated their plan to help the Palestinians establish self-rule in the Israeli-occupied West Bank and Gaza Strip, which was a political issue near and dear to the Arab leaders in the Middle East.

Because of America's special relationship with the State of Israel, the United States had a disadvantage when it came to the Israeli-Palestinian issue.

Interestingly, in one instance, the Americans even trumped the Europeans. They found an issue even more potent than the Palestinian issue. During the airplane sales to Saudia, the Saudi national airline, President Clinton's administration used the Bosnian Muslim issue when the EU position was less palatable to the Arabs.

Despite the European record of using their political leaders to sell the airplanes, in 1994, the EU and Airbus accused the United States of political interference. The Europeans accused President Clinton's administration of political interference in the Saudia deal even though, only a week before the EU complaint, President Mitterrand had flown to Saudi Arabia for his private meeting with the king. Besides President Mitterrand, Chancellor Helmut Kohl of Germany and Prime Minister John Major of Britain also had weighed in with the king. Interestingly enough, even Prince Charles had an audience with the king. Just by mere coincidence, the British prince happened to be in the area on a private visit.[53]

* * *

Airplane sales were often used as bargaining chips in international trade. Every time the US Congress wanted to question the most favored status for China, the value of the Chinese currency, or other trade issues, China spent a few billion dollars on new Boeing airplanes.

Similarly, whenever the Europeans questioned human rights abuse in China or other trade issues, China arranged the state visits of high-ranking officials and announced billions of dollars of Airbus airplane orders.

On the flip side, countries also used airplane orders to make a political statement, mostly against the world's remaining superpower, the United States of America. This affected Boeing more than Airbus.

Talks of US arms sale to Taiwan often results in Chinese threats of cancelation of Boeing airplane orders or announcement of new orders for the Airbus airplanes. In 2007, because President Putin of Russia did not like the American political overtures toward Russia, its national airline, Aeroflot, switched orders from the Boeing 787 to the European A350. But with the passage of time Aeroflot was able to order an equal number of the 787s.

Aircraft purchases also have been associated with controversy. In the 1970s, when Lockheed was still making commercial airplanes, it was caught bribing Japanese officials to buy its L1011 wide-body airliner. A Japanese prime minister was convicted of accepting bribes. Prince Bernhard of The Netherlands was disgraced for his involvement with Lockheed. This scandal led in 1977 to Congress passing the Foreign Corrupt Practices Act, which forbade American companies, their officers, or their representatives from bribing foreign officials. In 1982, Boeing pleaded guilty to making false statements about the commissions on airplane sales before 1977. But Airbus was not subject to such constraints for another 23 years.

France outlawed bribery of foreign public officials in 2000. Until then French companies were even allowed to openly claim a tax deduction for the bribes paid. Germany outlawed it in 1999. So it was perfectly legal for Airbus to offer bribes to clinch a deal as late as the year 2000.

In 2003, the British magazine *The Economist*[54] reported several instances when Airbus was accused or suspected of improper dealings. It covered allegations of corruption in the sale of Airbus airplanes that eventually led to the collapse of the Belgian airline Sabena, to Airbus agents offering bribes in 1994 to Saudi officials to secure the sale of Airbus airplanes to Saudia.

The Economist also reported that shortly after the first Gulf War and the freeing of Kuwait from the clutches of Saddam Hussein, US airplane manufacturers expected some sizable orders for airplanes from the grateful nation and its state-controlled airline, Kuwait Airways. But the chairman of Kuwait Airways stunned Boeing when he announced a deal with Airbus at the 1991 Paris Air Show. *The Economist* reported that the chairman, after he was fired from the airline, opened a shopping complex in Kuwait, which the locals nicknamed the "Airbus Centre."

In another case, Canadian and German law enforcement officials were involved in investigating bribes paid by Airbus in its first big sale in North America—a 34-aircraft deal to the then state-owned Air Canada in 1988. Investigation confirmed Airbus paid more than $22 million in "commissions," which the German court called Schmiergelder (grease monies).

Notwithstanding all the allegations of impropriety, no one had been criminally convicted, except for three Syrians. In October 2001, three Syrians were each sentenced to 22 ½ years of imprisonment (later reduced to 10 years) for "serious irregularities" in connection with state-owned Syrian Air's order for six Airbus A320s in 1996.

To put things in perspective, the instances cited by *The Economist* against Airbus or other allegations pale against the allegations of bribery and corruption in BAE dealings with Saudi officials. The allegations against BAE in the British media sounded more like something out of a James Bond movie. They included such things as fast cars and attractive women to payments into secret Swiss bank accounts. The allegations were related to a 1985 arms deal, worth £43 billion (nearly $90 billion). BAE was accused of secretly paying £1 billion (nearly $2 billion) to a Saudi prince. BAE called the payments a part of the marketing services.

In 2007, "to balance the need to maintain the rule of law against the wider public interest," the British Government suspended an active investigation of the allegations.[55]

According to the British press, in spite of the public sermons on corruption and bribery to the leaders of the developing nations, the British Government had to stop the investigation. It had the potential to expose the Saudi royal family's dealings and cause irreparable damage to the Saudi royal household. The Saudis had the petrodollars, and the British wanted them. Moreover, the Saudis were also dangling new orders for armaments worth billions of dollars. The Saudis also just happened to mention to the Brits that the French were very keen to get their hands on the new Saudi orders.

* * *

The power of the purse is not confined to the sale of armaments. In the world of commercial airplanes also, the airlines often use the weight of their purse to pit one manufacturer against another. They relish the fierce competition between the manufacturers.

Even in the 1950s, when Boeing hesitated to redesign the 707 to match the capability of the Douglas DC-8, Pan Am ordered 20 707s and 25 DC-8s. United immediately followed Pan Am with an order for 30

DC-8s. These were powerful shots across the bow. But Boeing did not relent until it found that American Airlines also was on the verge of ordering the DC-8s. Boeing got the message loud and clear. Boeing redesigned the 707, which, in hindsight, was a real blessing because it made the 707 a great airplane.

Airlines are continuously comparing offerings and do not hesitate to switch products in midstream. In November 1989, Continental Airlines announced orders for A330s and A340s, but ended up buying the 300-seater long-range 777-200ERs (Extended Range).

In 1990, Singapore Airlines confirmed an order for MD-11s, but after 18 months switched to A340-300s. Deliveries of the A340s to Singapore Airlines started in April 1996 but the airline, citing negative passenger comments and the airplane's performance issues, switched to the Boeing 777-200ER. Boeing received orders for 24 777-200ERs. Moreover, as a part of the deal, Boeing took the 17 A340-300s that the airline wanted to dispose of.

* * *

The European financial support and GIE arrangement helped Airbus reduce its costs and capture market share. Being a relative newcomer, Airbus also had an inherent advantage. Unlike Boeing, which inherited legacy systems and production methods from the days of the 707, Airbus started with a fresh canvas. According to industry experts, Airbus stream-lined its manufacturing processes watching the Japanese auto industry's production methods and best practices around the world, and thereby, reduced the costs of airplane production.

Although Airbus was a part of a public company, EADS, whose stocks were traded on the open market, European governments or their surrogates were still the major shareholders. The government collaboration greatly bolstered Airbus fortunes but it also created additional challenges. While optimizing its operations, Airbus had to be cognizant of the nationalistic interest of its major shareholders. Although success brought the Europeans together, failure prompted cross-border finger-pointing.

At the April 2005 ceremony in Toulouse to mark the airplane's maiden flight, French President Jacques Chirac called the A380, "a symbol of what Europeans can do together when they combine their strengths, their skills, their willpower and their creativity." [56] But the delay of the A380 exposed the historical, long-standing simmering rift between the French and the Germans. They blamed each other for the delay and for the financial mess of Airbus. It was reminiscent of the days of the Concorde; at meetings, people openly shared jokes such as the French brain was good as new and had never been used.

In March of 2007, the chief executive of Airbus at the time, Louis Gallois, told the media that the European government leaders were "haggling over the spoils of troubled aircraft maker Airbus without any thought for its future."[57] The fighting over national interests and the management infighting threatened the European partnership. The media reported: "EADS/Airbus, once viewed as a stellar example of European design and engineering excellence, became in recent years a laughing stock as Franco-German rivalry and bloodletting in the board-room tore it apart."[58]

The perceived threat from Boeing saved Airbus. The meteoric rise in the sale of the 787 prompted the French and the Germans to bury the hatchet and unify against the rising threat from their rival across the Atlantic. In March 2008, the EADS chairman declared that it was no longer mired in the "French and German battlefields."[59]

In 2009, Airbus accounted for nearly two-thirds of EADS' yearly revenues. Besides commercial airliners, EADS made and/or supported military airplanes, fighters, helicopters, rockets, satellites, and the Space Station, among others. EADS is striving to achieve a 50/50 balance between its commercial airplane business, Airbus, and its other parts.

Airbus has been, and for the foreseeable future will remain, a fierce competitor with Boeing.

2

AIRBUS STRATEGY

Launch of the A330/340 and the pincer strategy

Airbus needed a family of airplanes that covered a wide spectrum of payload and range to compete effectively with McDonnell Douglas and Boeing. Lockheed just had the Tristar L1011 and was not taken seriously. By the time Jean Pierson was the head of Airbus, he already had in the Airbus family the A300, the A310, and the A320.

The A310, which was supposed to compete with the 767, was not doing too well. Airbus had no way to foresee the newfound potential for the 767 when it launched the A310. When the 767 and the A310 were launched, neither Boeing nor Airbus had anticipated a new market for airplanes with two engines—the Atlantic.

Boeing had designed an airplane with large wings and the same powerful engines as the ones on the 747 except that it had only two engines. It was a powerful combination. The airplane was designed for non-stop US transcontinental flights, and had the range capability to operate across the Atlantic with full payload, and could be even used on selected Pacific routes. Reportedly, Lufthansa, a potential customer for the 767, believed Boeing had misjudged the market and that the airplane was not the best choice for the airlines' need. It felt the A310 with the smaller wing was optimal for its route structure. Lufthansa thought Airbus made the right decision and ordered the A310s.

Deregulation of the US aviation market in 1978 had far-reaching consequences, which no one in the industry had envisaged. It rekindled competition among the airlines. Since the airplane had the range, the US airlines operating the 767s on the domestic routes desired to operate the fuel-efficient twin carrying nearly 200 passengers over the Atlantic also. But there was just one hitch: aviation regulations did not permit twins to operate on direct optimal routing over the Atlantic.

*   *   *

Within a span of just over 30 years, Americans went from flying in a DC-3 at 10,000 feet (3,048 meters) to blasting off the Earth on massive rockets. Soon thereafter, they were hopping on the moon. But a regulation enacted nearly 30 years before in 1953, based on the experiences with the piston engines of the 1940s DC-3 era, was still in force in the 1980s even though Americans were jet-setting around the world in a 747, the jumbo jet, and space missions were routine.

In 1903, a little 12-hp piston engine introduced aviation and catapulted the Wright brothers' *Flyer* into the history books. By 1949, engines that had 300 times more horsepower than the little engine on the *Flyer* were powering airplanes.

The last propeller airplane built by Boeing, the 377 Stratocruiser, had four Pratt & Whitney engines, the biggest piston engine ever used on an airplane. The big engines had 112 high-compression cylinders and 224 spark plugs. These piston engines drove the propellers. The flight crew in the cockpit had to adjust many levers to ensure that the propellers operated at their most efficient setting. The bigger engines complicated things; there were too many moving parts, and the chance of something going wrong was always high. These engines could crank out 3,500 hp, three times more power than the engines that powered the world's most popular DC-3. But the little engines on the DC-3 were nearly seven times more reliable than the big piston engines that powered the Boeing Stratocruiser.

Therefore, it was very logical for the regulators to encourage manufacturers to build airplanes with several smaller piston engines, which would be much more reliable, than two massive ones to get the same total horsepower. However, if the industry insisted on using airplanes with just two piston-engines, the regulator required the airplane to stay within 60 minutes of an airport. This would ensure that there would be an airport nearby if there were a problem with the engine or the propeller.

The 707 with the jet engines changed history forever. Piston engines disappeared from the big commercial airplanes. The 727, the 737, and the 747 followed the Boeing success with the 707s. Unlike the piston engines, the reliability of the jet engine had no relationship with the size of the engine. Doubling or trebling the engine power output or the thrust level did not mean that the reliability would decrease. Engines with 60,000 pounds of thrust could be far more reliable than a 20,000-pound thrust engine.

* * *

The Soviet Union's Tu-104, introduced in 1956, was the first twinjet to be operated successfully in commercial service. Because it was mostly operated within the so-called "Iron Curtain," the Western World did not know much about it. French Sud Aviation's Caravelle, introduced in 1959, was the first Western twinjet. By the 1980s, airplanes with two engines were widely used in commercial aviation. Boeing had the whole range of twins—the 737, the 757, and the 767. Every Airbus airplane was a twin. The British had the BAC-111, and McDonnell Douglas had a twin—the DC-9; worldwide, at least three times more twins than quads were in commercial operation.

The fare-paying passengers on commercial airplanes expect their regulators to ensure the safety of aviation. In the United States, the Federal Aviation Administration (FAA) has the legal responsibility to make certain that all airplanes are designed and operated in accordance with the Federal Aviation Regulations (FAR). A fare-paying passenger expects an equivalent level of safety regardless of whether the airline operates a twin, a tri, or a quad on the route.

Since the introduction of the jet engine airplanes, the data showed that about 95% of accidents occurred during the phases of takeoff, climb, descent, approach, and landing. The cruise portion amounted to only around 5%. Hence, allowing the airplanes with jet engines to be farther away than 60 minutes from the nearest alternate would not make a significant dent in the safety of flight, because any extension of that 60 minutes would be in the cruise portion of the flight.

Regulators had not kept pace with the fast pace of aviation. Even in the 1980s, the regulations from 1953 governed the twins. It was time to look at the facts and data and make sound decisions that would further enhance the safety of operations while giving airplanes with two engines the flexibility to operate on routes that were beyond the 60-minute diversion time from the nearest alternate.

* * *

In 1985, a new standard was born—ETOPS. Actually, it was called EROPS then, although it meant the same thing. ETOPS meant extended range operations with two-engine airplanes, or operations of airplanes on routes with diversion times from the nearest airport extended beyond 60 minutes. Sometimes people called it Extended Twin Operations, Extended Range Operations, or just Extended Operations.

At an ETOPS conference in Seattle in November 1989, Tony Broderick, the associate administrator for regulation and certification at the FAA, said, "In the early 1980s, ETOPS began as a gleam in somebody's eye—I think it was Dick Taylor's [Vice President, Government and Technical Liaison, The Boeing Company]. When he approached us at FAA, we were quite cautious—some might say, skeptical, and he might even use a different word!"

Actually it appears the FAA was more than skeptical, "… FAA administrator Lynn Helms almost blew the proverbial gasket when Boeing's Dick Taylor first approached him in 1980 on the subject of modifying the twin-engine over-water requirement. 'It'll be a cold day in hell before I let twins fly long-haul, over-water routes,' he told Taylor. But Dick kept plugging away at the recalcitrant FAA chief."[1]

Taylor, with the help of Frank Fickeisen—a highly capable Boeing chief engineer with impeccable analytical ability—and a small group of subject experts, led this effort. The soft-spoken Taylor was an experienced Boeing senior executive who started his aviation career with Boeing in 1946 as a design engineer. In his more than 45 years of an illustrious career with Boeing he flew almost all the airplanes that Boeing had built, was a vice president, and managed many Boeing programs.

After several years of intense work between the regulators in the United States and Europe, International Civil Aviation Organization (ICAO), manufacturers, airlines, pilot unions, and other interested parties, the FAA issued a final set of standards in 1985. It allowed "two-engine jet airplanes" to operate up to 120 minutes from the nearest airport.

ICAO is a United Nations agency that was established in December 1944 to ensure that international civil aviation is developed in a safe and orderly manner. Its main objective is to provide for the safety, regularity, and efficiency of international civil aviation.

The FAA set stringent requirements for the manufacturers and for the operators to operate a twin under ETOPS. Two sets of approvals were required before an airline could operate a twin on ETOPS.

First, the manufacturer needed to show compliance with all the ETOPS requirements, then the particular combination of airframe-engine would be granted the approval; it was called the ETOPS Type Design Approval. The manufacturer had to prove, to the FAA's satisfaction, that the airframe-engined combination had the design features and the reliability stipulated under ETOPS standards. The rules required the engines to have a very low rate of in-flight shutdowns (IFSD) or failures. The rules also required highly reliable airplane systems such as the electrical, hydraulic, and pneumatic.

Second, the operator needed a separate FAA approval to operate the ETOPS Type Design approved airframe-engine. The airline's approval was called the ETOPS Operational Approval. The airline had to prove to the FAA that it had the flight operations and maintenance programs in place as required by ETOPS. Some of the airlines stamped "ETOPS" near the nose of the airplane to alert all those handling the airplane that it was an airplane for ETOPS operations and had to follow the more stringent ETOPS standards.

* * *

Twins, being more fuel efficient, significantly reduced the airline's operating costs. With the onset of ETOPS, airlines jumped on the Atlantic routes with the twins. The 767 became the ETOPS workhorse. Just as the Boeing 747 revolutionized air travel by reducing the cost of travel by up to 30%, the fuel-efficient twins further reduced the airline's cost of operations.

The concept of flying changed again!

Because the 767s and the 757s were much smaller in passenger capacity than the jumbo 747s, the airlines found that they could open new routes from many smaller cities in the United States to cities in Europe and still make money. This was the start of point-to-point operations between smaller cities. Not everyone had to fly through major hubs anymore.

Airbus fully supported the ETOPS initiatives and worked with Boeing on ETOPS issues.[2] After all, Airbus desired the same flexibility for its twins.

New markets opened for Airbus and Boeing twins. Airlines started to add extra frequency and operate 767s in place of a daily 747 flight. It did not take long for the 767 to dominate the transatlantic market.

In recognition of its importance to the future of the company, ETOPS received high-level attention within Boeing. On April 24, 1987, in an employee information newsletter, Boeing Commercial Airplane President Dean Thornton directed the company to form an ETOPS (called EROPS then) executive committee headed by Vice President Dick Taylor.

The committee included vice presidents from all the divisions. The committee was responsible for the coordination of company activities to get 180-minute ETOPS, support sales activities with customers who did not have ETOPS airplanes or operations, provide support to airlines big or small, and review in-service experience to ensure timely corrective action. The committee was also responsible for ensuring consistent communication through customer presentation material, media information, and so on.

Because of the excellent record of twin operations under ETOPS, in 1988 the FAA extended the maximum level of ETOPS authority from 120 to 180 minutes. This opened the US mainland to Hawaii market for the twins. Other regulatory agencies around the world closely followed the FAA's actions and extended ETOPS to 180 minutes. Even the ICAO updated its global standards.

While allowing the 180-minute ETOPS, the FAA further tightened the engine reliability requirements from the 120-minute ETOPS. For every 100,000 hours of engine operations, the engine failure target was ratcheted down to two—two IFSDs for every 100,000 engine-hours.

The manufacturers had to analyze the in-service data and make the necessary changes to the engines and airplane systems to qualify for the 180-minute ETOPS Type Design Approval. Similarly, the airlines had to examine the records of their ETOPS operations under 120 minutes and make changes as necessary. It required a new ETOPS Type Design

Approval and a new ETOPS Operational Approval before an airline could operate under this new level of ETOPS authority.

All the data showed that commercial twins were as safe as the tris and quads. If anything, the two-engine airliners were in many instances even safer than the three- and four-engine airliners they replaced in the airline fleet. The ETOPS standards further enhanced the safety of the twins.

* * *

ETOPS is literally an embodiment of culture of the Safety Management System (SMS)—a disciplined process that mitigates risk in every aspect of airline operations by using proactive, reactive, and predictive tools.

ETOPS requires the airframe and engine manufacturers to enhance the reliability levels of their products. ETOPS operational and maintenance standards levied on airlines ensure that the airlines plan for all eventualities and require the airlines to be proactive in monitoring the health of the airplane systems and engines.

ETOPS relies on a two-pronged approach: preclude and protect. First, do everything to preclude a diversion. Second, if the airplane has to divert, then protect that diversion.

Manufacturers design the airframe and engines to preclude diversions. Even after the failure of an engine or a system failure that could result in a diversion, the manufacturers ensure that the rest of the airplane design protects that diversion.

Similarly, in airline operations, the maintenance side takes steps to make sure that an engine or systems significant to ETOPS do not fail in flight. However, even if the engine or the systems fail in flight and if the flight has to divert, the airline makes sure that it protects that diversion by having enough fuel under the worst scenario for the airplane to make it to the diversion airport.

* * *

Even though the A310 was designed to compete against the 767, neither Boeing nor Airbus had anticipated the impact of the deregulation of commercial air transportation in the United States. The deregulation intensified the competition between the airlines. With the advent of

ETOPS, the 767, which had large wings and big engines and could fly the Atlantic with a full payload, became the airplane of choice for most of the airlines. Since the A310 was faltering in competition against the 767, Airbus had to build an airplane that could challenge the dominance of the 767 in the transatlantic market and compete with any future potential upgrades to the 767. Airbus was also convinced that Boeing would extend the 767 to cover the gap between its current 767 and the 747, that is, from 200 to 400 passenger seats. The A330 was the Airbus answer.

The initial version of the A330 would have a range of 4,700 nautical miles (nm) (8,700 kilometers [km]). A higher thrust engine with an extended range of 5,500 nm (10,400 km) would follow. The A330 was a twin-engine airplane that would seat up to 335 passengers in a two-class or 295 passengers in a three-class (first, business, and economy) configuration.

Based on market research and airline demand, the manufacturers decide the payload—the load that pays or makes money for the airline, that is, the number of seats and cargo—and the range for the airplane. The number of seats and cargo is used to determine the size of the fuselage—the body or the length and width of the tube. The range determines the amount of fuel the airplane has to carry and hence the size of the fuel tanks. During design, the manufacturers constantly trade between the payload and range. Even after the airplanes are designed and built, the airlines often do the same within the fixed design limits. Airlines may have a few luxurious seats with plenty of legroom and fly long ranges or they may pack in the passengers on the same airplane like sardines and operate on shorter ranges.

The Paris Air Show was the favorite venue for Airbus to launch new airplanes. At the 1987 Paris Air Show, Airbus launched not only the A330 but also a four-engine companion, the A340. By launching the A340, Airbus upped the ante. It was no longer satisfied with challenging the dominance of the 767 but was prepared to challenge the McDonnell Douglas three-engine MD-11 and the venerable 747 itself. The A340 had nearly the same range as the 747 but carried fewer passengers.

The media reported there were intense discussions within Airbus on whether it should launch a twin first or a four-engine airplane. Jean Pierson, Airbus managing director, rather than making a decision on which version to launch first, decided to launch both at the same time.

Boeing optimized the wing design for each of its airplanes; the A340 was essentially the same as the A330, except for the number of engines. By keeping the body and many systems the same, Airbus controlled costs. The A330 and the A340 used the same wings, with minor modifications.

To many Boeing aerodynamicists who took great pride in optimizing the wing design, the Airbus approach was a sacrilege!

Airbus relied on the European governments to fund the programs. "The decision to launch the A330 and A340 together meant a saving of half a billion dollars over the cost of launching them separately. Pierson says: 'There was a debate within Airbus. Some people said we should launch a twin, others a quad. Finally, the engineers promised they could do both aircraft with a common airframe for half a billion less. Let's go!' It was a lot easier, he adds, to sell a $3.5 billion double programme to the Governments than it would have been if he were to return to them in two years and ask for another $1.5 billion to launch a second aircraft."[3]

Because of the government launch money, Airbus could offer attractive pricing on the brand-new airplanes. As Pierson told the media after the airplane launch, the A330/340s "do not represent a technology goal. The goal is to increase market share."[4]

With the focus on the market share, industry experts believed Airbus was prepared to dump the airplanes in the market at a loss. Some even speculated that Airbus had a tacit understanding with the European governments that the "loans" would never be paid and the taxpayers would shoulder the cost.

* * *

In 1986, McDonnell Douglas had just launched a derivative of its DC-10, the MD-11. Airbus surprised McDonnell Douglas when it launched the A340 in 1987 for the same market as the MD-11. With the inherent pricing advantage, Airbus marketing went for a kill. The A340 outsold the MD-11, forcing McDonnell Douglas itself out of commercial aviation.

The Boeing 747 was next. It was in Airbus' proverbial "cross-hairs."

In the late 1980s or the early 1990s, Airbus was not in a position to challenge the venerable 747, but it would start nibbling at it.

"Adam Brown, head of planning at Airbus [and chief strategist] ... saw the Jumbo problem as the knottiest Airbus had faced. [Adam Brown said] 'Boeing took a heroic risk on the 747 and it almost broke them. But they are now a monopoly ... we cannot hope to compete head to head with the 747 ... so ...we thought ... of ... dealing with the 747 in a pincer movement.' The pincer movement was the riskiest and deadliest gambit Airbus had deployed in the war against Boeing: A tactic on the aeronautical chessboard, which threatened to checkmate Airbus's American opponent in two sweeping moves. The first was already in place: the A340. It challenged the 747 on range, but had fewer seats ... the second half of the pincer movement would be deployed: an Airbus Superjumbo. 'We have attacked them from below with the A340,' says Bernard Ziegler (Technical Director, Airbus). 'Now the idea is to come from over the shoulder with a high capacity plane.' With a Superjumbo, carrying 600 people or more, plus the A340, the 747 could be left floundering between the two. The monopoly would be broken, and so would the financial strength of Boeing."[5]

In his 25-year career at Airbus, Bernard Ziegler, son of the Airbus founder and its first president, Henri Ziegler, and one of Pierson's closed aides,[6] held various positions within the company, including senior vice president of flight and support, and senior vice president of engineering.

With the launch of the A330 and the A340, Airbus set in motion the 20-year gamble to checkmate its American opponent.

* * *

Lufthansa was the first to operate the A340-200, in February 1993. In January of 1994, Air France introduced the A330 into commercial operations.

Taking a cue from Boeing, Airbus kept the same fuselage for all its bigger airplanes—the A300, A310, A330, and A340. The length of the fuselage would vary but the diameter or the cross section was kept the same. To contain manufacturing costs, Boeing had used the same concept on its 707, 727, 737, and 757.

Airbus assembled the A330s and A340s at its Toulouse facility with major subassemblies flown in by the strange-looking Super Guppies, which were modified Boeing B377s. The Super Guppies were later replaced by equally strange-looking Belugas—the modified A300s.

When Airbus launched its A330/340, Boeing had its hands full with the development and certification of the 747-400. It could not proceed with a new aircraft, as engineering resources were fully committed to the 747-400. Besides, Boeing was not sure what it wanted to build.

Whatever Boeing launched, it had to be better than the A330/340. It had to leapfrog the competition. Because of the Airbus subsidy, it would be difficult for Boeing to compete on price.

To compensate for the pricing disadvantage, Boeing's new airplane had to be more fuel efficient and technologically superior to the Airbus offering. Further, Boeing could not allow the gap in the payload range between the 767 and the 747 and allow the A330/340 to capture that segment of the market.

Airbus had Boeing over a barrel!

* * *

After looking at various options, including a three-engine 7J7, by the late 1980s, Boeing concluded that, to attack both the A330 and the A340, its new airplane had to be a fuel-efficient big twin, called the 767-X in the interim.

The airplane would fill the niche between the nearly 200-passenger 767 and the over 400-passenger 747. But there were many major challenges.

One challenge was that the engines that could produce high levels of thrust to power the 767-X were not readily available. The 767-X required engines nearly 50% more powerful than what was readily available. Banking on developing a new engine that was much more powerful than anything in existence was a risky proposition.

Another major challenge was ETOPS.

Based on the payload range, the airlines were buying these airplanes to operate directly over the Atlantic and other international routes, which invariably required ETOPS capability. Boeing had to secure ETOPS approval for these big twins. But, there was a wrinkle.

The FAA requirements stressed the importance of in-service experience. After all, in 1985, ETOPS was an afterthought. By the early 1980s, the twins that were vying for ETOPS such as the 757/767 and the A300/310 were already out operating on routes around the world. The easiest way for the regulators to assess the worthiness of the airframe, engines, and the airlines' capabilities was to observe the data from actual in-service aircraft. The FAA and other regulators around the world required the airlines to operate the airframe-engine combination for one year to be eligible for 120-minute authority and an additional one year for the 180-minute authority.

Boeing was already a few years behind the A330/340 and could not afford to have the new airplane confined to the domestic routes, accumulating in-service experience. If it was going to have any chance of competing with the Airbus offerings, Boeing had to find a way to allow the new twins to operate on ETOPS sectors from the first day of revenue operations at the airline.

* * *

At least on the engine side, Boeing was successful in getting all three major engine manufacturers to agree to develop powerful engines for the 767-X. Each engine manufacturer was going to develop an engine of its own. This precluded Boeing from landing in the same situation as Airbus with the A340.

The A340 had suffered a setback right after the launch. The consortium that was going to develop the engines for the A340s backed out. As a result, Airbus used the family of engines that powered the smaller A320s. They had to extract just about every pound of thrust from those engines. These engines allowed Airbus to proceed with the airplane, but most observers felt the airplane was grossly underpowered.

* * *

The 767-X became the 777.

In October 1990, Boeing launched its new 777—an airplane family that would compete against both the A330 and the A340 families. It launched two models, one for medium range and one for long range: the 777-200 and the 777-200ER.

The 777-200 could fly 305 passengers in a three-class cabin configuration 5,210 nm (9,649 km) while the 777-200ER, also unofficially known as the 777IGW (Increased Growth Weight), carried nearly the same number of passengers but flew much farther, to 7,730 nm (14,316 km).

The 777 was a faster airplane than the A330 or the A340. Its optimal cruise speed was Mach 0.84 versus Mach 0.82 for the A330/340. Mach is a ratio of the speed of the airplane compared to the speed of sound. Mach 1 would signify the airplane flew at the speed of sound. Hence, Mach 0.84 would mean that the 777 flew at 84% of the speed of sound. The speed of sound on the ground is 762 miles per hour (1,226 km/hour).

Rather than being a jazzed-up version of the 767 to leapfrog the A330, the new 777 would challenge both the A330 and the A340. Moreover, it was a twin, which automatically would have better operating economics. Furthermore, the 777 had a faster optimal cruise speed.

Boeing declared the airlines would be able to operate the 777 on ETOPS at entry into service. Now, it was up to us to find a way to make it happen!

* * *

Conceptually, Airbus had some difficulty trying to market the A330s and the A340s, since they were advertised as being the same airplane with two engines or four.

Whether Airbus truly believed it, or it was just a marketing ploy, Airbus promoted the concept of efficiency crossover between twins and quads. Airbus said, "We developed an engineering and marketing strategy that covered this whole marketplace, where the long-range requirement is met by the 4-engine airplane and the medium-range requirement is met by the twin. There is an overlap. Just where the two join is a moot point. We reckon it falls at 5,500 nm, where the twin ceases to be economic, and a 4-engine airplane takes over, continuing to be attractive right out to very long ranges."[7]

It must have been a mere coincidence that in the mid-1990s, 5,600 nm (10,380 km) was about the maximum range for the A330.

Actually, the first time that I heard of this "crossover point" concept, it was at 4,700 nm, which, again, by coincidence happened to be the maximum range of the earlier versions of the A330s. But I had never seen the actual calculations that led to this conclusion until I attended a meeting in Rome.

As a member of the Boeing team, I was in Rome to talk about the Boeing 777s. When we showed charts that explained how the 777 could operate efficiently up to around 7,000 nm (13,000 km), the areas Airbus claimed for its quad, the A340, one of the airline representatives pulled out a folder and dropped it on the table. It looked like someone's doctoral thesis, full of double integrals and with the entire Greek alphabet. The airline representative said, "How can you say the 777 will be more economical than the A340 when Airbus has proven scientifically that quads are more efficient than twins above 5,600 nm?"

Obviously, the airline personnel were confused. After all, they were not the experts. As far as they were concerned both Airbus and Boeing were credible, so what we were saying did not agree with what Airbus had told them just a few days before. Besides, Airbus had given the airline personnel this scientific-looking study, even though the airline personnel could not decipher it.

Since I was there to talk about twins and ETOPS, all eyes were on me to respond. I looked at the pile of equations. I could not make heads or tails of it. It was the first time I had actually seen it, and even had I seen it before, I very likely would not have been able to figure it out. I was greatly relieved when one of the senior people in the Boeing group said, "We have the comparative data here, why don't we compare the actual airplanes, the 777 and the A340, rather than talk about some theoretical studies." To my great relief, the airline agreed.

Our data showed that twins were, on average, about 7% more economical than quads. This was based on the airplane/engine drag level, maintenance and ownership costs, operating empty weight, and specific fuel consumption. Airbus claimed that at 7,000 nm (13,000 km) twins were nearly 4% worse than quads.

In the early to mid-1990s, during my visits to the various airlines around the world, I was continually asked about this equation. The crossover equation disappeared when Airbus decided to extend the range of the A330 beyond 5,600 nm (10,380 km). Surprisingly, no one in the industry mentioned the "crossover point" after that, as if it had never existed. Out of intellectual curiosity, I would have loved to get my hands on a copy of that study but I was never able to get one.

Even though Airbus no longer mentioned the actual "crossover point" per se, it advocated the A330, the twin, for short-range to medium-range operations and the A340, the quad, for long-range operations. It aggressively promoted this product philosophy for the next 20 years.

Boeing and Airbus were ready for their strategic moves on the aviation chessboard!

3

BOEING RESPONSE

Boeing gambles its future on the 777 family

Airbus had to do what it needed to do to prevail over the 777. Besides asserting twins were uneconomical at long ranges, it argued that ETOPS at entry into service was unsafe.

Airbus regarded the promise of ETOPS at entry into service as the 777's Achilles heel. Airlines had bought the 777s, hoping to use them on international routes from the first entry into revenue operations. Most of the international routes needed ETOPS. Stopping the airplane's ETOPS approval at entry into revenue service would put a significant dent in the airlines' plans.

Getting the ETOPS approval at entry into revenue service was a big challenge, and Airbus knew it. All Airbus had to do was convince the regulators to maintain the status quo. If the regulatory authorities were to balk at changing the requirements, the 777 would not get the ETOPS approval. That would be a big blow to Boeing; greatly hurt the 777s, and could even be fatal.

Airbus believed the 777s with the newly designed or the upgraded engines, which produced nearly 50% more thrust than anything in existence, needed to be proved in actual in-service flight. Airbus advocated that it was too risky to allow them to fly on routes that required diversion with just one engine for three hours. Airbus believed Boeing should accumulate actual in-service data before getting 180-minute ETOPS authority.

We had to find a way to convince the industry and the regulators to change the requirements and give Boeing the opportunity to prove that its 777 could meet those new requirements.

* * *

The 777 was a customer-driven airplane. A couple of years before the launch of the airplane, Boeing formed a group of eight airlines, aptly called the "Gang of Eight." The "gang" included United, American, and Delta from the United States; British Airways from Europe; and Qantas, Cathay Pacific, Japan Airlines, and All Nippon Airways from the Pacific region. Boeing eagerly sought and received input.

The airlines wanted a wider airplane, 25 inches (63.5 cm) wider than the A330/340. Hence, a 767 derivative was out of the question. The Gang of Eight defined the 777.

The airplane had to be "service ready." It had to work as advertised from the first day of entry into the airline's operations. This required Boeing to add more time for the airplane program compared to its last new airplane programs, the 757 and the 767.

To make the airplane service ready, Boeing fundamentally changed the way it designed and manufactured airplanes. In the past, design engineers would design systems and figuratively throw the design over the fence to Manufacturing who, at times, would find it almost impossible to manufacture the component, requiring numerous revisions to the design. In the previous programs, it was quite common to see engineers reworking the designs even after manufacturing was in full swing, and making changes as problems showed up in the factories and on the flight lines during testing. Very often, Boeing found that the airlines could not easily maintain the system; either the access was poorly defined or not enough thought had been given to maintenance during design.

Maintenance tools, support equipment, and maintenance manuals had to be reworked; at times, this occurred after the airplane was in operation with the airlines. When the bigger jumbo jet with a stretched upper deck, the 747-400, began airline operation, Boeing had to assign additional personnel at the airline's maintenance bases to get rid of bugs that had not been spotted earlier.

Besides the aggravation, Boeing estimated that this "non-value-added" step cost up to $2.5 billion. If Boeing could get it right the first time, it could potentially save billions.[1]

Boeing was determined to put in the effort and money up front. Boeing aimed to make the 777 truly ready for service when it was delivered. In addition, Boeing would not have much hope of being granted

180-minute ETOPS if the airplane suffered early problems at entry into airline operations. ETOPS raised the reliability bar high for the manufacturers and the airlines.

For the 777, Boeing created the Design, Build, and Support Team (DBST) concept in which groups affected by the design worked together. This allowed the designers to get instant feedback on issues such as if the design was producible or easily maintainable by the airline. There were nearly 250 DBSTs.

The 777 program had many firsts. For the first time, Boeing was designing the airplane digitally. There would be no paper drawing—it was a "paperless" airplane. The famous saying in the manufacture of an airplane used to be when the weight of the paper drawing exceeded the airplane's actual maximum takeoff weight, it was time to stop designing and start building the airplane. This time, the designers would not be able to use this dictum.

The 777 was designed digitally in CATIA, which stands for Computer Aided Three-dimensional Interactive Applications. It had its origins in Dassault Aviation in France, where it was used to help build French fighter planes. IBM and Boeing enhanced the software to detect interference between parts that either did not fit or could not work with each other as intended. Just as the Airbus A330 and A340 were born inside the belly of the Super Guppy, which had its origins in America, the 777 was born inside a computer program that had its origins in France.

CATIA digitally displayed solid objects. The digital system showed how all the pieces fit together. If two parts clashed, for example, if a tube could not get around a spar, the problem would show up on the screen. CATIA practically eliminated the "shims," pieces of metal used to make structural pieces fit together, thereby eliminating weight. Unlike in the previous programs, parts did not have to be reworked to make them fit.

The DBSTs and the CATIA systems were not meant to speed delivery of the 777 but to make a highly reliable, service-ready airplane from the outset.

* * *

Boeing planned to incorporate ETOPS in the design, build, test, and support programs. Boeing named this the "Early ETOPS." Many called this the "ETOPS Out of the Box." The Early ETOPS program sought

ETOPS approval for its airframe-engine combinations around the same time as the basic certification for the airplane.

The Boeing plans were ambitious. In an interview with *Fortune* magazine in April 1992, Dean Thornton, president of the Boeing Commercial Airplane, said, "The 777 causes me to sit bolt upright in bed periodically. It's a hell of a gamble. There's a big risk in doing things totally differently. It's not going to fail, but the degree of success is uncertain. It depends on the market."[2]

The risk, indeed, was enormous. Designing the entire airplane digitally was new to Boeing. On Early ETOPS, there were no rules, regulations, or guidance allowing Boeing to do what it wanted to do.

Boeing had to convince the regulators of the concept of Early ETOPS itself. Airbus was not the only one opposed to it. Many in the industry did not support the Early ETOPS concept. We had to earn the support from the industry.

There was no guarantee that we would be able to convince the regulators or that the regulators would step up to enact new requirements allowing Early ETOPS. Even if the regulators were to enact the new requirements, there was no guarantee that Boeing would be able to design, manufacture, and test an airplane that would comply with the new requirements in time for the promised delivery of the airplanes to the customer airlines. It was indeed a great challenge, an audacious step!

Many in the media called Boeing's promise of Early ETOPS unprecedented and risky. Even the FAA's associate administrator for regulation and certification, Tony Broderick, the person who would be ultimately responsible for granting Boeing and the US airlines the ETOPS approval, echoed Dean Thornton's sentiments: "Boeing has taken on an enormous task; one that has never before been attempted in trying to get 180-minute ETOPS immediately for three different engine/airframe combinations."[3]

Some in the industry wondered why Boeing had taken such a risk. After all, Boeing dominated the airplane industry. In 1990, Airbus was barely making a dent.

Phil Condit, the executive vice president who ran the 777 program at the time, characterized the 777 strategy as an "offensive strategy" and not a "defensive one."[4]

Boeing hoped to secure its future with the 777. Opting for 180-minute Early ETOPS would force Boeing, engine manufacturers, and its other partners to design and build a very reliable airplane, an airframe-engine combination that would be easy to operate and maintain. It also required its support products to be mature.

* * *

In 1988, when Boeing was thinking of a 767 derivative to compete with the MD-11, A330, and A340, it launched an internal study to explore an alternative to the in-service experience requirement for ETOPS approval. The objective was to consider all aspects of airplane design, test, and customer support (documentation and training) to attain 180-minute ETOPS Type Design Approval for the airplane and the Operational Approval for the airline at initial entry. The study team concluded that 180 at entry would be feasible and documented that in the 767-X Early ETOPS Plan.

Boeing executives agreed with the team's findings. Accordingly, on July 6, 1989, Phil Condit issued a policy that any new or derivative twin-airplane program would support 180-minute ETOPS at entry.

By early 1990, we had developed detailed plans and proposals that would lead to 180-minute ETOPS at the initial delivery to airline. However, even though the airplane might be approved for 180-minute ETOPS, we were not sure if the airlines would seek 180-minute authority at entry or would apply for only 120 minutes and request 180 minutes after some months of operation.

* * *

Analysis of in-service data showed that achieving a certain level of reliability was not a technology issue but a design and test process issue. Analysis of the engine and the peripheral system data also showed that controlling the IFSD of an engine was not a design and test priority in the early 1980s. The engine failure rates could be low, average, or high. It was more the luck of the draw. Some engines achieved the level of IFSD required for ETOPS while others needed design changes after service entry. One would find out the level of reliability only by having the engines in actual operation. Therefore, it was logical for the regulators to focus on the in-service experience.

The 777 would start with a fundamental difference. It had some basic ground rules. No single failure in an engine would cause an IFSD of an engine, and no single failure of an airplane system would cause an "air interruption." An air interruption essentially means the flight did not get to its planned destination. It could have diverted to an alternate airport en route or turned back to the airport of departure.

We used the budgeting concept to manage the IFSD and air interruption rate. Similar to staying within a household budget, once we know how much money there is, we can figure out how to spend the money for different things and be within the allotted budget. In the same manner, engineers designing the engine knew what they had to meet, and they knew all the subsystems that contributed to that overall level and the components that made up the subsystems. Therefore, in the end, engineers could establish the reliability level they had to meet at the lowest component level.

The designers could meet the "failure budget" by making sure the component met the reliability criteria or by adding a backup component. But the backup component added weight and cost; engineers would add weight only if they could not improve the reliability of the existing component by enhancing the design.

At the initial design stage, we established the desired IFSD rates for the engines and air interruption rates for the airplane systems. For example, the total budget for IFSD could be two IFSDs for every 100,000 hours of engine operation, and, based on the lessons learned from previous airplanes, the allocation for the engine manufacturers could be 85% or 1.7 IFSDs for every 100,000 hours of engine operation.

Through analysis and test, engine manufacturers would be required to show that their design would meet the allotted IFSD budget. The remaining 15% or 0.3 IFSD would be allotted to airplane systems that could contribute to the shutting down of an engine. For example, out of 0.3, the budget for the flight deck could be 0.2 IFSD.

Similarly, the designers had to stay within an allocated budget for the air interruption rate. For example, the designers of the airplane's navigation system would be required to show that their system would not contribute to more than 30 air interruptions per million flights.

Boeing believed it could certify an airplane for 180-minute ETOPS at entry. But what it believed was not as important as what the regulators believed.

* * *

Because we were trying to win the industry support, we were upfront and shared what we knew. We had no secrets when it came to ETOPS. We never missed an opportunity to share the rationale behind the feasibility of 180-minute ETOPS at entry and how we planned to design and build an airplane that would meet the stringent requirements of ETOPS. Further, we discussed the changes in our support products and airline programs that would ensure the high standards required of ETOPS operators.

Boeing organized its first symposium on Early ETOPS at the Museum of Flight in Seattle for November 8 and 9, 1989. All the ETOPS experts attended. We shared our proposal for ETOPS at entry. The representatives from the pilot unions, various airlines, and the FAA spoke.

Normally, unions are associated with confronting management for more money, better benefits, or working conditions for their members. Pilot unions are no different. A former head of the Air Line Pilots Association (ALPA) supposedly told United Airlines during the union's negotiation, "We don't want to kill the golden goose. We just want to choke it by the neck until it gives us every last egg."[5]

The unions also ensure that any new rule or legislation does not adversely affect its membership. ALPA is the biggest pilot union in the United States. It had a significant impact in shaping ETOPS.

Although ALPA had opposed the basic concept of ETOPS when the idea was first proposed in the early 1980s, over the years ALPA had grown comfortable with the concept. Pilots liked the stringent dispatch requirements, planning for alternates, and the special attention given by the airline to the ETOPS fleet. ALPA strongly supported the FAA's existing requirement for in-service experience, what the pilot union called "prove and move."

While addressing "Pilots' Perspective on Future ETOPS," ALPA expressed confidence that Boeing could possibly design and deliver a "gold-plated" airplane. Nevertheless, it insisted that even the best gold-plated aircraft must "prove" itself in service before it could "move" forward on ETOPS.

It objected to any change in the "prove and move" concept with the airlines. It believed the airlines had to go through a learning curve within the lower risk environment before venturing to ETOPS. ALPA viewed in-service experience as the only true measure of an airline's ability to perform in the ETOPS environment. It was amenable to shortening the in-service requirement but not to zero.

Having acknowledged that Boeing could probably build an ETOPS-capable airliner, ALPA read a list of enhancements it wanted to see in Boeing's latest design. Because the symposium was in November, ALPA called it their "Christmas wish list." It called for enhancement in almost all airplane systems: communications, flight management computers (FMC), engine indicating and crew alerting systems, autopilot, engines, electrical, fuel systems, flight controls, air-conditioning and pressurization, and auxiliary power unit (APU).

Several airlines that had been conducting ETOPS for a number of years shared their early problems and suggested improvements. Airlines generally supported the our initiative of 180-minute Early ETOPS.

Tony Broderick led the FAA team. Even though he reported to the administrator, a political appointee, in reality Broderick would have the ultimate say on the 180-minute Early ETOPS. His people in the Certification Branch would be responsible for the ETOPS Type Design Approval, while the ones in the Flight Standards Branch would be responsible for the airline's ETOPS Operational Approval.

Broderick, a physics major, began his FAA career in the early 1970s and moved through the ranks at a fast pace. It was under his watch that ETOPS became a reality. Broderick was highly respected in the aviation industry and carried a lot of clout.

The FAA handled the Early ETOPS issue diplomatically. It did not give anything away but at the same time kept the door open.

The FAA told the audience that the FAA as a regulatory authority would keep an open mind toward developments in both technology and human factors programs, which could affect ETOPS criteria. The FAA acknowledged that the improvements in design, materials, testing, and personnel training could lead to changes in the criteria for granting airworthiness and Operational Approval to conduct ETOPS. It was important that the FAA not only recognize but also encourage such improvements. But the FAA cautioned that the overall goal of the approval process was to ensure that operations were conducted safely and with a high degree of reliability from their inception.

The FAA believed that the demonstrated performance was a basic tenet of the FARs. Before granting ETOPS, the FAA required a demonstration that the airframe-engine combination and the airline achieved the required levels of performance. By requiring a period of in-service experience, the FAA would be able to evaluate the performance in actual operations.

Broderick told the audience, "The FAA believes that in-service experience requirements have served us well over the past five years. Airframe-engine combination experience has enabled us to identify and rectify a number of problems prior to approving ETOPS operation. The majority of the problems can be categorized into six basic areas: control system malfunctions, crew indicating/alerting system malfunctions, fuel and lubrication system malfunctions, rotating machinery malfunctions (i.e., fan blades, bearings), miscellaneous engine buildup system malfunctions, and maintenance implicated problems. In each of these areas problems have been uncovered and solutions incorporated to improve reliability to levels which are adequate for ETOPS. We have observed this to be a normal maturing process for an engine and airplane design. Doing without this period of maturation is quite a challenge!"

He continued, "Operator in-service experience has also been instrumental in giving the FAA confidence that the operator's maintenance, dispatch, and flight crew training programs and operating procedures are satisfactory for ETOPS and that its personnel have acquired sufficient experience and expertise in dealing with aircraft systems and with programs designed to support ETOPS operations. Eliminating this phase cannot be done without thought, preparation, and analysis."

The symposium made it clear that we had a lot of work ahead.

* * *

Reliability of the engines was a major part of the ETOPS program. To improve its sales offering, Boeing was keen on having engines from all three major engine manufacturers: Pratt & Whitney, Rolls-Royce, and GE. Being a twin, the airplane required extremely powerful engines. A twin requires engines that are nearly three times more powerful than engines on a quad to lift the same weight off the ground.

The FAA's certification regulation requires the manufacturer to show that the airplanes can take off even when one engine fails at the most critical point during takeoff. Hence, for an airplane that needs a total of 90,000 pounds of thrust at takeoff, each engine on a quad must generate at least 30,000 pounds (or more to meet the climb requirement), and a twin would need at least 90,000 pounds for each engine. The twins that Boeing was planning to launch required engines that would generate thrust levels of nearly 80,000 pounds.

In the late 1980s, both Pratt & Whitney and Rolls-Royce had engines in operation with the growth potential to support the thrust levels required of the Boeing 777, but GE did not have an engine that had the potential for growth. But GE was prepared to launch a whole family of high-thrust engines, called the GE90 series, if Boeing went ahead with the 777.

In 1990, GE launched the GE90 series, an engine that would have 90,000 pounds of thrust as the basic capability. The engine's core was designed in such a way that, if required, the engine could be developed to generate around 120,000 pounds of thrust—a huge thrust level by any standard. GE badly wanted to participate in Boeing's new big twin, and was prepared to derate the GE90 to around 76,000 pounds of thrust to accommodate the initial versions of the new big twin.

GE designed its engines in anticipation of future growth of the 777. Neither Pratt & Whitney nor Rolls-Royce had the growth potential to extend the thrust levels significantly. If these engine manufacturers wanted to be in the extended versions of future Boeing twins, they would have to invest heavily in new designs or concede the market to GE.

* * *

The Early ETOPS symposiums were effective forums for the exchange of information. Boeing decided to have another one from May 15 through 17, 1990, at a hotel in downtown Seattle.

On May 16, 1990, Broderick opened his speech with a remark that had a profound impact on ETOPS. He told the audience, "ETOPS is, in my opinion, one of two programs in recent times which have significantly improved aviation safety. The other program deals with aging aircraft." Some of us who were intimately involved with ETOPS were aware of it, but having the most influential regulator in aviation say it in front of the industry was valuable. Undoubtedly, this was music to the ears of Boeing senior executives.

ETOPS and the Aging Aircraft program both had a cooperative approach to problem solving by continually and openly exchanging ideas and concepts. Broderick credited this cooperation among the airlines, manufacturers, labor unions, and regulatory authorities for creating a list of problems and developing early and effective solutions.

We shared the facts and data with the industry groups on a continuing basis, and had met with the FAA several times since the last symposium in November 1989. The FAA was still exploring the issue and had not come to any conclusion. At the May 1990 symposium, Broderick said, "The FAA is still very much in the study phase on Early ETOPS, and we are learning, like all of you ... I emphasize that the Early ETOPS concept has potential, though it is not without its special requirements."

When Boeing declared its intent to pursue 180-minute Early ETOPS at entry for the airlines in addition to the 180-minute Early ETOPS for the airframe-engine combination, Broderick indicated his surprise with the Boeing position. He was not quite ready to sign up to such an ambitious goal, but he left the door open.

He said, "In the spirit of open dialog and a willingness to work with our colleagues, I certainly will not rule out the possibility that, five years from now, we will be smart enough to know how to do it. But in 1990, I wouldn't sign any contracts to buy or sell an airplane with 180-minute ETOPS approval out of the box as a condition. We've got a lot more work to do before we cross that bridge, most of it focusing on operational issues and validation confidence."

* * *

United Airlines, with 34 firm orders and an equal number of options, was the launch customer. United wanted the ability to operate the 777 on 180-minute ETOPS routes from day one.

The airline selected Pratt & Whitney engines. These engines had some commonality with United engines on the 747-400s and the 767-300ERs. Some in United believed that this would help their engineers quickly resolve problems that might crop up at entry. The strategy had the potential to benefit the airline's 180-minute Early ETOPS approval.

To ensure that the 777 was service ready and qualified for Early ETOPS, Boeing and United changed the way they did business. Phil Condit, Boeing executive vice president and general manager, New Airplane Program; and James Guyette, United Airlines executive vice president of operations, signed a handwritten agreement on October 15, 1990, in Chicago. The leaders committed their teams to work together to design, produce, and introduce a service ready airplane with the best dispatch reliability and greatest customer appeal in the industry.

Boeing and United set the tone for all the 777 partners. DBSTs and concurrent engineering became the norm.

In support of the Boeing, Pratt & Whitney, and United "working together" relationship, United opened a dedicated facility, the 777 Coordination Center, at its Maintenance Operations Center near San Francisco International Airport. The center was akin to a nerve center within the airline. It managed and controlled the early planning necessary to ensure that the 777 was service ready and reliable from the day of delivery of the airplane to the airline. The center, through the "working together" teams, worked closely with Boeing and Pratt & Whitney.

* * *

Having engines from all three engine manufacturers increased the marketability of the 777.

British Airways opted for the GE90, and Cathay Pacific selected Rolls-Royce to power its 777s. British sought 180-minute Early ETOPS, because it would be competing with United on the same transatlantic market, and it did not want to be constrained by a lower ETOPS approval time.

Cathay, at the time of the airplane order, did not have immediate plans to introduce the airplane on ETOPS. The routes where it wanted to operate the 777s initially did not require ETOPS, but Cathay had plans to fly the airplane on its Australian route where 120-minute ETOPS would suffice. Cathay was interested in having a service-ready airplane and wanted to work together with Boeing and Rolls-Royce as if it were going to begin 180-minute ETOPS routes from day one.

* * *

Boeing, like Airbus, used more "fly by wire." It decreased weight by eliminating long cables and pulleys. But unlike Airbus, Boeing retained the pilot's situational awareness in the flight deck.

Although, in addition to saving weight, Airbus approach opened up more space around the pilot's seating area, the Airbus fly-by-wire system provided no mechanical feedback to the flight crew. For example, with the move of the side-stick, the computers automatically moved flight controls without moving the control levers in the flight deck. Further, since the two side-sticks for the two pilots were not linked, the system did not provide cues of the other pilot's inputs.

But, Boeing strongly believed in the importance of giving the flight crew direct visual awareness of the activity of the fly-by-wire computers. Boeing spent time and money to design systems that would back-drive the control columns, rudder pedals, and throttles and feed back information to the flight crew as if they were operating with the old cable and pulley system.

Additionally, while the Airbus design did not allow the pilots to override the airplane computer's protection envelope, Boeing made it harder for this to occur. But the pilots could override the computers and had the ultimate full authority on the airplane's capability in an emergency.

The electrical system of the 777 had sufficient built-in capability to power all essential systems during any foreseeable electrical system failure. The backup electrical generator had four times more capability than the one on the 767. This additional capability allowed more functionality if both the electrical generators failed.

In the cockpit, the 777 had new flat panels for the main digital displays instead of the conventional cathode ray tubes. The new panels were thinner and stayed cooler.

To increase brake life, the airplane was designed so that only four of the six wheels would brake at any one time during taxi operations. The system automatically rotated braking among the six wheels.

* * *

We incorporated Early ETOPS requirements into the basic airframe and engine design requirements. We placed an unprecedented emphasis on the total system design issues and early identification and resolution of potential problems.

We considered historic failure modes and operational concerns. We thoroughly analyzed lessons from previous programs, early problems, and other in-service problems. The database included lessons from other airplanes besides the ones built by Boeing. We added redundancies and capabilities to basic designs to comply with Early ETOPS demands.

The engines received a great deal of attention. For example, Pratt & Whitney analyzed IFSD data points to identify the causes, which were grouped separately. The analysis showed percentage contributions from the oil systems, engine fuel and control systems, core engine, and equipment around the engine. These in-depth analyses led to design upgrades on the Pratt & Whitney engine. As an example, to cut down the number of diversions due to false indications of IFSD, the designers added such things as dual redundant oil pressure transmitters, dual redundant oil temperature probes, dual oil filter elements, and oil indication fault discriminators.

Engines are important, but other airplane systems are also equally important. We addressed each and every one of the lessons learned. Every lesson learned in the database showed what had happened, the cause, and how that problem was addressed in the 777 design.

For example, the lessons from the 767 Integrated Drive Generators (IDG) failures resulted in many changes to the 777 IDG design. Boeing designed the 777 IDG to operate at lower operating temperatures. It had a vented oil system and a crack-resistant terminal block cover. Based on the lessons learned, engineers designed different-sized connectors so that maintenance personnel could not make a wrong connection. In some cases, the designers made the connector of different lengths so it would be physically impossible to make a wrong connection.

* * *

ETOPS approval under the in-service method required accumulation of 250,000 engine hours on the world fleet. Based on the projected use rate of the early 777s, to replicate a high cycle engine, the engine manufacturers added a 3,000-cycle engine test program. This testing would be done with the complete propulsion system, which included the basic engine from the engine manufacturer and all the peripherals. Boeing or its other partners designed the peripheral systems that attached to the basic engine.

During development testing and the 3,000-cycle tests, engine rotors were intentionally unbalanced to twice the acceptable production limits to replicate wear and tear after a few years of actual operation. The engines were exposed to high-vibration environments.

ETOPS rules required a backup power source in the unlikely event of an electrical power failure; the APU was used as one of the sources of the backup power on the 777. The APU is a little engine normally used on the ground for air-conditioning, keeping the passengers comfortable when there is no other source of power on the airplane. On the twins, the design allows the APU also to be used in flight, if needed.

The APU incorporated advances in design to address the in-service problems encountered in previous models. Based on lessons learned, it incorporated new design features. To duplicate years of in-service experience, the APU had to undergo 3,000 cycles of testing, mostly at a cold Alaskan test site. For example, to ensure that the APU would start in flight at normal cruising altitudes after being cold soaked for several hours in frigid temperatures, it underwent hundreds of cold soak starts at the test site. The APU was designed for 99% in-flight start reliability.

* * *

Analysis of lessons learned data showed if the problem originated with design, manufacturing, assembly, or maintenance, and which kind of test would have exposed the problem early on.

All airplane systems underwent scrutinized tests in various test vehicles. Boeing heavily invested in the test vehicles.

Besides the independent test vehicles, the Integrated Airplane Systems Laboratory (IASL) included four integration laboratories for testing a number of systems working together: the System Integration Laboratory (SIL), Flight Controls Test Rig (FCTR), Engineering Simulator Cabs, and Electrical Power Systems Laboratory. These integrated laboratories tested the actual airplane systems working together, fully integrated, as they would be on the airplane. Boeing also had an integrated Cabin Management Systems and Passenger Cabin Engineering laboratories.

First, we tested the airplane systems individually. Then we tested them together with other systems to duplicate the way systems would interact with one another in an actual airplane. For example, if the system passed the stand-alone test, it would go to the SIL. To make the testing realistic, complete aircraft AC/DC power was available for use in the SIL.

Besides the six airplanes on normal flight test for the three airframe-engine programs, one airplane was dedicated to each airframe-engine combination just to validate the Early ETOPS program. Each airplane dedicated to the Early ETOPS program underwent a 1,000-Cycle Validation Program (CVP).

These CVPs were a mix of long and short flights operated at various altitudes in different weather conditions, in hot and cold areas, and with different types of fuel and oil. The CVP also included APU altitude starts, including long cold soak.

Each airplane on the program flew for at least 500 cycles with engines that had undergone at least 2,000 cycles of testing on the ground, which represented operation with a worn-out engine. We also conducted tests with engines that were intentionally unbalanced to duplicate one year's exposure to vibration in service. For a number of cycles, the airplanes were operated with only the backup electrical system, simulating the failure of both generators.

Based on the lessons learned from the initial five years of the 767 ETOPS operations, each 777 airframe-engine combination conducted eight cycles of 180-minute diversions with one engine at maximum continuous thrust (MCT). MCT is the higher thrust that is set on the remaining engine when one of the engines on the airplane fails.

To the best of my knowledge, this level of investment in testing the airplane, engines, and their systems and components had never been done on any airplane program, at Boeing or at any other airplane manufacturer.

* * *

Besides the hardware, we also had to ensure that all the support products would be mature and service ready to support the airline's Early ETOPS program. We incorporated lessons learned from previous programs to improve the support products in a manner similar to the use of lessons learned to design better systems.

On the previous programs, the manufacturer validated only a small portion of its support products before handing them over to the airline.

It was not unusual for Boeing to revise many procedures, tools, and support equipment based on the input from the airlines.

On the 777, to make sure everything worked as advertised, we validated procedures, tools, and equipment that the airline would use in the first couple of years. Because the Boeing and airline support teams were integral parts of the 777 DBSTs, they were jointly responsible for ensuring better maintainability, dispatch flexibility, and ease of operation of the airplane.

An example of dispatch flexibility is the MEL. Airlines are allowed to dispatch a flight with an airplane system inoperative if the MEL permits it. Whenever possible, the airlines try to fix the problems, but if they are under a time constraint, they will dispatch the flight under the MEL and schedule the repair later. Hence, it is in the airline's best interest to have a flexible MEL. Boeing considered the MEL flexibility during the basic design itself and validated the majority of the critical procedures during the test phase.

The airlines worked closely with Boeing to develop the flight crew training program and procedures. The pilot qualification program included rigorous task analysis and much validation of the procedures. We used engineering simulators, FMC Labs (laboratories), the SIL, FCTR, and flight-test airplanes, including the airplanes on the 1,000 CVP, to validate the procedures. Whenever feasible, to ensure similarity with the airplane, Boeing incorporated actual airplane hardware into the airplane simulators.

Similar to the flight crew training program, we developed a maintenance training curriculum with the airline. We designed the courseware so that airlines could use it with minimal or no customization. We increased the emphasis on hands-on training, which could be done by computer-based training (CBT), maintenance simulators, and even on the airplanes used for 1,000 CVP.

We trained Boeing mechanics who maintained the 1,000 CVP airplanes, using the same training program that would be used by the airline. The 1,000 CVP included 90 cycles during which the airline would fly and maintain the airplane.

During the 90 CVP, United flew to several US destinations; the British flew to European, Middle Eastern, and South American destinations; and Cathay flew to Asian and Australian destinations.

Boeing had learned from previous programs that it spent considerable time after the first delivery correcting the maintenance procedures. While trying to maintain the airplane or engine, the airlines would find that a procedure did not work. For the airlines to gain 180-minute Early ETOPS and service readiness, it was important that the maintenance manuals contained minimal or no errors. At a minimum, Boeing planned to validate all the procedures the airlines were likely to perform during the first two years.

We verified maintenance procedures, most of which were simple. Those that were more intricate were physically validated. The engineers determined the best vehicle to validate the procedure, which could be any of the test vehicles, including the actual airplane at Boeing, the actual engine at the engine manufacturer, or the actual system at the supplier. The procedures included maintenance test, maintenance practices, and various procedures such as removal and installation, servicing, inspection and check, and fault isolation.

The program placed a great emphasis on the maintainability of the airplane. For the first time in the history of Boeing, a position of "chief mechanic" was created similar to a "chief pilot." The Boeing chief mechanic was the airline's advocate for maintainability.

* * *

CATIA made a huge difference in the maintainability of the 777. For example, it discovered that a human mechanic would not be able to reach the red navigation light on the roof of the airplane to change the bulb. Without this feature, Boeing would not have found out about the bulb until late in the airplane program. It could have been found during a mockup or in the final assembly. It could have even gone unnoticed until some airline called to say, "We have a plane with 300 passengers stuck in Paris because we cannot change a light bulb."

CATIA could evaluate the access of a component and ensure relatively trouble-free maintenance for the airline. The CATIA-human model could climb inside the three-dimensional images and act as a mechanic. The model simulated the physical motion. It could construct an area inside the airplane to show the component removal path, which did not interfere with any other components or structure and reserved the required maintenance access space in design.

A variety of tools could be modeled in CATIA. Tools could be placed in any location and orientation on the airplane. The required sweep of the tool could be analyzed to ensure adequate space during design.

Neither the airline nor Boeing wanted to repeat some of the surprises from previous airplane programs. For instance, while attempting to replace a valve in the engine pylon in one of the airplanes, airlines discovered that the access hole was large enough for the valve or a hand, but not both. On the 777 program, CATIA caught such anomalies.

Boeing was proud of CATIA. Part of winning the ETOPS battle was convincing the detractors that Early ETOPS would result in an airplane equal to or better than the one that went through the in-service experience. Early participation of the airlines was immensely beneficial to the program.

Because the 777 has a much bigger engine than the 747, the wings had to be raised so that the engines cleared the ground with adequate margin. As a result, the fueling station on the wing of the 777 was located 30 inches higher than the similar station on the 747. The designers did not think much of it until an airline person pointed out that this would force his company to replace all its fuel trucks. This would be an expensive proposition. Because it was caught early in the design, the engineers found another location for the fueling station on the 777 wing that would be at the same height as on the 747.

Whenever possible, the airlines prompted the 777 designers to use the tools and support equipment that they already had to service other airplanes in their fleet.

Even a simple design change can make a big difference for maintainability. Mechanics working in the most congested part of airplanes—the electronics and electrical bay under the cockpit—complained that they had to hold a flashlight between their teeth because the bay door blocked the light. Installing simple latches to keep the door open and repositioning the lights eliminated this potential problem on the 777.

The classic problem, which the media reported on extensively, was when American Airlines persuaded Boeing to redesign the cover plates for reading lamps. If a reading light over a passenger's seat was burned out, nothing could be done except by a mechanic with a screwdriver. With the redesign in the 777, anyone, including the cabin crew, could change the bulb.

The media also was transfixed with the 777 program's superlatives—its digital design, CATIA, and the use of the largest cluster of mainframe computers in the world. The finished plane would roll out through doors almost as big as a football field. The enormous factory itself, at Everett, Washington, which already had the 747 and the 767, would increase to the size of 76 football fields to accommodate the 777 assembly line. Its twin engines would be the largest and most powerful ever built. The cowl of the GE90 engines would be as big as the girth of a 737 fuselage. Each engine was nearly 50% more powerful than the engines on the most popular big commercial airplane of the time, the jumbo 747.

The media attention on the 777 and Boeing's claims of superior designs probably did not amuse Airbus. After all, Airbus had declared that the A330s and the A340s did not represent a technology goal; the goal was to increase market share. To the best of my knowledge, Airbus did not invest in the intense scrubbing of the lessons-learned data to enhance the design, maintainability, or service readiness to the same extent as Boeing on the 777.

* * *

Airbus publicly attacked the 777 Early ETOPS program. Its slogan was, "Experience simply cannot be manufactured in a laboratory."

Airbus was out to convince the pilot unions, passenger organizations, airlines, and, undoubtedly, the regulators that, to qualify for the 180-minute ETOPS authority, Boeing should accumulate a couple of years of in-service data and prove the engine and system reliability.

Airbus claimed that the proposed 777 test programs would not be able to duplicate problems that happen on actual flights. For example, it argued that Boeing would not be able to simulate the actual vibration or gust effects, problems associated with fluid or dust contamination, system problems associated with temperature variations or icing conditions, and lightning or electromagnetic interference effects.

It also claimed that Boeing would not be able to duplicate the chafing of wiring, premature bearing wear, and potential airline-related maintenance problems. Airbus insinuated that the airplanes on the 1,000 CVP would be nursed with kid gloves, which, it claimed, would be a far cry from the rough and tumble airline operational environment.

Airbus tried to create concern in the pilot community by attacking Boeing's lack of experience in the fly-by-wire technology. In addition, the 777 used new flat panels for the main digital displays instead of the conventional cathode ray tubes. Airbus told the pilot unions that the new flat panel displays were not a mature technology and that Boeing would be unwise to rely so heavily on an unproven technology.

We did not take Airbus lightly. We looked carefully into every comment Airbus made and fine-tuned the program if we found such action justified.

Because the A330 was for medium range, Airbus continued its attack on the feasibility of twins—namely the 777—for long-range operations. It released studies that claimed that on long-ranges a twin would cost more for engine maintenance, more for airframe maintenance, and that total direct operating cost for a twin would be higher than for a quad. It concluded that the numbers vindicated the decision by Airbus to produce a twin-engine A330 for medium ranges and the four-engine A340 for long ranges, each carefully optimized for its respective mission. It criticized Boeing for distorting the truth.

Airbus reminded the industry that Boeing originally rejected the need for a widebody twin in the early A300 days, and then built the 767. Boeing rejected the need for a 300-seater aircraft when the A330, the A340, and the MD-11s were launched, and then built the 777. It left the industry guessing by adding, Boeing today rejects the need for four engines on long-range aircraft…

* * *

While Airbus tried to convince the industry and the regulators to deny ETOPS to the 777, it was vying for ETOPS approval at entry into service for its own twin, the A330. Even though the A330/340 program had a three-year lead, Airbus decided to bring the A340 into service first. This delayed the A330 introduction. Hence, Airbus also sought changes to the ETOPS requirements to allow the A330 180-minute ETOPS approval at the time of 777 certification.

Obviously, Airbus believed that its approach was more reasonable and safer.

Airbus promoted what it called the "technology transfer" process to accelerate the ETOPS approval for its A330. It claimed, since the A340 and the A330 were practically the same airplane except for the number and type of engines, the A340 experience could be transferred to the A330. The A340 was going to be in airline operation for a year before the A330 entered service. The in-service experience of the A340 would be credited toward the ETOPS approval of its A330.

Airbus went for a step approach. It requested 90-minute ETOPS approval for its airframe-engine at service entry, followed by 120-minute after 25,000 fleetwide engine hours, and 180-minute after 50,000 fleet-wide engine hours.

Regarding the engines, it argued that the engines on the A330 were close derivatives of other engines in the Airbus family and thus did not need extensive experience.

Its earliest customers either did not need ETOPS or would not need the longer authority until the end of 1994 or beyond. Generally, Airbus marketing and sales policy with the airlines was to promote the four-engine A340 on routes that required longer ETOPS.

Although we were aware of the inadequacies of the A330 ETOPS by the process of "technology transfer" from the A340 to the A330, we felt attacking the A330 ETOPS program could further inflame the situation and that would not be in Boeing's best interest. Rather than responding to the Airbus public attacks, we continued to reiterate the facts about the 777 program and the reasons why it qualified for 180-minute Early ETOPS. But it did not stop the media from looking to stir up the discord. That is what sold newspapers.

* * *

Many Boeing personnel cringed every time they saw Byron Acohido's reporting in *The Seattle Times*. He knew how to make the headlines catchy and push Boeing executives' blood pressure to the stratosphere.

In "Boeing's Lobbying over 777 Blasted," Acohido wrote that the Boeing Early ETOPS campaign had "touched off a storm of protest in the aviation community." Quoting representatives from different organizations, he said, "Not coincidentally, the proposed changes should help boost 777 sales. This grates pilots and passenger-safety advocates, who contend the flying public's margin of safety is being eroded primarily to boost the aerospace companies' profits. ... 'They are pushing the edge of the envelope, and it's a pure marketing ploy on their part,' ...

'The quicker you can make the case that the 777 can fly from Seattle to Tokyo, the bigger the market becomes,' … 'No amount of testing can take the place of real life, day-in and day-out use. Before we go putting a couple of hundred people out over some ocean, we think it's important that everything possible is done to assure the aircraft will, in fact, be reliable on those routes.'"[6]

In April 1991, in another equally catchy article titled "Boeing Co. Pushing the 'Envelope'- Could Early ETOPS Erode 777's Margin of Safety?" Acohido blasted the 777. He wrote that the eagerness by Boeing to fast-track a 180-minute ETOPS rating was pushing the airplane to the edge of the safety envelope. Having the airplane designed in CATIA would further add to the uncertainty. The article stressed the importance of in-service experience with an airline.

In the same article, Acohido quoted ALPA generously: "What Boeing is doing with backup systems, enhanced cockpit systems and just taking to heart the laundry list of ideas we've given them, and many other people have given them, is just phenomenal [but] … We're still very skeptical … No one doubts that Boeing is quite capable of building a highly reliable airplane. But the airplane hasn't been built yet that hasn't developed some problems after going into actual service … Boeing is trying to anticipate all the problems and come up to the FAA and say, 'We think we've anticipated all the problems, how about giving us credit?' … That's difficult, if not impossible, to do … They're going to put one golden test airplane through the test program, but who knows what that tells you about the first few planes off the production floor."[7]

Acohido's coverage in *The Seattle Times* based on the quotes from selected industry representatives had an eerie similarity to the Airbus message. In addition, we soon found that the article had made its way around the world, through either the courtesy of Airbus or the local publications that carried the article from Boeing's home base. This was not good for Boeing.

Boeing was pleasantly surprised when ALPA refuted Acohido's 777 coverage in *The Seattle Times*.

In May 1991, a couple of weeks after the Acohido article, *The Seattle Times* printed the letter from ALPA. In the letter, titled "Negative Slant— Setting the Record Straight on Boeing's New 777 Airliner," ALPA took strong exception to the tone of Acohido's April 21 article on Boeing and its new 777 airliner. ALPA said, "Certainly, Boeing is attempting, with early Extended Twin Operations (ETOPS) certification, to achieve an aircraft maturity and reliability earlier than previous models. Present federal regulations set guidelines for a much more elaborate in-service evaluation. However, these same regulations allow for reductions in such requirements based on credible experience and technical performance. Boeing is doing nothing that we deem inappropriate or smacks of 'corporate bravado,' a term used in the article." ALPA added, "... he [Byron Acohido] left the reader with the impression Boeing is moving in a direction contrary to the best interests of the industry and the wishes of groups such as ALPA. That is not the case."

The ALPA letter went on to say, "There is no 'storm of protest' over the issue of Early ETOPS, as the article indicated. There is only a genuine concern that Boeing heeds all the issues involved. We also do not view the proposed process 'derisively' as the article suggests. We are pleased with the unprecedented early involvement of major parties to the certification process. What Boeing is attempting to do is very difficult and it remains to be seen if it will be successful in achieving full, Early ETOPS certification. We at ALPA and others in the industry will continue to provide input to the process. With Early ETOPS as a goal, the 777 certification process will be more thorough and the 777 will consequently be a far better product for the effort."[8]

Even though the letter did not get the same level of coverage as the original article, it helped set the record straight.

* * *

An annual symposium on 777 ETOPS had become standard. As usual, Boeing invited members across the aviation industry to its June 1991 ETOPS symposium.

By 1991, we had made much progress on the 777 and ETOPS. Airlines were jumping on ETOPS with twins all around the world. US airlines were opening all kinds of routes from the mainland to Europe, and twins had taken over the Atlantic market.

Symposiums allowed Boeing to make sure we had not overlooked anything that we would come to regret later. Diverse opinions, even though critical to Boeing, were welcome.

At the symposium, Tom Edwards, Jr., who is probably one of the world's leading experts on the airplane maintenance issues, presented a paper on behalf of United on how it had instituted ETOPS practices on the quads, the 747s, and how it was able to dramatically decrease the number of IFSDs it had on the airplane. With facts and data, Tom showed how ETOPS enhanced the overall safety and the reliability of airplane operations. I believe the data was helpful in assuaging the regulators' apprehension with Early ETOPS.

Various pilot unions attended the symposiums. ALPA reiterated its proposal for a step-by-step approach. Instead of the familiar "prove and move," this time ALPA wanted us to "walk with 120-minute ETOPS before we ran with the 180-minute." ALPA commended the 777 designs and what we were doing with the testing and support products. It believed this effort would lead to a product that would be better than any previous aircraft, but ALPA objected to ETOPS approval without minimal in-service experience.

The International Federation of Air Line Pilots Association (IFALPA), an international umbrella group for the world's pilot associations, said that even though IFALPA was initially opposed to the idea of ETOPS in the 1980s, pilots were generally comfortable with ETOPS. IFALPA attributed this comfort with ETOPS to the gradual and prudent extension of ETOPS authority. IFALPA appeared to echo Airbus sentiments and told the audience the 777 was a completely new aircraft, not a derivative, and was Boeing's first fly-by-wire aircraft. It even repeated the Airbus humor that the only similarity with existing Boeing aircraft was that the diameter of the engine cowling for the 777 would be comparable to the fuselage diameter of the 757. IFALPA expressed its disappointment with the regulatory authorities, principally the FAA and the European Joint Aviation Authorities (JAA).

At the launch of the A330/340 program, the goal of Airbus was to get 90-minute ETOPS at entry, followed by 120-minute and 180-minute after some in-service experience. But after 1991, Airbus changed its goal to 120-minute ETOPS at entry. The JAA was amenable to the request by Airbus for 120-minute ETOPS approval at entry followed by 180-minute after some in-service experience.

IFALPA concluded its speech by saying, "Although, at present, exact positions are unknown, it is understood that the FAA is considering 180-minute approval at entry into service. On the other hand, the JAA has indicated that it will probably approve 120 minutes. The Federation [IFALPA] believes that the JAA's proposal for 120-minute

ETOPS approval at entry into service is excessive and is truly shocked at the FAA's suggestion."

* * *

Unrelated to Boeing 777 efforts, a parallel activity had been going on between the US airlines and the FAA regarding new approaches for the operational in-service requirement for 180-minute ETOPS approval. America West wanted to start 757 operations to Hawaii from the mainland, but that required 180-minute ETOPS approval. According to the FAA requirement, an airline would be eligible for 180-minute ETOPS only after one year of experience at 120-minute ETOPS. America West was a domestic airline with many years of 757 experience, but it did not have any route where it could operate at 120-minute ETOPS.

To get around this classic Catch-22 situation, in the early 1990s the FAA issued an alternative to this one year of 120-minute ETOPS operational in-service requirements. It created a new approach called "Simulated ETOPS." This new approach allowed an airline to simulate ETOPS flight and maintenance processes and procedures while operating domestically on non-ETOPS routes.

Incidentally, even though America West was the initiator of the Simulated ETOPS method, United Airlines became the first to take advantage of this method to gain 180-minute ETOPS approval for its 757 for the Hawaii route. United was kind enough to invite me on the 757 final proving flight to Honolulu.

The acceptance of Simulated ETOPS was an early indication that the FAA was open to exploring alternative options.

* * *

Normally, in any organization the top management sets the tone for the entire enterprise. Broderick set that tone for the FAA on the 777 and Early ETOPS. Industry greatly admired his vision. His message at the 1991 symposium was: "FAA must continue to acknowledge and encourage developments which have been proven to enhance reliability at an early stage. ...We at the FAA are willing to listen. We are willing to observe and learn from experience. At the same time we also intend to fulfill our role as regulator."

The FAA had accepted the possibility of Early ETOPS, but it raised the bar very high. The FAA was working on requirements that were very stringent.

* * *

The final meeting of the operational side of ETOPS with the FAA in Washington, D.C., before we agreed on the plan for United's Early ETOPS was memorable. The FAA had given us a list of requirements to comply with in the next four years to ensure that Boeing products were mature enough to support United's 180-minute Early ETOPS. Since the meeting affected the future of Boeing and United, we had good representation from the airline. Additional attendees included FAA people from Denver and San Francisco, the two regions that controlled United's flight operations and maintenance; Seattle FAA, which would look at Boeing programs; FAA New England, who were responsible for Pratt engines; and the FAA representatives from the headquarters, who would make the ultimate decision. As the Boeing manager responsible for the operational side of ETOPS, I was in the hot seat. All eyes were on me, including my director's, who was there for moral support.

Roy Grimes, who had been active on the operational side of ETOPS, led the FAA team. Despite being a history major, Roy was very knowledgeable about aviation matters. Although he often had strong views, he was always open to new ideas. He would not hesitate to discard his proposal and embrace new approaches if he thought they made sense. The industry knew if we could convince Roy of the merits of our plan, we would succeed with the FAA. Roy had that much influence.

After giving an overview of the total program, I went through every item from the FAA's list and showed them how we were going to comply and what method of compliance we would use. Our process was very disciplined, with more than 80 "review gates." A review gate was a milestone-tracking plan; it allowed for the orderly tracking and documentation of specific requirements and their completion. It also minimized any last-minute surprises from either side.

After two days of the FAA's grilling, trying to pick the plan apart, Roy agreed that we had a good plan for the 180-minute Early ETOPS Operational Approval and that the FAA, Boeing, and United could proceed with the proposed plan.

We were very happy with the FAA's decision; we had cleared the first hurdle. My management was ecstatic. I was recognized as the "Employee of the Quarter." At the luncheon to celebrate the recognition, my director told the group of my peers that for my performance with the FAA in Washington, D.C., I actually deserved an Oscar!

We used the plan we had prepared for the FAA as a template to establish similar programs with the UK Civil Aviation Authority (CAA), the British equivalent to the US FAA, and with British Airways, the launch customer for the 777 with GE engines. We did the same with the Hong Kong Civil Aviation Department (CAD), Hong Kong's equivalent to the US FAA, and with Cathay Pacific, the launch customer for the 777 with Rolls-Royce engines.

* * *

Despite the FAA's decision, ALPA opposed 180-minute Early ETOPS for the airlines. It preferred United to fly non-ETOPS for six months, followed by six months at 120-minute ETOPS before going on to 180 minutes.

ALPA praised the JAA's approach for the A330 of allowing only 120 minutes at entry even though it would deny United the 120 minutes for the first six months.

ALPA believed Boeing could design and qualify the 777 for 180-minute Early ETOPS, but its concern was about the airline, in this instance, United Airlines—the 777 launch customer.

Some airline representatives felt that the ALPA stance on the 180-minute Early ETOPS for United Airlines might have more to do with dollars and cents than anything else. Apparently, there had been instances in the past when the concern for the safety of flight disappeared with an increase in flight allowances or a better pay packet. The conjecture was that ALPA wanted to keep the issue alive and did not want to forgo the chance to use the safety of Early ETOPS as a bargaining chip in future negotiations with United's management.

Aviation media supported the ALPA position. An *Aviation Week & Space Technology* (April 20, 1992) editorial pleaded, "Don't rush early ETOPS."

* * *

On the certification side, after considering the inputs from all the affected parties, the FAA concluded that 180-minute Early ETOPS for the airplane was technically feasible. On May 5, 1993, the FAA issued a set of requirements called "special conditions," which would permit the 777 up to 180-minute Early ETOPS if the manufacturer were able to show compliance. The requirements were stringent and had a few surprises, especially in the engine test arena.

Even after concluding that the 180-minute Early ETOPS for the airplane was technically feasible, Broderick was not confident that Boeing would be able to deliver 180-minute Early ETOPS as promised to customers.

Broderick said, "I will be surprised if by, say 1997, when you go through all three engines and all the initial delivery customers whether they [Boeing] will achieve all their goals. ... Remember, this isn't just Boeing. It's Boeing and General Electric and Pratt & Whitney and Rolls-Royce, not to mention all the thousands of suppliers they have. So I will be very surprised if it all works perfectly. On the other hand, if it does, I will be very pleasantly surprised."[9]

Boeing submitted its compliance plans. All that remained was for Boeing to prove it could accomplish what it promised. All Boeing wanted was a chance to prove it could do it, and now it had the chance.

* * *

At least on the US side, there was a path to the 180-minute Early ETOPS. Although the Europeans had created a path for the A330 to gain ETOPS from the outset, reportedly due to the intense Airbus pressure, they were reluctant to do the same for Boeing.

The FAA's decision must have rattled Airbus. It ratcheted its lobbying to the European regulators, pilot unions, and passenger organizations against Boeing's Early ETOPS program. Its basic message was that in-service experience could not be duplicated in test programs, and that Boeing's program was unsafe.

Because British Airways had selected the brand-new GE engines to power its 777s, Airbus found a fertile ground with the British Air Lines Pilots Association (BALPA). Here was an engine that would produce around 90,000 pounds of thrust and, according to Airbus, had no pedigree.

To combat the Airbus challenge, we accelerated our efforts in Europe. We had to convince the European regulators, the pilot unions, and the passenger organizations that what Boeing was attempting to do might be difficult and challenging, but it did not compromise safety in any way.

* * *

Unlike in the United States, IFALPA had a strong voice in Europe. Being an umbrella organization, it represented BALPA also. We were in London every few months to meet with IFALPA. GE accompanied us. Even though it was an IFALPA meeting, most of the attendees were actually from BALPA. The meetings were held at the BALPA offices at Heathrow.

The first meeting was tense. IFALPA intently listened to our presentations, but we did not make much progress. It appeared as if there was a credibility issue. It was probably at our second meeting when one of the members asked why Boeing had reservations about sharing IFSD data. That was a bit of a surprise to us; we had no reservations about sharing data. We had been open with the industry and regulators. Of course, whenever we shared data we blanked the data so an airline could not be identified. What was important was what happened when, how, and the findings or resolutions. Apparently, unknown to us, a few years earlier IFALPA had asked to see our record on IFSDs and Boeing had declined to share the data. Obviously, IFALPA concluded that Boeing was trying to hide something, and hence, the credibility issue arose.

With no hesitation, we agreed to provide the IFSD data that IFALPA wanted. There was suddenly warmth in the room.

In addition to meeting with us, IFALPA frequently met with Airbus. IFALPA was trying to understand the issues better and to separate facts from fiction.

IFALPA representatives visited Seattle a few times to ride the engineering simulators and witness the tests on various test vehicles and in the FMC Labs, SIL, and other facilities. IFALPA scrutinized Boeing plans and programs.

By early 1993, IFALPA was impressed with the rigor and depth of the 777 Early ETOPS program. The only concern it had was if Boeing would be able to pull it off. At its June 29–July 1, 1993, annual meeting in Brighton, England, IFALPA stated to its membership that Boeing had taken a tremendous gamble in trying to achieve 180-minute ETOPS at entry into service and that the FAA requirements in the "special conditions" were stringent.

Boeing had succeeded in conveying its message to IFALPA. Fortunately for Boeing, Airbus did not prevail.

* * *

Boeing also worked closely with other international groups that could influence the 777 Early ETOPS outcome. The International Airline Passengers Association (IAPA) was one of them.

The IAPA, a group formed in 1960 to protect airline passenger rights with supposedly around half a million regular and associate members from more than 150 countries, was concerned with the media coverage of Early ETOPS. In a letter to the JAA on January 8, 1993, Dr. Hans Krakauer, senior vice president of IAPA based out of Lisbon, Portugal, voiced his organization's objection to the concept of Early ETOPS. Based on their information, IAPA considered the requests by Boeing and Airbus to permit ETOPS operations from the first day forward to be a significant breach of safety. IAPA threatened to call for a public hearing and advise its members to avoid any aircraft subject to "premature" ETOPS approval.

Later when we met with IAPA, we learned that, in an effort to understand the issue better, IAPA also had contacted IFALPA and Airbus. We also learned from IAPA that on January 9, 1993, the president of IFALPA, even though he sympathized with IAPA's concerns, actually supported the Boeing program by saying that the Boeing program looked good and was a serious attempt to build ETOPS philosophy into a design. Interestingly, to the best of my knowledge, IFALPA did not make such mention of the Airbus program.

As expected, the response from Airbus was different. We were informed that the vice president of product integrity at Airbus agreed with some of IAPA's concerns. But in a letter dated February 10, 1993, to Dr. Krakauer, Airbus tried to differentiate its program from that of Boeing by saying its systematic program retained a high level of safety, an underpinning of ETOPS. Airbus added there was no method that could eliminate the requirement for in-service experience, especially in the case of a completely new design. Airbus confirmed that it had not eliminated the need for in-service experience, but merely taken credit for the service experience from the A340.

* * *

Boeing had been working to convince the JAA members to develop requirements that would permit 180-minute Early ETOPS. The UK CAA was leading the group that favored 180-minute Early ETOPS.

British Airways wanted 180-minute Early ETOPS authority on its 777. Even though British Airways had selected GE engines, Rolls-Royce also supported the UK CAA position on Early ETOPS. Rolls-Royce support was related to Cathay Pacific; the airline had chosen the Rolls-Royce engines for its 777s. Even though the inspectors from the UK CAA mostly staffed the Hong Kong CAD, there was some concern that CAD would opt to follow the more restrictive of the FAA and JAA positions.

As expected, Airbus opposed the 180-minute Early ETOPS for the 777. The group led by French Direction Generale de l'Aviation Civile, generally known as the French DGAC—a counterpart to the UK CAA or the US FAA—was leading the group of regulators that opposed the 777 Early ETOPS.

The battle lines were drawn!

In the end, in July 1993, the regulators reached a compromise. If Boeing were able to comply with the JAA's stringent requirements, the regulators would permit 120-minute Early ETOPS for the 777. After 20,000 hours of satisfactory in-service experience with the derivative engines, or 50,000 hours with a new engine, the 777 could achieve the 180-minute ETOPS approval.

The upshot was that the JAA would uphold the same standards for the 777 and the A330.

Byron Acohido, the reporter for Boeing's hometown newspaper *The Seattle Times*, never missed a chance to come up with a catchy headline. This time it was, "European Ruling a Blow for Boeing 777 – Fate of Orders left Hanging; Airbus Could Gain an Edge."[10] The article stated that the JAA ruling would make it easier for Airbus to sell the A340s. The article also speculated that United would back out of the 777 order if Boeing failed to deliver 180-minute Early ETOPS.

Notwithstanding the headlines in the media, it was the best outcome Boeing could expect. Airbus had aggressively lobbied the European decision-makers against the Boeing proposal.

However, British Airways was disappointed. In effect, the European decision restricted the British Airways 777 ETOPS to a maximum of 120 minutes at entry. Because the FAA had no such restriction, British Airways' competitor United Airlines could have an advantage for the transatlantic market. The 180-minute Early ETOPS on the 777 could give United route flexibility in the Atlantic.

* * *

Despite the JAA decision, IAPA was still concerned with the Early ETOPS and wanted to meet with Boeing. Lars Andersen and I, together with our public relations person, met with Dr. Krakauer in New York on August 16 and 17, 1993.

Lars, who retired in 2007 as the vice president and general manager of the 777 group, was managing ETOPS from the engineering side at the time. He was responsible for making sure the 777s would be approved for 180-minute Early ETOPS. Lars was very thorough, well prepared with facts and data, hard working, and dedicated, just the right person to lead the project. But on one occasion Lars had to squirm for a few seconds.

I think it was probably in 1991. Even though Phil Condit headed the 777 program, Alan Mulally, a charismatic leader with a charming smile who became the president and chief executive officer of Boeing Commercial Airplanes, ran the show. Alan used to have weekly meetings of his chiefs, the chief engineers and chief project engineers, in Renton, a city on the outskirts of Seattle. One special feature in the room was that, for some reason, every chair had very thick lamb's wool for seat covers.

Even though Boeing pretty much knew it had to get 180-minute Early ETOPS to compete effectively with the A330/340, some of the chiefs were reluctant to sign up for it. They understood the reasons why Boeing had to go for it, but they had to think about the awesome responsibility that they had to accept for their group. It was a high-risk initiative. Even though failure was not an option, success was not necessarily guaranteed. After all, no one wanted to be in charge of an airplane system such as electrical, hydraulic, or pneumatic that would be blamed for holding up the Early ETOPS approval, which could be a very career-limiting situation for the person in charge.

At the chiefs meeting that week, at the top of the agenda was a presentation from Lars on the 777 180-minute Early ETOPS plan. He needed their commitment of support.

Lars came with a stack of vufoils, transparencies that could be projected on the screen. As Lars sat down and was ready to make his hourlong presentation, Mulally turned to him and said, "Lars, why don't you pick just three vufoils and make your case." Talk about pressure; it was a good thing that Lars did not suffer from a heart condition!

Lars was a bit stunned for a few seconds. Of course, he quickly recovered and picked three charts from the pile and made his case. He covered why the 180-minute Early ETOPS was important to the success of the 777 and the proposed steps to achieve it. It probably took less than 15 minutes.

Mulally did not waste time asking questions nor did he ask any of his chiefs if they had any questions. Instead, he turned to his chiefs and said, "If any of you still have any doubt about 180-minute Early ETOPS, let me know. I will help you find another assignment." Suddenly the room was very quiet.

The time for debate was over; somebody had to make the final decision. For the 777, it was Mulally's job. The chiefs and everyone on the 777 program had their marching orders to support the 180-minute Early ETOPS.

We met with Dr. Krakauer in a New York hotel suite. He told us that he was a naturalized American and had served in Vietnam. When we met him, he was in his late sixties.

It was during the initial pleasantries that we learned of his communications with IFALPA and Airbus that I mentioned earlier. Even though we had not seen these communications with Airbus before, there were no surprises. Dr. Krakauer also told us that before his trip to New York, Airbus had filled his head with a lot of technical information and he was not sure how much spare room he had in his head for more technical matters.

Lars meticulously went through the details of the program and showed how intensive the program was and how it compensated for the lack of a couple of years of in-service experience. We spent the entire morning on Lars' presentation. Just before we broke for lunch, Dr. Krakauer, looking at Lars, said, "You're just like my son." This was a little surprising to us. Even though he was a fatherly figure, it was the first time anyone had made a comment like that in a professional meeting. Dr. Krakauer, referring to one of his sons who was a professor at one of the prestigious US universities, continued, "My son goes on some subject for hours, and at the end, I have no idea what he said." We all took Dr. Krakauer's comments in stride, had a hearty laugh, and went to lunch.

During my presentation, which was on airline operations, I justified why the three 777 launch customers of the three engine types deserved 180-minute Early ETOPS. The New York meeting helped break the ice. We kept in touch with Dr. Krakauer over the years. I was in Europe or passing through Europe to go somewhere almost every other month, so it was no problem for me to drop by Lisbon and update him on the 777 progress. After several briefings and program updates over the years, IAPA felt comfortable with the Boeing ETOPS plans.

Incidentally, we also found that our 777 supported IAPA's "The Airline Passengers Bill of Rights," which listed its expectations of an airline. Primarily they were to regulate fares and resolve problems, but one right pertained to the capability of the airplane: "To fly on the most direct route and to have the fewest number of stops and changes of planes." The Boeing goal for the 777 was to have the most economical "point-to-point operations."

Besides having a professional relationship, Dr. Krakauer and I became good friends. The last time I was in Lisbon, he and his wife took me on a coastal drive and we had some wonderful meals in the little villages. When he passed away in February 2001 at the age of 75, Boeing and I lost a good friend. He had a very high regard for Boeing and its people.

* * *

After four years of endless review gates, the operational side of the Early ETOPS program was the first to receive a formal approval from the FAA. In the letter formally issued to Boeing, the FAA wrote, "BCAG [Boeing Commercial Airplane Group] has successfully complied with all the requirements of the ETOPS Operational Approval Plan and has demonstrated that those products produced by BCAG to support airline operations and maintenance are sufficiently mature to support 180-min ETOPS operations." The Director of Flight Standards Service signed it on May 24, 1995. The letter ended with, "Congratulations on a job well done."

On May 30, 1995, the Airplane Certification side of the FAA approved the 777 with Pratt & Whitney engines for 180-minute Early ETOPS.

Boeing took a big calculated risk and succeeded. These were jubilant days for Boeing, Pratt & Whitney, and United.

At the Boeing 777 ETOPS approval ceremony on May 30, 1995, Broderick represented the FAA; he called the 777 "the finest, most reliable and safest airplane ever delivered." David Stempler, IAPA executive director, referring to the FAA's special condition requirements for 180-minute Early ETOPS, said, "As the representative of passengers, I am pleased to say that Boeing has met and exceeded those requirements. We had all raised the 'high jump bar' very high, but Boeing soared over it." Dr. Krakauer could not personally attend the ceremony; Stempler, who was based in Washington, D.C., represented IAPA.

I believe, by challenging the industry to meet the highest standard of Early ETOPS, visionary leaders such as Broderick contributed greatly to the enhancement of aviation safety. By strictly enforcing the stringent requirements, people like Steve Clark and his colleagues in the FAA's Certification Branch helped make the 777 one of the safest and most reliable airplane ever delivered.

On June 1, 1995, Seattle's daily newspaper, *Seattle Post-Intelligencer*,[11] said, "If Boeing's new 777 jetliner were a Broadway play, the rave reviews on its debut would keep it on the boards for years." The paper called it an astounding success and mentioned all the accolades Boeing had received from all quarters. It said that Boeing did what it promised and with excellence. It quoted the chairman of Airworthiness and Performance for ALPA, Capt. Don Cornwall, who referred to the 777 as "leading-edge technology." Quoting Stempler, the paper wrote that IAPA, which initially had been skeptical of Early ETOPS approval, has "great confidence in the safety of the Boeing 777 as it enters airline service because it was subjected to the most extensive and expensive flight test program of any aircraft."

A few weeks before the final certification of the 777, IFALPA wrote in a letter that the IFALPA pilots were very impressed with the in-flight handling and system response of the 777, and with the ease with which they were able to perform both normal and non-normal flight procedures.

IFALPA added that it was impressed by the confidence Boeing had in its product by allowing IFALPA the latitude to set its own agenda on the demonstration flight. Absence of any problem during the flight further boosted its confidence in the program. IFALPA wrote that Boeing delivered the product it promised. The letter also mentioned how the relationship between IFALPA and Boeing had improved over the years.

* * *

While granting the 180-minute ETOPS Operational Approval, the FAA announced that United Airlines had successfully complied with the requirements of its ETOPS plan and had demonstrated the ability to operate and maintain the 777 in a manner consistent with that required for 180-minute ETOPS operations. On June 7, 1995, the airline started its 777 revenue operations; it was a transatlantic ETOPS flight.

Despite having the authority to operate up to 180-minute ETOPS, to appease the pilots who were members of ALPA, United Airlines voluntarily restricted its ETOPS operations to 120 minutes for the first few months.

* * *

By 1995, Airbus also had received 180-minute ETOPS authority but it did not get the same level of media attention as the 777. Actually, in a way, Airbus probably considered it a blessing that the media was not hovering over it because, as I understand it, the introduction of the A330 had some early problems that never made the headlines.

Aer Lingus was the first airline to operate the A330 on ETOPS, and it sought 90-minute ETOPS approval. I have been led to believe that the airline had technical problems from its first A330. On the delivery flight from Hamburg to Dublin, the landing gear would not retract and the flight diverted to Toulouse, where the problem was supposedly fixed. The problem reoccurred in Ireland, which prompted the airline to return the airplane to Airbus the day after delivery.

As a part of the ETOPS approval process, the Irish regulatory authority flew on the proving flight. The regulators found that the

APU could not be started after a cold soak in flight. Even after landing at Sondrestrom, Greenland, the APU could not be started due to ice buildup in the APU line.

* * *

For Boeing, getting the first airframe-engine combination approved for 180-minute Early ETOPS was the challenge. It was akin to a "proof of concept." The other programs, the 777s with GE and Rolls-Royce engines, were important but did not get the same level of industry or media visibility as the first one. In October 1996, the FAA granted 180-minute ETOPS approval on the 777 with GE90-76B engines and on the 777 with Rolls-Royce Trent 800 engines.

The European JAA policy was to only issue 120-minute ETOPS Type Design Approval for the 777. Because the Operational Approval could not exceed the airplane's Type Design Approval limit, the UK CAA had to limit British Airways' Operational Approval to 120 minutes.

Shortly after the airline started 777 transatlantic services in October 1996, several storms inundated the North Atlantic. The storms had the potential to close the diversion airports en route, which would adversely affect British Airways' 120-minute ETOPS operations.

Under certain provisions, even when the ETOPS type design for the airplane was limited to 120 minutes, ETOPS standards allowed for a 15% extension on 120-minute Operational Approval, which would be 138 minutes. The 138 minutes would allow optimal operations over the transatlantic even during adverse weather conditions. After discussing the issue at a European meeting, the UK CAA granted British Airways 138-minute ETOPS operational authority on its 777.

The 138-minute ETOPS gave the airline the flexibility it wanted on the transatlantic route. In reality, because of the 138-minute ETOPS, I do not believe the policy of JAA not to grant 180-minute ETOPS on the airframe-engine combination had any significant adverse operational impact on British Airways 777s over the Atlantic.

Even though, in reality, the JAA's 120-minute policy did not cause great pains at British Airways, we had attempted to change the policy before the airplane delivery to the airline.

JAA had formed an ETOPS working group, an industry group with regulators, airlines, and unions that met about every six months in one of the European capitals to discuss ETOPS issues. I represented the operational side of ETOPS for Boeing at this European forum. At a meeting of this forum on October 11 and 12, 1995, we proposed changing the JAA 120-minute ETOPS at entry policy. Airbus and the French DGAC strongly objected to changing the JAA position. They believed there was insufficient data to show the effectiveness of the Early ETOPS program even though the FAA had approved the 777 and United had been operating the airplane on the transatlantic route. After making several other attempts, we realized that we would not be able to change the JAA policy until Airbus had a reason to change it.

With the disappointing sales of the original medium-range A330-300, Airbus developed the A330-200, which offered increased range. The first flight of this version was in August 1997; Canada 3000, a Canadian operator, was its first customer. The operator wanted 180-minute ETOPS at entry, so we thought the JAA would change the policy to allow Airbus to certify the A330-200 without any in-service experience, and thus open the door for the 777s.

Actually, it was interesting how Airbus approached this issue, probably a reflection of its paranoia with the 777. Even though Airbus had to change the JAA policy to allow 180-minute ETOPS at entry for the A330-200, it still did not want the 777 to qualify for the same authority.

To our great surprise, Airbus came up with the concept of a "close derivative," which would permit the JAA to revise its policy and allow A330-200 certification while restricting the 777 certification. Airbus argued that the A330-200 engines and systems were a "close derivative" of the A330-300.

I was impressed by the Airbus ingenuity. They had outmaneuvered us.

The JAA sent the proposal to the chairman of the JAA ETOPS Working Group, and asked him to provide the comments.

Rather than wait to discuss the proposal after a month at the group's next meeting in Geneva on April 22 and 23, 1998, the chairman of the group issued a letter asking the members to comment. We proposed that rather than start splitting hairs on "close" and "not so close," we should allow 180-minute ETOPS at entry as long as the Authority was totally satisfied with all aspects of the approval plan.

The chairman of the group informed the JAA that it had received four comments, and that the majority accepted the close derivative proposal and endorsed the change. I understand the other three comments supporting the proposal were from the French side of the Working Group: DGAC France, Airbus, and ATR, a Toulouse-based manufacturer of turbo-prop airplanes.

Surprisingly, at the Geneva meeting, Airbus formally introduced the paper that discussed the concept of the close derivative. The chairman again solicited the group's comments. Most of us knew that the JAA had already decided to revise the policy and we were just going through the motion. As expected, the next day, on April 24, the JAA revised the policy to allow180-minute ETOPS at entry for close derivatives.

We made no further attempt to change the JAA policy. It was time to accept the reality and move on.

4

THE COLLABORATION

Working together for common good

Although Boeing and Airbus were fierce competitors, they collaborated on projects that were mutually beneficial. While Airbus was trying to kill the 777's 180-minute Early ETOPS program, Boeing and Airbus collaborated on the Canadian Atlantic Storms Program, which was sponsored by the Atmospheric Environment Service of Canada. This study ran from January 15 to March 15, 1992. Boeing concentrated on accumulation during icing encounters, and Airbus focused on the effects of airspeed on the accretion of ice and sublimation. Most of such collaborations were on technical issues that had little or no direct marketing impact.

Interestingly, there was one initiative on which Airbus collaborated with us to get what it wanted. However, unknown to us, Airbus was planning to stop Boeing from taking full advantage of the outcome. The initiative was the "Accelerated ETOPS Operational Approval."

However, at the end we outmaneuvered Airbus. Having supported an initiative that ended up greatly bolstering the 777's market potential, Airbus must have deeply regretted collaborating with Boeing on this initiative!

* * *

By 1993, Boeing had the requirements in place to permit the ETOPS Type Design Approval for the 777 and ETOPS Operational Approval at entry for the three airlines that would participate in the Boeing 1,000 CVP. But Boeing had other 777 customer airlines that could not participate in the 1,000 CVP but wanted ETOPS at entry just like United, British, or Cathay.

In the early 1990s, most of the industry groups were comfortable with accelerating the ETOPS approval process for the airlines. Normally an airline was required to operate the new twin for one year before being eligible for 120-minute ETOPS. After operating under 120-minute ETOPS for one year, the airline could apply for the 180-minute ETOPS approval. Essentially, it would take two years before an airline could start operating a new twin on the 180-minute ETOPS route. Even some of the more vocal groups—the pilot unions—supported decreasing the time, but they insisted on some minimal level of operator in-service experience with the new airframe-engine combination.

Airbus also had customer airlines that wanted to use their twins on ETOPS routes without waiting for the one-year time frame. Airbus had a proposal on the table that had many steps: 75, 90, 120, 138, and 180 minutes, and would get to 180-minute ETOPS in a year. The idea was for an airline to step to the next level as it gained more in-service experience. Whether it was based on the Airbus study or it was just a ploy to appease the pilot unions or the regulators, the Airbus proposal also included what it referred to as "conservative operations and maintenance practices." It included the dispatch reliability level that the airline had to achieve before it could step up to the next level of ETOPS authority. It also required additional fuel contingency and a stricter MEL.

By early 1993, to support the needs of the European airlines, the JAA prepared a draft titled "Accelerated ETOPS Operational Approval," a set of requirements that would be used to accelerate an airline's ETOPS approval process. The draft appeared to incorporate almost all the Airbus inputs.

The FAA was also looking into the Accelerated ETOPS Operational Approval. It had compiled a list of items to consider. Actually, it was more like a skeleton. It looked as if the FAA extracted the skeleton from the JAA's proposal; it had a stepped approach starting at 75-minute ETOPS and getting to 180-minute after 12 months. The FAA approached the issue with an open mind, and asked the industry for proposals. It also announced that it would call a meeting with the US airlines, manufacturers, and the pilot unions to develop an industry position on Accelerated ETOPS.

* * *

Despite the requirements for in-service experience before gaining approval to operate ETOPS, a handful of countries around the world had granted ETOPS authority to their airlines with reduced or no in-service experience. Unless other countries blacklist an airline from operating in their airspace or airports, theoretically, an independent nation can permit its airline to operate any way it wants.

Doug Kihm, who was an engineering manager at the time, analyzed the data to see if there was any correlation between the level of in-service experience and the level of safety. Consistent with our expectation, we found that the airlines that started ETOPS with little or no in-service experience had no higher incidences of IFSDs or system problems compared to the airlines that accumulated a year's experience for 120-minute or an additional year for 180-minute ETOPS.

As Boeing representatives, Doug and I participated in many ETOPS-related meetings in the United States and Europe. He had an in-depth knowledge of the airplane certification requirements. With his certification background and my knowledge in the operational arena, our joint team was formidable.

Because the 777 Early ETOPS 1,000-cycle program for each engine type included 90 cycles when the launch customer airline that participated in the DBSTs could actually operate the airplane and accumulate hands-on experience, there was an opinion within Boeing that we should embrace some level of in-service experience. I was one of those who believed it did not add value and argued against retaining such a requirement. The upshot was that I was volunteered to write about what I was preaching, and to draft a Boeing proposal.

In December 1993, I drafted an Accelerated ETOPS Operational Approval proposal, which was radically different from the JAA's draft and the FAA's skeleton. The proposal was not specific to the 777. It would apply to all twins. I circulated the draft within Boeing for comments and left for a three-week vacation to Florida.

Boeing does not give employees time off during the year for all the national holidays; however, the company policy is to combine most of them and give employees nearly two weeks off at the end of the year. Typically, Boeing closes from around Christmas Eve to January 2. By adding a week of vacation during this time, every year I used to take off for three weeks; that is what I did that year also.

On my return after New Year's Day in 1994, I found that the FAA had asked the Airline Transport Association (ATA), an association of US airlines, to call a meeting with the airlines, pilot unions and the manufacturers to discuss various ETOPS issues, including the FAA's Accelerated ETOPS Operational Approval skeleton. The meeting was set for January 19 and 20 at the ATA headquarters in Washington, D.C. This was the start of the ATA ETOPS Subcommittee, which was one of the most productive industry groups ever. Many of its recommendations became the guidance material or policies for the FAA, and, in some instances, for the JAA.

The draft I circulated before the holidays received some comments, most of which were from Chet Ekstrand, who was a director of flight training. We refined the proposal and were ready for the meeting.

I had reported to Chet since 1991 and continued to report to him for the next 16 years. Chet had taken an active interest in ETOPS. He actually led the Boeing team during the IFALPA meetings in London. Chet's piloting background added to his credibility with IFALPA. When Chet became the vice president of the regulatory group, he also had the overall responsibility for the Boeing ETOPS policy. Chet worked closely with Boeing's top executives and industry leaders on the policy issues.

Chet had great confidence in me and trusted my judgment. As his director, I was allowed to manage the operational side of ETOPS the way I saw fit. I thoroughly enjoyed working for Chet and am grateful for the latitude he gave me to run the program.

Chet, Doug, and I represented Boeing at the ATA meeting. One of the four agenda items was the FAA's Accelerated ETOPS Operational Approval skeleton. The group did not know that Boeing also had a proposal. We formally introduced our proposal. Because this was very different from what the industry had seen thus far, the group needed time to study the proposal in detail. We felt that the FAA was receptive to our proposal. Due to inclement weather on the day of the meeting, ALPA was not in attendance.

The FAA and the JAA tried to agree whenever possible. The next harmonization meeting between the regulators on the two sides of the Atlantic was set for March 23 and 24, 1994. Normally, the harmonization meeting was held in one of the European capitals, but this one, for the first time in the history of FAA/JAA ETOPS harmonization, was to be held in Hong Kong at the invitation of the local CAD.

The Europeans had their proposal on Accelerated ETOPS Operational Approval, which they wanted to discuss at the harmonization meeting. The US side had no formal proposal at that time. The ATA ETOPS Subcommittee decided to call a dedicated meeting on Accelerated ETOPS Operational Approval for March 9, 1994, in Washington, D.C. Because ALPA could not attend the meeting, Boeing was requested to conduct a separate meeting with them before the March 9 meeting.

On March 1, the JAA ETOPS Working Group met in Vienna, Austria. Doug and I were at the meeting. Because our proposal was submitted at the ATA meeting in January, most of the Europeans already had a chance to study it. We presented our Accelerated ETOPS Operational Approval proposal, discussed the rationale, and showed the analysis that Boeing had made on the impact of in-service experience on the success of ETOPS.

Incidentally, Airbus also had compiled similar data and had analyzed the Airbus operator data to see if there was any correlation between the level of in-service experience and the success of ETOPS. Airbus findings were consistent with ours.

Some in the industry were disappointed to see Boeing and Airbus working together. Some of these groups looked for a wedge between these two titans, so that they could slip in their agendas.

Regardless of our best efforts and the Airbus cooperation, the JAA did not budge. It rejected our proposal. The JAA ETOPS Working Group stuck to its step approach; it also required airlines to carry additional fuel and increased the restrictions on the MEL.

* * *

Since we were requested to meet with ALPA before the March 9 meeting of the Subcommittee, on March 7 we met with a group from ALPA. The FAA joined us at the meeting. ALPA had a change of players. The ALPA focal who had been involved with ETOPS practically from its inception in the mid-1980s had been replaced by Dale Istwan. Dale had been with Ozark before TWA absorbed it. In 1994, he was flying the 767 for TWA and had extensive experience flying ETOPS.

Boeing made its presentation. ALPA acknowledged that the data appeared to support the Boeing proposal, and it was willing to participate in further development of the concept. ALPA commented that it was supportive of this concept for airlines planning to introduce mature airplanes like the 757 and the 767 but felt the 777 needed to reach a level of reliability comparable to mature airplanes before being eligible for such approval. This was a positive sign.

We had worried that ALPA might discard our proposal outright as untenable. After all, we had been through the ALPA speeches on Early ETOPS and the importance it placed on an operator's in-service experience. Regarding the issue of reliability on the 777, we told ALPA that the entire concept of the Early ETOPS approval of the 777 was to prove beyond doubt that the airplane would have the reliability at entry into service comparable to mature airplanes. ALPA did not bring up this issue again.

Although we were pleasantly surprised by the ALPA position, we were taken aback by what the FAA had to say. Roy Grimes, FAA ETOPS focal, who had led the 777 Early ETOPS team from the FAA side, presented a draft proposal. It would allow 120-minute Accelerated ETOPS only to those airlines that had ETOPS experience on other airplanes. The airline would be required to fly for three months and 100 cycles at 120-minute ETOPS before being considered for 180-minute ETOPS. For airlines with no ETOPS experience, the approval would start at 90-minute ETOPS, then, only after three months of satisfactory operations, would the airline be eligible for 120-minute ETOPS.

This was different from our understanding of the FAA position on January 20. Even ALPA was surprised by the FAA proposal to limit operations initially to 90-minute, because they saw no safety benefit by restricting ETOPS diversion to 90-minute in the North Atlantic area, where most US airlines operated ETOPS at the time. ALPA believed the 90-minute would force airlines to consider diversion airports that might be marginal.

After some discussion, it became evident that, internally, the FAA lacked consensus. The FAA had not even assigned a focal to lead this project. ALPA, the FAA, and Boeing all recognized that the forthcoming meeting on March 9 could be jeopardized by the FAA's internal disagreements.

Boeing requested an immediate meeting with the FAA leadership. Chet met with Tony Broderick and his senior managers. The FAA agreed to look into the issue.

On March 9, the ATA ETOPS Subcommittee meeting was dedicated to Accelerated ETOPS Operational Approval. US airlines, pilot unions, Boeing, Airbus, the engine manufacturers, and the FAA were at the meeting. We presented our paper, the rationale, and all the analysis we had compiled. Airbus presented the data it had presented the previous week in Vienna. The airlines supported the Boeing proposal. Except for some word changes, ALPA also had no problem. The FAA introduced a new draft proposal that essentially supported the Boeing concept, but was silent on the level of authorized diversion time at entry into service. The FAA had nominated Roy to lead the internal FAA team for this initiative.

We incorporated the various inputs from the group into the original proposal. At the end, the industry agreed on the amended Boeing proposal, which essentially became the ATA ETOPS Subcommittee proposal.

AC120-42A was an Advisory Circular (AC) that listed all the requirements on ETOPS. The AC had five appendixes. The sixth one was reserved for a process developed in the early 1990s called Simulated ETOPS. The ATA ETOPS Subcommittee called this new proposal Appendix 7. The group requested that the FAA propose it as the US proposal at the FAA/JAA harmonization meeting.

We always preferred to elevate the source. When Boeing accepted my draft proposal, it became a Boeing proposal and, when the ATA ETOPS Subcommittee accepted it, then it became their proposal. Even though the FAA had not approved it, now we were asking the FAA to call it the US proposal at the harmonization meeting just like the Europeans called their proposal the "JAA proposal" even though the JAA had not approved it.

After some internal deliberations, the FAA agreed to present the ATA ETOPS Subcommittee proposal as the US proposal at the harmonization meeting. Maybe because the US proposal was radically different from the European proposal, the FAA kept repeating to us privately that the JAA would never agree to it.

While submitting the proposal to the FAA, the ATA ETOPS Subcommittee requested that the FAA permit the Subcommittee to review the changes, if any, made by the Harmonization Group before the FAA took further actions on the proposed new Appendix 7.

Many Boeing executives were anxiously waiting for the outcome of the FAA/JAA harmonization meeting.

* * *

On March 23, the FAA, the JAA, and other industry groups met at the CAD, Hong Kong for the two-day ETOPS harmonization meeting. CAD formally welcomed us at the meeting. After a few initial pleasantries, we got into technical issues.

Because it was the first time such a harmonization meeting was held outside Europe or the United States, word of the meeting had spread among the civil aviation authorities in the Pacific zone. The agenda, as always, was fairly heavy; it included a presentation from the New Zealand regulatory authority just before the Accelerated ETOPS Operational Approval. The New Zealand regulatory authority delivered a presentation on Total Quality Management (TQM).

I had been to several of these meetings but it was the first time I had seen a non-ETOPS topic on the agenda and the first time that it came from someone outside the United States or Europe.

The New Zealand presenter was dynamic. He explained how the New Zealand CAA was adopting the principles of TQM and would actually pursue ISO 9000 certification. ISO, which is a French acronym, stands for International Organization for Standardization. At the time, ISO 9000 was a badge of honor in quality circles. Even though the standard was released in 1987, many multinationals had started to adopt the ISO 9000 quality management system only in the early 1990s.

Every other word in the TQM presentation was "process." The presenter explained how controlling the process would guarantee quality. The regulators were spellbound. It was a real revelation to many.

The FAA asked me to make the presentation on the proposed Appendix 7. It just happened that the proposal I was presenting was also all about "processes." In fact, we had gone one step further—we were talking about "proven" or "mature" processes.

After my presentation, we went through the other data, which included the analysis of the operators' experience on the success of

ETOPS. Airbus shared its data, which it had presented earlier in Vienna and Washington, D.C.

Our presentation fit perfectly with the TQM concept. It had all the elements: plan, do, check, and act. At Boeing, we constantly went through various quality programs. Some employees used to disparagingly refer to them as the "flavor of the month." We had adopted the TQM concept into our proposal. We even had a built-in feedback loop to ensure that the process worked and was mature. We extended the concept of formal review gates even after the airline was approved for ETOPS and went into actual operation. This was to ensure that the processes worked as intended in real operations. This step allowed the airlines to refine their processes based on actual operations.

It was the first time the chairman of the JAA ETOPS Working Group had seen my presentation. He was not able to attend the Vienna meeting. Although he had received a briefing on the Boeing presentation in Vienna, it was not the same as hearing first hand the rationale and data behind it.

By 1994, the industry had been operating ETOPS for more than nine years and had sufficient data. There were many questions after our presentations, but we had answers for all of them. The FAA's comments were positive but noncommittal.

The JAA presented its proposal. There were many questions on the rationale behind the JAA proposal. The questions revolved around the value that the additional steps would add to the safety of operations. Bob Grange, chairman of the JAA ETOPS Working Group, led the European side.

Grange came from the UK CAA. For some strange reason, he reminded me of England's famous King Henry VIII. Maybe it was the beard or just a force of personality. Grange was an effective leader and commanded respect in the JAA ETOPS Working Group.

At the end of the day, Grange told the group, "We will accept the US proposal." That was music to our ears. We never expected the JAA to discard its proposal and fully adopt the proposal that Boeing had initiated. Even though Grange's decision must have surprised the FAA representatives, they did not show it. We could not wait to go back to the hotel and share the news with our team back in Seattle. This was before the days of cell phones.

Even though we always believed our proposal was logical, rational, and well substantiated, I think it was the TQM presentation from the New Zealand CAA that literally changed the European position. That was the first and last time I saw that gentleman from the New Zealand CAA.

Despite the Airbus support during the meeting, I was a little surprised with the parting comment that the Airbus representative made to me at the end of the two-day meeting that Airbus thought that ALPA would not agree with the outcome of the harmonization meeting. I was not sure what that meant, because after all, both ALPA and the ATA had fully supported the proposal at the March meeting in Washington, D.C. Obviously, I had no idea of the relationship, if any, between ALPA and Airbus. There might have been new developments going on behind the scenes, which we were not privy to. But this was not the time to worry about the Airbus representative's remarks. It was a time for celebration over a few drinks.

It was only when I returned to Seattle that I learned what the Airbus representative meant by the comment about ALPA.

* * *

The Airbus representative was also the secretary to the JAA ETOPS Working Group. Obviously, Airbus wasted no time faxing the minutes from the Hong Kong harmonization meeting. They were faxed on the 25th.

In the meeting minutes, Airbus wrote that ALPA might oppose the proposal agreed to at the meeting. It said ALPA opposed application of Accelerated ETOPS Operational Approval for the airplanes that had been certified under Early ETOPS. The implication was that 777 operators would not be able to use the Accelerated ETOPS Operational Approval. It added that Boeing would contact ALPA to clarify the situation and would report at the next European meeting.

This was news to us; we were not aware of any comments of this nature from ALPA. I had no plans to contact ALPA. As far as I was concerned, the suggestion was ludicrous.

Airbus wanted Accelerated ETOPS Operational Approval. Obviously, Airbus liked what we proposed even more than its own proposal, which the JAA ETOPS Working Group had adopted. Therefore, they supported us, but they were going to play the Early ETOPS card to stop the 777 operators from taking advantage of the Accelerated ETOPS Operational Approval. Airbus was possibly dangling the bait to see if ALPA would bite. But ALPA did not take the bait.

Maybe something that Airbus wrote in the meeting minutes irritated Grange or he may have felt a genuine desire to communicate with the group. Nevertheless, six days later, on March 31, 1994, he sent a long letter to all the JAA ETOPS Working Group members. He was very frank and told the group why he discarded the JAA Working Group paper and accepted, in his words, the American proposal. He said the American side of the Harmonization Group had produced a paper that was based on an analysis of data. And the data convincingly showed that the process-based approach for obtaining ETOPS approval was safe and satisfactory.

He was rather blunt in his comments on the shortcoming of the European approach. He told the group that the stepped approach, the restrictive MEL, or additional fuel did not add value. He also told the group that the European position lacked any new thinking.

Grange added that the American process-based method required a very structured self-audit process to be in place, with decision-making review gates and specific penalties for poor performance. He reminded the group that processes based on a quality assurance system were intrinsic to the JAA and Europe. He was referring to JAA's operational rules, which required the Air Operator Certificate holders to establish a quality system, develop procedures required to ensure safe operational practices, and maintain monitoring that must include a feedback system to ensure corrective action as necessary.

He strongly recommended JAA adoption of the American version of the Accelerated ETOPS Operational Approval. But he gave a fair opportunity to the Working Group. He asked the Working Group the following question: if it accepted the process-based method, and if the proposal from the American side was a satisfactory guide, could the startup airline and the airlines that operate airplanes approved under Early ETOPS use this method? Grange asked the group members to submit dissenting views with justification, if any, by June 1. He wanted the comments well ahead of the next meeting of the JAA ETOPS Working Group, which was scheduled in London for July 26 and 27, 1994.

* * *

Before we went to the Hong Kong harmonization meeting, the ATA ETOPS Subcommittee had agreed to meet on April 11 and 12, in Washington, D.C., to review the outcome of the harmonization meeting. The Harmonization Group had made some minor changes to the original proposal. The Subcommittee accepted the changes made by the Harmonization Group. The group requested that the FAA adopt the new Appendix 7.

Because Appendix 6, "Simulated ETOPS Operational Approval," still retained some of the elements from the in-service concept, it looked cumbersome compared to Appendix 7. The ATA ETOPS Subcommittee also recommended delaying the adoption of the proposed Appendix 6.

Adoption of the Accelerated ETOPS Operational Approval method was a reflection of the willingness of the aviation industry to examine data and retain only those requirements that added value to the safety of operations.

At the next meeting of the ATA ETOPS Subcommittee, on July 19, the FAA announced that it had accepted Appendix 7, and declared its intent to publish it in the Federal Register. The FAA also declared its intent to process the application for ETOPS approval based on Appendix 7 effective immediately. The FAA had already received an application from Continental Airlines for ETOPS approval on the new 757s it was about to receive from Boeing.

The news of the FAA's decision spread quickly in Europe. The European airlines did not want to be left out. They wanted the same level of flexibility as the airlines in the United States. After all, they were competing in the same transatlantic market.

The JAA ETOPS Working Group, at its London meeting of July 26 and 27, accepted Grange's recommendation to adopt the harmonized Accelerated ETOPS Operational Approval proposal. On August 3, 1994, Grange, as the chairman of the group, formally requested that the JAA incorporate Appendix 7.

The race was on between the FAA and the JAA to see who would be the first to incorporate the appendix into its regulatory structure. We loved this race!

* * *

Boeing had worked closely with Continental Airlines in preparing its application for Accelerated ETOPS Operational Approval. In support of Continental, Boeing prepared an application template. I later turned it into a generic document that could be used by any airline around the world. It became a very popular template.

Continental was the first airline to receive the ETOPS authority under Appendix 7. On September 1, 1994, it was granted 120-minute ETOPS on the 757, followed by 180-minute on November 25. The floodgate had opened. The Accelerated ETOPS Operational Approval method became the most widely used method to gain ETOPS approval for airlines around the world.

Again, ALPA had a change of volunteers. For personal reasons, Dale Istwan no longer volunteered for ALPA. The ALPA focal, who had been intimately involved with ETOPS since its inception in the 1980s, except for a short period when Dale filled in, was back. He was not too enamored with the Accelerated ETOPS Operational Approval, as it did not require minimal in-service experience even to jump to 180-minute ETOPS from day one. He made his views known to the FAA and the industry. But it was too late. Because ALPA, as an organization, had earlier supported the proposal at the ATA ETOPS Subcommittee, this new input had no real impact.

I have always wondered how the Accelerated ETOPS Operational Approval concept would have looked if we did not have Dale Istwan representing ALPA at the time, and the New Zealand CAA at the harmonization meeting in Hong Kong and Grange agreeing to adopt the US proposal. Of course, because I am an engineer to the core, I keep wondering about the probability of such concurrent events!

* * *

Typically, under the Accelerated ETOPS Operational Approval, the regulators started to approve the airlines for 120-minute, followed by 180-minute in a matter of a few months. Airbus started to take note.

Feeling threatened by the 777 operators' ETOPS approval under the Accelerated ETOPS Operational Approval method, Airbus again attempted to deny the 777 operators the use of the Accelerated ETOPS Operational Approval method.

Grange had moved on to better opportunities; there was a new chairman of the JAA ETOPS Working Group. Even though he also came from the UK CAA, he was more low-keyed and avoided confrontational situations as much as possible.

Working with some members of IFALPA, Airbus attempted to revive the proposal to deny airplanes approved under Early ETOPS—namely the 777—to use the Accelerated ETOPS Operational Approval. Airbus proposed that airlines planning to operate airplanes approved under Early ETOPS should start with 90-minute, then it would take the airline about a year to reach 180-minute.

We never missed an opportunity to set the record straight. Some of the European meetings were very lively.

In the end, Airbus did not succeed.

We succeeded in implementing our plans. Just like any other twin operator, any 777 operator could potentially start ETOPS at entry into service. It was no longer the exclusive privilege of United, British, and Cathay, the three airlines that participated in the 1,000 CVP of the 777.

Boeing had outmaneuvered Airbus. To Airbus' great regret, the initiative that Airbus had supported ended up greatly bolstering the market potential of the 777.

* * *

China Southern was one of the first 777 operators to use the Accelerated ETOPS Operational Approval method to gain approval for its ETOPS. The airline had purchased the 777s with GE engines. In early 1997, it was getting its first 300-seater long-range 777-200ER airplane and, within a few months of the delivery, it wanted to fly the shiny new 777-200ERs to the United States.

The first time I met with a high-level delegation from the Chinese regulatory authority on ETOPS was in March of 1995. It was at our new state-of-the-art training facility at Longacres, just south of Seattle. At the meeting, the delegates were pleasantly surprised to find that their new Chinese Civil Aviation Regulations had provisions for Accelerated ETOPS Operational Approval. They had those provisions in their regulations well ahead of the United States and the Europeans. In the United States and Europe, it was only "guidance material," a much lower status than a regulation.

In the early 1990s, China did not have comprehensive aviation regulations in place. Boeing had offered to help by contracting a consulting group in Washington, D.C., that specialized in rule preparation to draft a comprehensive set of regulations that paralleled the FAA requirements.

In early 1994, this consulting group asked me to review the section that pertained to ETOPS. Besides providing comments, I suggested that they include a provision on Accelerated ETOPS Operational Approval, which they did. The People's Republic of China adopted most of the recommendations from this consulting group, including all the material on ETOPS.

Having the regulation in the rulebooks did not mean that the authority personnel knew how to enforce it. Therefore, I had the unenviable assignment of guiding the authority and the airline at the same time.

The chief pilot at China Southern, who later became a minister in the People's Republic of China, referred to these two groups—the airlines and the regulators—as my left and right hands. We put together teams and worked closely with the different groups for over a year to ensure that all the steps were fully in place and proved. In 1996 alone, I traveled to China probably about five or six times.

I still vividly remember the comment from the same China Southern chief pilot just before the airline received its ETOPS approval. He came close to me and said, "You told us, your left hand, what to do to meet the standard; now, can you tell your right hand to approve it." I thought that was cool!

China Southern received 120-minute ETOPS approval on April 22, 1997, and it started 777 flights to the United States. It became the first airline to operate a 777 over the Pacific.

During this time I also worked with other airlines that were about to get their 777s to establish plans that would allow them ETOPS at entry or shortly thereafter. By the middle of 1997, Malaysian Airlines, Singapore Airlines, Emirates, and Egypt Air received their ETOPS approval using the Accelerated ETOPS Operational Approval method. We even celebrated Egypt Air's approval with a light and sound show at the Sphinx, under the shadows of the pyramids, and a dinner at a nice restaurant in Cairo.

* * *

I was already doing a fair amount of travel by 1994, but the onset of Accelerated ETOPS Operational Approval really accelerated the pace. Because I had a finger in everything ETOPS operational, besides participating in US and European rule-making meetings, I started to be heavily engaged in the 777 and other twin sales campaigns.

Airlines wanted assurances that if they purchased any Boeing twin, they could operate on ETOPS routes from the first day of revenue operations. Potential 777 customers also required assurance that the airplanes would get 180-minute Early ETOPS on the airframe-engines. They wanted to be convinced with facts and data. I also had to dispel the Airbus propaganda that an airline needed a four-engine airplane such as the A340 for longer range operations. During the next decade, I felt like I spent more time outside, somewhere in the world, than at my office in Seattle.

Even though I had occasional visits on Boeing business to South America, Australia, Africa, and the Middle East, most of my time outside the United States was in the European capitals or the Asian countries in the Pacific corridor.

I have been to around 70 countries and have circumnavigated the globe more than a dozen times. Because of the various meetings in Europe, I have been in some European capitals more than 30 or 40 times! Besides Washington, D.C., my business travel inside the United States was mostly to the cities in which the major US airlines were located.

I had developed a passion for my work. It had all the elements of what some called "meaningful work."[1] Boeing had full confidence in my abilities to lead the project the way I saw fit and shape its future. ETOPS had the complexity to make it mentally challenging. Furthermore, we could instantly see how our efforts influenced the ETOPS operations around the world.

Besides letting me admire the natural beauties of the world from 35,000 feet (10,700 m), and explore the various cities, my work gave me the opportunity to work with people of different cultures around the world, which I relished.

For a kid born in Nepal, it was a great honor and privilege to be able to represent Boeing in the international forums. As a child who started his formal schooling at the age of eight and who went to England at the age of 18 to study Aeronautical Engineering, I could not even dream that one day I would be so fortunate as to play such a role in global aviation!

* * *

The Pacific oceanic region had become the battleground for the 777s and the A340s. New bilateral aviation agreements and open-skies agreements between the United States and the Asian countries around the Pacific Rim allowed operators to increase the flight frequency between existing city pairs and inaugurate new city pairs.

Besides having the latest technologies, the 777s, being twins, had the operating cost advantage over the A340s. But the operators required ETOPS approval to operate on the transpacific routes. Despite the success of the 777, Airbus continued to treat ETOPS as the Achilles heel of the 777.

According to the feedback we received from some of the airlines in the Pacific Rim, Airbus told the airlines considering purchase of the 777s that ETOPS approval would require the airlines to wait for a year before they could operate the 777s on the transpacific route.

Just before Christmas 1995, during the Malaysian Airlines 777 versus the A340 sales campaign, ETOPS became a central issue. Malaysian Airlines had been operating the Airbus A330 for nearly nine months, and the airline had been struggling to get 90-minute ETOPS approval. The airline was apprehensive when Boeing Sales told the airline that if it bought the 777s, it could operate on 180-minute ETOPS from the start. Sales wanted me in Kuala Lumpur as fast as I could get there.

I landed in Kuala Lumpur in the evening, and the meeting with the airline was the next morning. I made my presentation on the 180-minute ETOPS approval for the airframe-engine, and then talked about how the airline could get 180-minute approval from the first day of revenue operations using the Accelerated ETOPS Operational Approval method. They were sympathetic to what I had to say but were not convinced. Actually, the airline said all it wanted was 120-minute ETOPS on the 777s.

The airline could not believe its regulator would grant it 120-minute on the 777s with no in-service experience when it could not even get 90-minute ETOPS on its A330s with in-service experience. When I repeated my rationale, the airline put me up to the challenge—they wanted me to go with them to their regulatory authority and get a commitment from the regulators. I agreed. The next morning, we were sitting in front of the decision-makers at the regulatory authority.

Our sales director and the three airline personnel accompanied me. I went through a presentation similar to what I had presented to the airline just a day earlier. The crux of my presentation was, with the processes in place, Malaysian Airlines should be approved for 180-minute ETOPS at entry.

I also talked in detail about the support we had given other airlines in establishing mature processes. I gave examples of airlines that had been approved for ETOPS with the Accelerated ETOPS Operational Approval method.

The main official at the Civil Aviation, responsible for granting ETOPS to Malaysian Airlines, had some very piercing questions. He was very detail oriented and thorough. Even though the meeting was scheduled for an hour, we probably spent more than a couple of hours at his office. After he had exhausted all his questions, he turned to the airline personnel and asked them, "Why do you need 180-minute ETOPS at entry; why can't you live with 120 minutes?"

The senior-most person from the airline looked at the regulator and told him very politely, "Yes sir, we could live with 120-minute ETOPS at entry." The regulator thanked the airline for agreeing to 120-minute and thanked us for a very informative session.

The Boeing sales director could hardly contain himself; he was ecstatic. I think he recognized he was close to nailing the deal. That was a very good day for Boeing.

Within a few weeks of that meeting, Malaysian Airlines announced a $4 billion order for 15 Boeing 777s and 10 Boeing 747-400s. The first 777 was delivered on April 23, 1997, and the airline received its 120-minute ETOPS approval on June 5.

The loss of the Malaysian deal shocked Airbus. ETOPS did not become the Achilles heel of the 777.

The 777 threatened the future of the A340, and in the process, possibly endangered the Airbus long-term strategy to topple the Boeing 747 from its pedestal.

The airline's ability to get ETOPS approval on the 777 at entry into revenue service by following the Accelerated ETOPS Operational

Approval method was threatening the A340. Airbus had started to hemorrhage. If uncontained, it could potentially lose billions of dollars from the lost sales.

Airbus had to confront the 777 challenge.

5

BATTLE OF THE PACIFIC

Struggles for regional dominance

The Malaysian Airlines 777 order added insult to injury. While the Airbus A330 already in service with the airline was struggling to qualify for 90-minute ETOPS operation, the airline had received the regulator's assurance of 120-minute ETOPS approval at entry into revenue service of the 777.

The Accelerated ETOPS Operational Approval became a double-edged sword for Airbus. While it allowed the operators of Airbus twins to start ETOPS at entry into service, it provided the same flexibility to the 777.

In the late 1995, Airbus could do nothing about the ETOPS Type Design Approval of the 777. Early ETOPS was a done deal. The 777 with Pratt & Whitney engines had already been approved and was operating under United Airlines colors. The FAA's 180-minute ETOPS Type Design Approval process for the 777s with GE and Rolls-Royce engines was on track.

The only thing Airbus could do was stop the ETOPS Operational Approval for the airlines. Airbus' only hope was to put impediments on the airline's use of the Accelerated ETOPS Operational Approval method for the 777 operation.

* * *

Once again, Airbus would attempt to regulate the 777 operators in using the Accelerated ETOPS Operational Approval method. It was an agenda item for the April 24, 1996, JAA ETOPS Working Group meeting in Toulouse, France.

Possibly to portray it as an industry concern rather than just a competitive Airbus issue, Airbus had convinced a member of a European pilot union to present the proposal this time. The proposal would question the safety of these 777 operations.

Most of the pilot union representatives to the Working Group were volunteers. At any time up to three or four pilots represented the various European pilot unions. Just like us, Airbus also could always count on a couple of the representatives to sympathize with it.

Actually, it was some of our friends at the European pilot unions who warned us of Airbus' plan.

In the name of safety, Airbus had devised a matrix that showed the minimum experience the airlines had to accumulate before they gained ETOPS approval. The bottom line was that airplanes approved for ETOPS with Early ETOPS—namely the 777s—would not qualify for an airline's Accelerated ETOPS Operational Approval at entry into revenue operation.

Even though Boeing believed the argument lacked supporting facts and data, and Airbus would not be able to mount a serious challenge against the 777, we did not want to take a chance. After all, many airlines had bought the 777s to start on international operations from day one. Any requirement of in-service experience before the start of ETOPS could cripple the 777.

Having advance information of Airbus and the pilot union's plan, we contacted the airlines that normally participated in the JAA Working Group and sought their support.

Accelerated ETOPS Operational Approval had been in place for a year and half, and the European airlines were not going to allow anyone to tinker with it. The airlines came to the meeting fully prepared.

Airbus did not prevail at the European JAA ETOPS Working Group. The airlines stopped the pilot union.

Possibly realizing the futility, Airbus abandoned the idea of getting the JAA ETOPS Working Group to impose restrictions on the use of the Accelerated ETOPS by the 777 operators. Besides, there were new challenges to the A340 and the pincer strategy lurking on the horizon.

* * *

By 1996, twins virtually dominated the transatlantic market. The 777 had joined the ETOPS workhorse, the Boeing 767. With the introduction by China Southern Airline of the 777 between China and the United States, the focus had shifted to the transpacific market. United Airlines, Continental Airlines, and American Airlines all aspired to deploy the longer range 777-200ERs in this market. It was just a matter of time. Even though several airlines had used the Boeing 767 in the transpacific market, the industry did not regard the 767 as the airplane that would alter the dynamics in this market. The 777-200ER had the range and the payload to change the transpacific market forever, just like the 767 did for the transatlantic market.

The 180-minute ETOPS is adequate for transpacific routes. But at certain times of the year, the airline may have to delay or cancel a flight because en route alternates are not available. Although diversion to an en route alternate during the cruise phase of flight is rare, ETOPS flight planning rules require availability of a sufficient number of alternates en route. At certain times of the year, the airports around the Aleutian chain, in the North Pacific, can get heavy snow, fog, or strong winds, which would make the airport unsuitable for ETOPS.

The US airlines wanted Boeing to pursue 240-minute ETOPS. This level of authority would permit airlines more route flexibility and would even allow them to skip the marginal en route alternates even though it could require the airlines to carry more fuel on board to comply with the ETOPS fuel requirements.

In late 1996, we began discussing the possibility of 240-minute ETOPS on the transpacific. But Airbus had different plans for the area.

* * *

In 1994, John Leahy, the 44-year-old New Yorker who was the "super-salesman" for Airbus, became its chief commercial officer. A Piper Aircraft marketer before joining Airbus North America in January 1985, Leahy had quickly risen up the ranks to become the head of sales and president of Airbus North America. Penetrating the strategic North American market for Airbus was his claim to fame.

According to published reports, in 1995, the energetic Leahy, who apparently never took "no" for an answer, set a commercial goal for Airbus to boost the 19% market share to 50% by the year 2000.

Airbus was well positioned. Its A320 family was popular. When sales of the A330-300 became disappointing, Airbus launched the A330-200 in 1995. It offered increased payload capacity and more range. The A330-200 trounced the Boeing 767. The flagging sales of the A340 prompted Airbus to launch the A340-500 and the A340-600 in 1997. The 300-seater A340-500 was the world's longest range commercial airliner. The A340-600 could carry nearly 380 passengers at a range of 7,500 nm (13,900 km). It was coming very close to the Boeing 747 in performance.

Besides updating the product line and optimizing its production methods, Airbus fully exploited the intrinsic advantages of its unique legal structure and financial arrangements. Reportedly, the GIE structure allowed Airbus to pursue market share with little regard for profit; the price of the Airbus airplane was whatever it took to make the sale. Apparently, Airbus also guaranteed a residual or resale value.

The Wall Street Journal, while describing the inner working of an airplane sale to Spain's Iberia Airlines in 2003, wrote, "On the Airbus side, Mr. Leahy also was feeling pressured because a past sales tactic was coming back to haunt him. In 1995, when Iberia was buying 18 smaller A340s and Mr. Dupuy [Chairman of Iberia] expressed concern about their future value, Mr. Leahy helped seal the deal by guaranteeing him a minimum resale price. ... If Iberia wants to sell them, Airbus must cover any difference between the market price of the used planes and the guaranteed floor price. The guarantee is one of the tools that Mr. Leahy has used to boost Airbus's share of world sales to about 50% today from 20% in 1995. Boeing rarely guarantees resale values."[1]

If the 777 triumph over the A340 at Malaysian Airlines was an early indication of events to follow, it was not good for Airbus. Obviously, the well-honed techniques such as slashing the price to the bone or guaranteeing the residual value for market share somehow did not work this time. The chairman of the airline, while announcing Malaysian Airlines' $4 billion order for 15 Boeing 777s and 10 Boeing 747-400s, told the media that the Boeing airplanes were "slightly more costly, but they fit in more with our proposed destinations."[2]

* * *

Leahy's vision of a 50% market share required a change of plans, a strategic shift on ETOPS

In October 1996, when the FAA granted 180-minute ETOPS Type Design Approvals on the 777s with Rolls and GE engines, Airbus resorted to subtle advertisements in the print media that cast doubt on long-range twins. It released an advertisement that showed an Airbus A340 in flight with a caption that read, "Why do pilots prefer the A340? Put two and two together."

Airbus also vehemently started to oppose any extension of ETOPS beyond 180 minutes. Its declared goal was to stop twin operations in the Pacific, polar routes, and routes between Africa and Australia. Airbus called this area "extreme." The obvious implication was that the airplanes operating in these areas encountered extreme operating conditions. Airbus declared that only the quads were capable of operating in these areas.

Boeing saw this as an Airbus attempt to exclude the 777s from long-range operations. Despite having said, "The increasing importance of ETOPS operations, with associated maintenance and logistic procedures, illustrate that ETOPS is the way of flying for today and also for the future,"[3] Airbus ratcheted the anti-ETOPS rhetoric.

Challenging ETOPS became a corporate strategy. It was no longer just the sales and marketing people such as Leahy and his team who made public statements against the 777 ETOPS. The issue was elevated to the highest level at Airbus. Even Noel Forgeard, who had taken over the helm as the managing director of Airbus in April 1998, got into the fray. The Airbus media campaign became even more aggressive.

In 1998, when Iberia announced its intention to acquire additional A340-300s, Forgeard announced, "Iberia's additional A340 order is the proof that our four-engine aircraft and their ETOPS-free ultra longhaul operations represent the ideal tool for long-range routes."[4]

From then on, just about every A340 sale or delivery would include some comment about ETOPS. Often, the comment was attributed to the head of the airline, Forgeard, or Leahy. When Olympic Airways took delivery of its first A340-300, the chief executive officer of the airline said, "Not only will the A340 offer a more economical tool on ultralong flights than current fleet but it also boasts state of the art technology and the highest levels of passenger comfort, while being free of any ETOPS constraints."[5]

Argentina's flag carrier cited ETOPS restrictions while ordering the Airbus A340. Forgeard added, "[Aerolineas Argentinas] understands the clear advantages of four-engine aircraft on long-haul routes over water and remote areas where ETOPS imposes severe operational limitations."[6]

The ritual went on for nearly a decade. "Like all four-engined aircraft, the A340-300E is free from extended range twin-engine operations (ETOPS) constraints. This helps airlines such as Air Tahiti Nui to fly the shortest and most direct routings."[7] "For South African Airways, four engines is the best solution for ultra-long haul flights, especially if they involve flights over desolate terrain or oceans. The A340-600 offers total freedom of flight, unrestricted by ETOPS regulations. This allows airlines to fly more direct routes, saving travel time, cutting fuel consumption and reducing costs."[8] "With its unique four-engine operational capability, the A340 ensures [Air Mauritius] ETOPS free operations in the particularly demanding routes over extremely long stretches of ocean to India, Asia and Australia. With four engines for the best economy on ultra-long-haul routes, Airbus A340s give unmatched operational flexibility on non-stop flights over remote areas—such as oceans, mountain ranges and the polar regions."[9]

It was a revelation that Air Mauritius, a small airline located near the Equator in the middle of the Indian Ocean, was contemplating operations over the polar regions!

On February 7, 2007, when Airbus sold a VIP version of the A340-500, it repeated the same mantra as if the "four-engine for remote areas" slogan was on autopilot. Attributing the statement to Leahy, Airbus issued a press release that said, "...the Airbus A340-500 has exactly what a VIP customer wants – a very large and attractive cabin, four-engined freedom for routings over the remotest regions, and the range to fly nonstop to the world."[10] Obviously, it was an oversight, because by 2007 Airbus was aggressively promoting its own long-range twin, the A350XWB. To the best of my knowledge, this was the last time Airbus publicly mentioned "four-engined freedom."

* * *

By the end of 1996, Boeing-Airbus battlefield had shifted. Now it was the 240-minute ETOPS on the transpacific. Boeing working with the US airlines was planning to draft a proposal.

But Boeing was taken aback when it saw Airbus take the lead by presenting a 240-minute ETOPS proposal at the JAA ETOPS Working Group meeting in Toulouse on April 24 and 25, 1996. We were very surprised that Airbus, of all the groups, would be the one to petition for this level of ETOPS authority.

Airbus justified the need to extend ETOPS to 240 minutes and created a list of system improvements that would be required. Obviously, just like us, Airbus talked to the airlines; it knew the airlines' desires. The proposal was a pre-emptive strike. By appearing to support the extension, it was planting the seed for enhanced system capabilities. System modifications after the airplanes were already in operation could be potentially expensive. At the Toulouse meeting, we made no comments on the Airbus proposal.

When we officially made a proposal in 1997, Airbus supported our efforts. Airbus motives were transparent. I had been working with Airbus for several years. Both of us had worked together on projects, but at times we vehemently opposed each other. The 240-minute ETOPS was not the issue on which I expected Airbus to work with us. This extension of ETOPS, if it materialized, would severely cripple the A340 family, and there was no way Airbus would allow it. The Airbus support made me suspicious. I was waiting for the other shoe to drop!

I did not have to wait too long. Shortly after our 240-minute proposal, Airbus unveiled its proposal for LROPS, which stood for Long-Range Operations. Airbus launched a massive campaign that it had obviously been working on for some time. It had very detailed in-depth studies on different aspects of long-range operations. Airbus representatives fanned around the world to spread the LROPS message. Airbus freely distributed a comprehensive CD-ROM on the subject, which was updated four times a year.

The 240-minute ETOPS proposal that Airbus had presented at the April 24 and 25, 1996, meeting in Toulouse was in effect a subset of the LROPS proposal.

* * *

Boeing could never afford to underestimate Airbus. It did its homework. It had the resources and it used them strategically. It funded studies with the universities in Europe to substantiate its approach and gain instant credibility. It recruited industry experts to plead its case. It had great support from certain factions of the aviation industry.

It was up to us to find holes in the Airbus argument and make our case with facts, data, and logical arguments. It was an intellectual challenge, and I loved every bit of it. I also had access to the tremendous informational resources at Boeing.

Airbus called LROPS an international regulatory framework that would ensure a safe operating environment for all long-range operations. While acknowledging the resounding success of ETOPS, it argued that the ETOPS requirements did not ensure the "appropriate level of safety" that would be needed in the areas of the world it called "extreme areas of operation." Because the Pacific oceanic areas were in this new extreme bucket, according to the Airbus argument, any extension of ETOPS authority in this arena would be totally out of the question.

Obviously, Airbus was entitled to its opinion. Boeing had not seen the data that supported these claims.

Airbus in its publication said, "LROPS can best be defined as a regulation that will encompass the design, certification and operation of all aircraft (irrespective of the number of installed engines) on long-range missions involving flight over remote and operationally challenging zones. Such missions would include any flight further than three hours flying time from an adequate airfield and any flight irrespective of diversion time, where the operating conditions at existing airports present a serious risk. ... Whereas ETOPS is based on the idea that diversion airfields are safe, LROPS will be based on the idea that diversions would not be needed at all. ... twin-engine aircraft ... will be prohibited from operating in the extreme areas. ... All A340 and A380 aircraft will be certified for LROPS."[11]

LROPS was a strategic move on the part of Airbus. Recognizing the 777 threat, it was even prepared to subjugate the A340s and the A380s, the quads, to additional requirements if it could stop the 777s at 180-minute ETOPS. Airbus saw this as a way to disrupt the 777 operations over the Pacific, polar routes, and routes between Africa and Australia—the areas it called "extreme."

Even though we knew that some of the arguments were technically flawed, the Airbus proposal had media appeal. By dragging the three-

and four-engine airplanes into the fray, Airbus also tried to give the impression that it was not fighting the "quad" A340 versus the "twin" 777 battle with Boeing.

Although the media often implied that Boeing was responsible for requiring quads to comply with some of the stringent requirements of ETOPS twins, actually it was Airbus in 1996 and 1997 that, to its later regret, came up with that strategy.

LROPS included flights that were as long as 20 hours or more. LROPS also covered crew duty time and crew rest associated with 20-hour flights.

I found that on every continent I traveled to, LROPS was a topic of conversation that I could not avoid. It had become a part of aviation industry jargon. Airbus had done a superb job of spreading its message and the CD-ROM.

* * *

Three US airlines were getting close to formalizing their plans to start the 777 on the transpacific route. Because of the 777, the airlines looked up to Boeing to take the lead on the 240-minute ETOPS.

Airbus knew the game. Its goal was to kill any proposal that would permit unrestricted use of the 777s in the areas it considered the domain of the A340. If it could not kill the proposal outright, it would try to complicate the issue such that the proposal would be in "perpetual discussion" for years.

By throwing in tris and quads, crew duty time, crew rest, and other hot-button issues, Airbus was probably hoping to keep the discussion going for the next 10 years. But we did not have that luxury. I had to find a way to expedite the process.

I had an alternative proposal and wanted to bounce it off the airlines, so I called United Airlines.

* * *

Gene Cameron was the chief flight dispatcher based out of Chicago. He is probably one of the most knowledgeable people in the aviation industry on flight dispatch issues. We discussed if we really needed to push for 240-minute ETOPS right away or, in the interim, if we should propose a

15% extension on 180-minute. This level of authority would be used on an as-needed basis.

The 180-minute ETOPS was adequate to support all transpacific 777 operations except for those instances when the airports in the Aleutian Island chain or some of the Russian airports were not available due to inclement weather conditions. Based on the route analysis, we found that, even at the worst scenario, depending on the performance capabilities of airplanes, we probably would need somewhere between 7 to 13 additional minutes of diversion time beyond the 180 minutes. Fifteen percent extension on 180-minute would give an additional 27 minutes.

I chose the 15% based on precedence.

In 1985, when the whole idea of ETOPS evolved, ETOPS was limited to 120 minutes. However, because of occasional inclement weather over the Atlantic which threatened the availability of enroute alternates, the regulators also permitted a 15% extension on an as-needed basis for transatlantic operations. The airlines could extend ETOPS to 138 minutes when needed. It was not a level of authority to be used on a daily basis throughout the year.

Therefore, if, at the time of dispatch due to the unavailability of some airports en route, the airline could not fly the planned route based on 120-minute ETOPS, the airline could find other airports that were within 138 minutes and conduct the operations.

If a similar concept were to be used for 180-minute ETOPS, a 15% extension would result in 207 minutes. This level of authority would address the concerns that the airlines had for those times of the year when the en route airports would not be available.

In rulemaking, precedence can be a powerful tool. United agreed that the 207-minute ETOPS would address the airline's concern. I agreed with United that we wanted to pursue the 240-minute and beyond, but that could wait. We would tackle the LROPS another day. The immediate need was to operate the 777s on the transpacific route with no potential for disruption, and 207-minute ETOPS would do it.

The next airline I called was Continental Airlines. Capt. Jim Starley, who was a senior director in 2009, was a director of flight operations at the time. I had known Jim since 1992. In 1993, when I was about to draft the Accelerated ETOPS Operational Approval method, it was Jim who asked me to make sure the proposal covered all twins, not only the 777s.

Continental had ordered new Boeing 757s and it wanted to operate the airplane on ETOPS at entry. The airline wanted to use the new method that I was about to draft, which is what happened. Continental was the first airline to operate ETOPS under the Accelerated ETOPS Operational Approval method.

When I suggested my desire to pursue 207-minute immediately and delay the 240-minute to a later date, Jim agreed right away. There was no hesitation whatsoever. Having worked together on ETOPS issues for so long, Jim and I had developed a mutual respect for each other.

Then I called American Airlines, who was a bit more persistent in pursuing 240-minute. With the introduction of the 777s, American had plans to expand its twin operations in the Pacific, and it was concerned with the potential closure of a critical airport in the mid-Pacific, Midway. After some discussion American also supported the proposal to proceed with 207-minute.

Getting a commitment from the airlines was far easier than getting a commitment from the Boeing senior executives. Thinking it had a better chance of being accepted by the industry and the FAA, some favored the 207-minute, while others preferred the 240-minute because it would also address the potential issue with Midway.

Before 1997, Midway Atoll—an island in the middle of the Pacific with an airport capable of handling big commercial jets—was under the control of the US Navy and was available as an emergency alternate airport en route. In 1997, the Navy vacated the island and turned control over to the US Fish and Wildlife Service, which would maintain the island as a refuge for endangered species. Under a cooperative agreement, the Fish and Wildlife Service granted a commercial enterprise, Midway Phoenix Corp., to engage in eco-tourism, and to maintain and operate the airport and the island infrastructure.

The Navy's departure created a concern within the airlines. Midway was a crucial airport in the mid-Pacific, an en route diversion airport that was important for ETOPS operations. The airlines questioned the long-term viability of Midway as a diversionary airport under the US Fish and Wildlife Service, an agency with a charter to protect the flora and fauna of the island. With the 240-minute, the airlines could skip Midway, and it would no longer be crucial for twin operations over the Pacific.

Eventually, after a few weeks of looking at various scenarios, Boeing upper management also lined up behind the 207-minute ETOPS. Having

Boeing management support and the support from the three major US airlines, I was ready to propose the 207-minute ETOPS policy to the ATA ETOPS Subcommittee.

* * *

When Boeing first made the 240-minute proposal in late 1996 at the ATA ETOPS Subcommittee meeting, the pilot unions had some concerns with the proposal. The three pilot groups that were mostly concerned were ALPA, Independent Association of Continental Pilots (IACP), and Allied Pilots Association (APA). APA represented the American Airlines pilots. Several representatives from ALPA, IACP, and APA had joined to form a pilot union group. The group had 25 issues it wanted Boeing to address on the 777 before it would consider the 240-minute ETOPS.

ALPA had 10 members on the team. Bob Reich headed the ALPA team. Bob was a Naval Academy graduate with a Master's degree in Aeronautical Engineering. He had flown for the Navy before joining United Airlines. Even though I had met Bob in the early 1990s, I had never worked directly with him. This was my first opportunity to work closely with him. The 240-minute initiative required us to meet often to exchange facts and data. Bob and I did not always agree on everything, but we developed a mutual respect for each other. As ALPA's ETOPS focal, Bob greatly influenced the ETOPS outcome. I do not believe ETOPS would be where it is today in 2010 had it not been for the wisdom and foresight Bob brought to the ETOPS deliberations. Bob helped the US regulator move to a new ETOPS frontier when he joined the FAA in 2005.

The pilot unions also were concerned with Midway. But the reason for their concern was different from that of the airlines. They did not want to extend the ETOPS authority to 240-minute and indirectly encourage the closure of Midway.

Obviously, the pilot unions were receptive to the idea of the industry pursuing the 207-minute first and then pursuing the 240-minute down the line. Although we were no longer pursuing the 240-minute, we felt it was important for us to still address all the 25 issues of the unions about the 777. The issues the unions had raised required us to launch several internal studies, and we shared the outcome with the pilot groups.

I drafted a 207-minute proposal and submitted it to the ATA ETOPS Subcommittee. The Subcommittee met several times to scrub the 207-minute proposal. Airlines brought additional data to justify the proposal. United even launched a simulation exercise to see how often the airline would need the 207-minute extension. We incorporated the industry comments, including almost the entire wish list of the pilot unions.

Airbus also was a member of the Subcommittee. The JAA ETOPS Working Group decided not to act on the 207-minute proposal, because this proposal focused on transpacific operations.

Some of my European colleagues privately told me that Airbus was impressed with our ingenuity. Our new proposal essentially postponed the "perpetual discussion" Airbus had planned with LROPS. We latched onto the precedence.

* * *

Boeing anticipated that the 777 would change the transpacific market just as the 767 had changed the transatlantic market. The 207-minute would accelerate that change.

By the third quarter of 1998, we thought we were getting closer to getting an agreement between the airlines and the pilot unions on the 207-minute extension. But developments outside the Subcommittee threatened the possibility of such an agreement.

The merger of Reno Air with American Airlines created a rift between the APA and airline management. Even though the rift had nothing to do with ETOPS, the APA decided to withdraw its support from the 207-minute ETOPS. Over the years, some of the pilot unions had used ETOPS as a bargaining tool in labor negotiations, so this was not a real surprise to the ATA ETOPS Subcommittee.

APA and its parent organization, the Coalition of Airline Pilots Association (CAPA), openly started to espouse the Airbus position and challenged ETOPS beyond 180 minutes. The media picked up the stories.

Under the headline "Pilots Coalition Argues Against Easing ETOPS Rules," *Aviation Week & Space Technology* reported that the union sought meetings with the FAA administrator to present its opposition and review the risks of extending the 180-minute ETOPS. It reported that the union wanted to stall any efforts to ease the ETOPS rule. The article indicated that the FAA was expected to attend the November 23 and 24, 1998, ATA ETOPS Subcommittee meeting. CAPA feared that the FAA might be inclined to approve the extension.[12]

The Subcommittee proceeded with its work. On February 4, 1999, at a meeting of the ATA ETOPS Subcommittee, a final proposal emerged that was acceptable to the Subcommittee. The ATA ETOPS Subcommittee endorsed the proposal and recommended that it be submitted to the FAA.

Capt. Sam McWilliams, a senior management pilot from United Airlines, chaired the ATA ETOPS Subcommittee. Most of the meetings were held at the ATA headquarters in Washington, D.C. It would not be a stretch to say Sam was one of the early pioneers of multitasking. His office in Denver looked more like a stockbroker's office with Sam talking on a couple of phones while carrying on conversations with a few of his pilots around the table. His leadership made the ATA ETOPS Subcommittee one of the most productive committees or working groups that I have attended.

The senior vice president of the ATA, the executive air safety chairman of ALPA, and the president of the IACP jointly signed the final submittal to the FAA.

* * *

The 207-minute proposal received wide media coverage.

Aviation Week & Space Technology wrote, "American and United Airlines plan to join Continental and other carriers using new Boeing 777s on transpacific routes in a trend that follows recent dominance of twin-engine transports on scheduled transatlantic flights. The shift, although just beginning, could affect the viability of proposed 'super-jumbo' transports such as Airbus' 600-passenger A3XX and stretched Boeing 747 derivatives. Boeing has long held that transpacific routes would develop similarly to the North Atlantic's, with passengers preferring frequent, nonstop flights rather than multi-segment trips through major hubs."[13]

Airbus and the APA took exception to the developments taking place on ETOPS. Airbus started to refer to the 207-minute as "ETOPS by stealth."

On March 3, 1999, *Aviation Daily* reported, "President of Americans' Allied Pilots Association (APA), told FAA Administrator Jane Garvey yesterday that his union 'is strongly opposed to any increase in ETOPS diversion times,' He said APA also ' objects to the process used to produce the proposed policy letter' justifying the 27-minute increase. And he said there is 'no valid reason' why ETOPS is an FAA policy and not a regulation."

The *Daily* also reported that the APA and the CAPA said neither group endorsed the 207-minute, refuting some published reports that pilot unions supported it. "[The APA and CAPA representative] said, 'There is no question that the 777 is a superior aircraft, and I am sure we are ready to agree to that,' but the pilot groups he represents were not involved in the latest meetings on the issue. 'Boeing, ATA and ALPA apparently had an important meeting on this subject in January to which the rest of us were not invited.'"[14]

It appeared the statements offended ALPA. It issued a news release the next day with the headline "ALPA Supports 207-minute ETOPS after Thorough Review." The ALPA's news release of March 4, 1999, said,

> The Air Line Pilots Association, International, the nation's largest and oldest airline pilots union, today reiterated its support for a proposal that would allow a 15 percent extension to the 180-minute limit on extended twin-engine operations (ETOPS) on long-range flights.
>
> "ALPA, which represents 53,000 airline pilots at 51 airlines in the U.S. and Canada, has been working closely with government and industry representatives for nearly two years to address safety concerns with the Air Transport Association proposal to increase the ETOPS limits," said Captain Duane Woerth, president of ALPA. "Over the past two years, the FAA, the airlines, and the manufacturers addressed to ALPA's satisfaction a total of 25 different concerns raised by the union. The union is now prepared to formally endorse the proposed policy letter to increase the ETOPS limit from 180-minute to 207-minute on an exception basis," Woerth said.
>
> However, ALPA officials now are concerned by a last-minute effort by one or two unaffiliated pilot groups to

derail the carefully crafted agreement. In statements printed in the Mar. 3 Aviation Daily, the Allied Pilots Association (APA), which represents American Airlines pilots, attempted to cast doubt on both the ETOPS change and the method used to build the consensus.

The APA also claimed that the Coalition of Airline Pilots Association (CAPA), of which APA is a member, opposed the change and that the APA was shut out of the process. However, APA representatives were invited to, and attended, all of the ATA ETOPS Subcommittee meetings dealing with this issue. The only meeting they specifically were not invited to was a closed-door briefing requested by ALPA, at ALPA, from the FAA, Boeing, and ATA, so that ALPA political leaders and safety representatives could have their questions answered by the principal parties. APA was free to request a similar briefing for their leaders but apparently did not do so.

ALPA was initially skeptical of the proposal, so the union formed its own ETOPS Working Group to study the issue. The group included pilot safety officials from all of ALPA's ETOPS carriers, the chairmen of ALPA's accident survival committee and the airworthiness, performance and evaluation committees, and members of ALPA's professional engineering staff.

In accordance with ALPA safety policies, the union supported and participated in the lengthy investigation and analysis required for the ETOPS change. When all the issues of concern to ALPA had been addressed, the union presented the final draft document to the pilot leadership and safety coordinators at all the ALPA carriers.

The proposal would only allow the 207-minute limit to be authorized as needed on an "exception" basis, if and only if a normally available diversion airport required for 180-minute operations is not available and there is another diversion airport within the 207-minute radius. There also is a mechanism for FAA and industry review in order to keep the use of the exception to an accept-able minimum.

It is ALPA's view that any further extension of ETOPS limits will require an overhaul of current rules. ALPA also got specific agreement from Boeing and ATA that the 207-minute authority would not be used as a basis to close transpacific diversionary airports, which could have been done under a 240-minute rule. Keeping those airports open will provide an available diversion not only for ETOPS emergencies, but also for any kind of inflight emergency for any model of aircraft. ATA, Boeing, and ALPA also agreed to send a joint letter to FAA Administrator Garvey asking FAA to do all that it can to ensure that those airports remain open for all long-range operations.[15]

The joint letter to Garvey on the airports was sent on March 26, 1999. Even though the APA objected to the 207-minute ETOPS proposal, it participated in sending the joint letter.

* * *

Contrary to some of the media reports, Boeing advocated keeping all the diversionary airports open; for Boeing it was not a twin, tri, or quad issue although the rules required them only for the twins. The fact that Boeing pursued the 207-minute authority to be used only when needed, and agreed to keep the usage to an acceptable minimum, meant for the most part that the ETOPS would be conducted under 180-minute authority. This showed that Boeing had no intention of promoting the closure of the diversionary airports.

Although it is extremely rare for airplane manufacturers or airlines to provide financial support to keep airports open, in one instance Boeing actually paid to keep an airport open.

When Midway Phoenix Corp., which was operating Midway under a cooperative arrangement with the Fish and Wildlife Service, found out that it could not make a profit, it threatened to close its operations in Midway, including the operation of the airport. To ensure the availability of Midway as an ETOPS alternate, Boeing stepped in and subsidized Midway Phoenix for nearly five years.

This was during the initial campaigns to introduce the 777 into the North Pacific. If Boeing had not stepped in and helped during the transition, the long-term viability of Midway and the prospects for the 777 in the Pacific could have been compromised.

Boeing also expended a great deal of resources in organizing industry assessments of airports in the mid- and North Pacific and Siberia. Until the breakup of the USSR, we did not even know that some of these Siberian airports existed. Recognizing the lack of operational information, Boeing formed a team to survey these Siberian and other airports important for ETOPS. To add to the credibility, Boeing made sure the survey team included members from the FAA, US and non-US airlines, and, for airports in Russian territory, the Russian regulator.

The assessment reports were widely used by the airlines operating in the North Pacific and the polar regions. The assessment started in 1997; by 2001, two dozen airports had been comprehensively assessed.

Boeing's efforts to assess the airports and the financial support it made to keep Midway open for all operations gained credibility for Boeing with the pilot unions.

* * *

After the ALPA press release appeared, the ATA issued a press release the next day, March 5, 1999. The ATA fully supported 207-minute ETOPS. The ATA was the nation's oldest and largest airline trade organization. It had 23 US and 5 non-US associated members. Its member airlines transported more than 95% of all passengers and cargo traffic in the United States. The press release said:

> The effort to extend ETOPS limits was precipitated by weather and operational constraints of the current limits and is supported by the long-time excellent safety record of reliable ETOPS operations and an extensive review process. ATA member airlines, manufacturers, pilot associations and other interested parties participated in the ETOPS review process, through the ATA ETOPS Subcommittee.[16]

* * *

In the mid-1990s, Eric Van Opstal, flight standards national resource specialist, had taken over the responsibility for ETOPS operational issues at the FAA. Eric, in his younger years, was an Army aviator who flew helicopters in Vietnam. He had been with the FAA since 1979 and had pilot ratings in several Airbus and Boeing airplanes. Eric also represented the FAA at various European committees on which I also participated. It was always a pleasure to work with Eric.

During his ten years at the ETOPS helm, Eric worked on various ETOPS operational policy issues and contributed greatly in the success of ETOPS. As the ETOPS program manager, Eric would be the one responding to the ATA's 207-minute request.

Airbus and the APA did not want the FAA to grant the ATA request without a full public review.Because the industry had proposed the 207-minute ETOPS, the FAA decided to publish the proposal in the Federal Register for public comments. The FAA was wise not to endorse the proposal. There was no point in aggravating Airbus, the APA, or the others who might disagree with the proposal. The FAA would make its findings based on all the comments it would receive from the public review process. The FAA did not hold anything back. On April 27, 1999, it published the entire submittal, including the cover letter, and allowed 45 days for comment.

The ATA's letter of submittal, which was published in the Federal Register, stated:

> In conjunction with the planning and implementation of Extended Range Operations with Two-Engine Aircraft (ETOPS) in the North Pacific area of operations, the Air Transport Association (ATA) member airlines determined that a need exists for expanded ETOPS authority beyond 180 minutes. The ETOPS Subcommittee established a process where associated airlines, the Pilots associations, Boeing, Federal Aviation Administration representatives and other parties worked together to determine the criteria to support the establishment of a proposed 15 percent operational extension of 180-minute ETOPS. The result of the effort is the attached

draft proposal, including the associated application and approval criteria, for an ETOPS policy letter providing for 207-minute ETOPS authority.

As reflected in the proposed policy letter, it was determined that there would be additional requirements associated with the new authority. Most of these requirements are self-evident. However, to assist in your analysis and review of this proposal, we have included an Executive Summary of the Boeing Reliability Study, which was conducted in support of this effort.

There are many issues associated with 207-minute ETOPS, especially in the North Pacific area of operations. One example is the availability and support functions of Alternate and Emergency airports. ATA ETOPS operators have conducted airport visits and inspections of selected airports in Alaska and Russia, and are establishing plans to expand these and foreign governments to ensure airport availability to support all international air transport operations.

In conclusion, we request your consideration and approval of the attached policy letter establishing 207-minute ETOPS authority. Since there are airlines conducting ETOPS in the North Pacific now and three more airlines plan to start operations in that area this year, we respectfully request accelerated processing of this proposal.[17]

The 207-minute ETOPS did not open any routes in the North Pacific. Airlines would continue to operate the same routes they operated around the year under 180-minute ETOPS authority. All the 207-minute did was allow some flexibility.

ETOPS required en route alternates to meet a higher weather minimum at the time of flight dispatch. If an en route alternate that the airline commonly used could not meet the ETOPS weather minimum, the airline would be able to find an en route alternate that might be farther than 180 minutes but within 207 minutes and dispatch the flight. But it did not come cheap.

For this flexibility, the airlines had to step up to more stringent dispatch requirements. Additionally, the airplane manufacturer had to ensure that the airframe-engine had more capability than required under the 180-minute approval.

Airbus advocated that the first-generation ETOPS aircraft should not be permitted to operate on ETOPS beyond 180 minutes. The pilot unions picked this up and sided with Airbus.

The ability of a backup electrical system to power at least one fuel boost pump in each main fuel tank was one of the new requirements. This provision quashed any hope for the 767 or the 757 to gain 207-minute approval without a major expensive redesign. The operator that was directly affected by this decision was United Parcel Service (UPS), which was hoping to have the 207-minute ETOPS flexibility for its 767s. Based on Boeing and Airbus analyses, only the 777 and the A330 would be able to comply with the new requirement.

* * *

Some of us on the Subcommittee were hoping for an amicable settlement of the labor dispute between the APA and American Airlines, which could open the possibility for the APA to withdraw its objection to the 207-minute proposal. But things did not go as some of us had hoped. On April 15, 1999, a US district judge fined the APA $45.5 million and held some of the officers personally liable for their actions during the labor disputes with American Airlines, which dashed any hope of reaching an agreement with the APA.

Reminiscent of the Early ETOPS media coverage in the early 1990s, a *Flight International* editorial referring to the 207-minute ETOPS asked the question, "Can or Should?" The editorial said, "ETOPS has been evolutionary so far for good reasons. From its origins in the days of big piston engines, when shutting down one out of four engines on a trans-atlantic crossing was a routine occurrence. ...The fact that this subject continually excites such emotion is not a point that should be lost on those who have to make decisions. Science and statistics are an essential part of ETOPS extension decisions, but perceptions and values must be heard too. Just because you can do something it does not mean that you should."[18]

* * *

At the International Airline CEO Conference in Miami, on May 3, 1999, the chief executive officers (CEOs) of the airlines acknowledged a shift in the type of aircraft that was increasing competition and improving efficiency. The CEOs noted that as the 767 replaced the 747 in the Atlantic, the 777 was starting to replace the 747 in the Pacific and, to a small degree, in South America. The Japan expansion for Delta, Continental, and American all focused on the 777. The CEOs also remarked that the Dallas–Tokyo route was economical in a 777, and soon American would start a San Jose–Tokyo route for the same reason.

Even with the wide application of twins on the transatlantic route and other parts of the world, the FAA did not have ETOPS rules and regulations. The FAA permitted the operations under an "exception" basis. The FAA regulations contain provisions such as "unless approved by the Administrator," which allows the FAA to permit an operation without changing the regulations. Typically, the FAA develops guidance material or policies to allow such operations. ETOPS was a good example of operations under the FAA's "exception" basis.

The FAA Docket received many comments, including one from Boeing that requested the FAA to develop ETOPS rules and regulations. The difference between the supporters and the detractors of the 207-minute ETOPS was that the supporters wanted the FAA to issue the 207-minute operations policy and then launch the activity to update the Federal Aviation Regulations (FAR), and the detractors did not want the FAA to consider the 207-minute proposal until the FARs were updated.

Updating the FARs to incorporate ETOPS would be a major effort. ETOPS would affect the certification of engines, the airplane and its systems, and the Operational Approval of the operators.

The 777 operations in the Pacific and potentially the future of the 777 family could be affected if the detractors could convince the FAA to shelve the 207-minute proposal until the FARs were updated.

Updating the regulations can be a long and arduous process and can easily take years. The stakes were high. It could also affect billions of dollars of future sales of the 777s and the A340s.

We anticipated Airbus to strongly object the 207-minute proposal published in the Federal Register. Moreover, Airbus had some excellent help!

Tony Broderick, the FAA's ETOPS patriarch, who kept an open mind and challenged Boeing to meet the very high standards of Early ETOPS, had retired and joined Airbus as a consultant. Nearly a month after the May 11, 1996, Value Jet DC-9 accident that killed 110 people on board, Broderick decided to retire from the position of FAA's associate administrator for regulations and certification. As an Airbus consultant, the quick-witted Broderick became the very credible and highly recognizable new American face espousing Forgeard and Leahy's stances on ETOPS.

Like Anakin Skywalker, who had gone to the dark side and become Darth Vader in the *Star Wars* movie, some Boeing diehards felt that Broderick had gone to the "dark side." Apparently, Airbus offered a very lucrative contract.

* * *

On the US side, the main objection came from the APA and its parent organization, the CAPA. They told the FAA that it should not proceed with the 207-minute proposal.

The other objections came from the DGAC, France, and the Association Européene des Constructéurs de Materiel Aerospatial (AECMA). The DGAC pointed to the lack of harmonization on the two sides of the Atlantic. The fact that the JAA ETOPS Working Group had decided not to even entertain the 207-minute proposal was lost in translation.

AECMA is the European association of aerospace industries. Airbus was AECMA's most influential member. AECMA strongly opposed the 207-minute proposal.

The Europeans also added that the International Civil Aviation Organization (ICAO), a branch of the United Nations that specializes in international aviation, should be the one recommending such extensions.

All the US airlines, a few international airlines, ALPA, all three engine manufacturers (Pratt & Whitney, GE, and Rolls-Royce), and Boeing supported the proposal. Supporters cited the excellent reliability and safety of twins on ETOPS.

A non-US airline group commented that while the US airlines would be able to take advantage of this flexibility, it might not be available to their member airlines.

Boeing was pleased to see Dr. Hans Krakauer's and David Stempler's organization, the IAPA, support the proposal: "IAPA supports the concepts of ETOPS approval and, in principle, the 15% extension to a 180-minute approval on the lines proposed." [19]

The industry virtually anticipated who would be on which side of the fence. There was really no surprise, except for one. It was the first time we, in the world of ETOPS, had heard of the group called International Air Crash Victims Families Group, which submitted to the Docket, that "... the present application for extension of separation from 180-minute to 207-minute be held in abeyance, pending further studies. That a Public Hearing be held. That the ETOPS work group be enlarged to include representation from all interested parties." [20]

Boeing submitted its comments to the Docket. Our comments showed essentially our overwhelming support of the FAA proposal.

Airbus waited until the last hour of the last day of the comment period to submit its 35 pages of comments blasting the 207-minute ETOPS proposal.

Boeing perceived the Airbus comments to be inaccurate about ETOPS and Boeing airplanes. It felt compelled to submit a second set of comments. Even though the comment period had closed, Boeing decided to submit them anyway. It was up to the FAA to ignore any late submittals.

Boeing comments were recorded in the FAA Docket on July 8, 1999. Boeing said, "Enclosed please find an additional submittal to the docket. While we are aware the stated period of time for such submittals has passed we are hopeful you will accept and fully consider our comments. ... Boeing has had an opportunity to review the comments received by the FAA during the comment period for 207-minute ETOPS (Docket No. 29547). In our view, many of the comments are not germane to 207minutes in the North Pacific. Additionally, some of the comments include inaccuracies about Boeing airplanes, factual errors or misrepresentations. Boeing submits the following for purposes of clarification and accuracy." [21]

Boeing's second submittal allowed the FAA to look at the issue from both sides. We hoped it would help the FAA reach a rational conclusion.

We learned from industry sources that Boeing's second round of submittals rattled Airbus. Apparently, Airbus had not anticipated that

Boeing would submit a direct rebuttal to the Airbus comments after the comment period had ended.

* * *

The news of our submittal on July 8 was overshadowed by the shock waves that Singapore Airlines sent around the world.

In the middle of July 1999, Singapore Airlines decided to dispose of the 300-seater long-range A340-300s in favor of the 300-seater long-range 777-200ERs. Some of the A340s had not yet been delivered from the factory to Singapore Airlines.

The media speculated, "SIA may also be expecting that ETOPS will be extended to 207-minute allowing the 777 to be used with greater flexibility, particularly if it converts some orders and options to the -200X/-300X."[22]

Undoubtedly, it was a shock to Airbus and to its newly installed leader, Noel Forgeard. After all, just a few months back, on November 10, 1998, after declaring that airlines preferred the four-engine A340s for long-range routes to the 777, Forgeard had told the French media, "The A340 has relegated the 777 to the role of a regional transporter."[23]

Forgeard's pronouncement of the 777's death from the long-range market was, obviously, premature.

Incidentally, by February 2010, airlines had ordered nearly three times more 777s than A340s.

* * *

Boeing was considering the launch of the 777-200LR and the 777-300ER. These airplanes would seat anywhere from 300 to 400 passengers and could cover up to a range of 9,400 nm (17,400 km). Combined with the 207-minute ETOPS flexibility, these airplanes had the potential to eliminate the A340s from the Pacific market.

Airbus must have felt severely threatened or felt it had no options left, because it did something that was very unusual. It blatantly played the safety card in an advertisement. Until that time, even though Airbus advertised a preference for the A340 over the 777 and quads over twins, Airbus did not openly question the safety of these operations.

In early October 1999, Airbus launched a print advertisement in aviation trade magazines, as well as in such business publications as *The Economist, Fortune, Financial Times*, and the European and Asian editions of *The Wall Street Journal.*

The ad showed wave-tossed waters as if something big had just splashed into it, with ominous dark clouds above and, in the far corner, an image of the four-engine Airbus A340 flying away. The text read, "If you're over the middle of the Pacific, you want to be in the middle of four engines." This was followed by a smaller set of texts on the side that read, "It's always reassuring to have the redundancy option of four engines rather than two. Especially when you're a long, long, long way from home."

The industry called it the "splash ad," a reference to a twin splashing in the waters and creating the waves while a quad, the A340, safely continued its flight.

Airbus had a reputation for being overly aggressive in its media campaigns. "The Airbus Industrie publicity machine quickly established a reputation as a very skillful, if not ruthless, operation, devoted to harassing and harrying the opposition, particularly Boeing, at every opportunity. … Many years later (in 1996) [Henri] Ziegler (the first President of Airbus Industrie) was to admit that the Airbus style was perhaps too aggressive."[24]

However, this time Airbus broke the taboo!

Normally, the airlines and the airplane manufacturers shun blatant safety comparisons in advertisements. Scaring the traveling public is considered a no-win proposition for all. The industry regards it as fear mongering. Because the data did not support safety concerns, some in the industry considered it a sign of desperation in the Airbus camp.

* * *

Most of us in aviation know that commercial air transportation is one of the safest means of transportation. As an example, for the years 1999 through 2003, Department of Transportation (DOT) data on US accidental deaths show that the five-year average for motor vehicles is 36,676 per year; recreational boating, 714; bicycles, 695; and air carriers, including the people who died on the airplanes on 9/11, 138. If we were to exclude the deliberate mayhem at the hands of the terrorists on the four airplanes on 9/11, the yearly average for the five years would be 87. This is nearly 400 times fewer fatalities than from motor vehicles!

Actually, for many years there has not been a single fatality in commercial aviation in the United States. Often, fatalities from horse-drawn carts, like the ones in the Amish community in Pennsylvania, are greater than from commercial aviation in the United States.

In spite of these numbers, we feel more comfortable being on the ground than in the air. Most of us feel safer in a motor vehicle or on a bike ride than on an airplane. Many of us pray when we get on an airplane or encounter turbulence on the flight. Praying is the last thing on our mind while on a recreational boat ride or cruising down the highway.

Fear is based on gut feel. We do not fear cars. Cars are nothing more than carts with four wheels driven by an engine. Carts have been with us for many centuries. The only difference is we can go faster and do not have to clean up after the horses!

It is different with flying. In every culture around the globe, there are fascinating stories of winged horses, flying chariots, magic carpets, and so on. For centuries, man has attempted to fly like a bird but failed. Despite flying being humankind's oldest dream, we still fear flying.

We may have learned at school that airplane wings create lift, which sustains the airplane in the air, but somehow we cannot relate to it. Besides, we can think of so many things that can go wrong. Occasional video footage from an airplane accident somewhere in the world helps validate our fear.

Most of us do not know the rigor the engineers have to go through during airplane design. For example, to ensure that an airplane will have the necessary hydraulic power for the brakes or the control surfaces to maneuver the airplane under even the worst situation, today's airplanes may have several independent hydraulic systems with sufficient physical separation such that if something blows up, it does not totally compromise the operation of the brakes or the control surfaces.

Some of us worry about the number of engines on the airplane. With twins, we worry about an engine failure and having to be with 200 other people sitting white-knuckled while the airplane is chugging along with one operative engine.

The data on twins shows that diversion due to an engine failure in flight is extremely rare. The average rate for an airplane like the 777 is

around one diversion for every 100,000 flights. Moreover, the FAA certi-
fies the twins to operate on one engine. Besides, it is just a diversion to
an airport. It may be inconvenient but the passengers are safe.

Actually, an engine failure on a modern twin is so rare that many
pilots retire after a lifetime of commercial flying without experienc-
ing an engine failure in flight. Until the fateful day, even Capt. "Sully"
Sullenberger III, who became an instant American hero after ditching
the US Airways A320 in the Hudson River off Manhattan in New York
on January 15, 2009 after bird strikes disabled both engines, had never
encountered loss of an engine in flight in his 27,000 hours of flying in
40 years.

Furthermore, in aviation, the manufacturers are continually refin-
ing the product reliability based on the lessons learned. The industry anticipates the diversion rate to go even lower with better system
designs.

Engineers design and test the engines to make sure the in-flight failures are extremely rare. The possibility of the second engine failing on a
twinjet after the first one has failed is almost impossible. On a Western-
built twin, there never has been an accident in which both engines failed
for independent cause. There have been instances of all engines failing
for a common cause—because the airplane flew right through a cloud
of volcanic ash, or as in the case of Capt. Sullenberger encountered a
flock of birds, or the airplane ran out of fuel, at which point the number
of engines makes no difference!

All of us know that the level of risk in motor vehicles, boats, or bicycles does not significantly change with distance. The risk is nearly the
same for every mile traveled. The risk is no greater at the start of the trip
than at the middle or the end of the trip. But it is different in aviation.

Nearly 95% of the risk in commercial aviation is at the beginning
and at the end of the trip—takeoff, climb and descent, and the landing phases. The cruise phase accounts for about 5% only. Therefore,
extending the cruise phase by flying long ranges does not significantly
increase the overall risk.

Besides, aviation regulations, including those of the FAA, ensure
that all commercial airplanes have a comparable level of safety and comply with all the stringent requirements. Rigor in design ensures that
the probability of failure of critical systems in commercial airplanes is
extremely low, often less than one in a billion.

Even though counter-intuitive, all the data show that twins are as safe as the quads. It all has to do with the level of effort put in designing the high levels of reliability into the airplane systems and the engine. In fact, the data show that the modern twins are even safer than the three- and four-engine airliners they replaced.

The facts and data overwhelmingly support the safety of twins at all ranges.

Just because the fear is not rational or not supported by data does not mean we do not fear. For many of us, these statistics do not mean much. Most of us have some innate fear of flying. But many long-timers in the aviation industry were shocked when Airbus decided to exploit the intrinsic fear of flying by questioning the safety of twins on long ranges.

* * *

The reaction to the "splash ad" was swift and critical. The heads of several airlines openly criticized Airbus. For example, on October 18, 1999, the chief executive of Continental Airlines, Gordon Bethune, fired off a letter to Noel Forgeard to express his utter disappointment. He asked Airbus to drop its ad campaign. Even though, Bethune had copied his letter only to the editor of *Aviation Week*, the ATA board of directors, and the Aviation Safety Alliance board of directors, copies of the letter were widely circulated in the industry.

Boeing also formally expressed to Airbus its displeasure with the ad.

The Wall Street Journal said Airbus dismissed any controversy. "'It's all about operations,' says Michel Guerard (Airbus Vice President for Corporate Communications), who says he has received positive reactions to the ad. 'We believe that over certain remote areas, it makes sense to have a four-engine aircraft.' The ad 'is not about safety,' he says. 'We're certainly not trying to inspire fear.'... Indeed, Mr. Guerard is proud of the ad. 'It has had a lot of impact. If there were an award for impact in aviation advertising, this would win it.'"[25]

* * *

On January 21, 2000, the FAA published a notice in the Federal Register.[26] After responding to public comments on the ATA's 207-minute proposal, the FAA informed the public of its decision to establish the conditions for a limited authorization for up to 207-minute ETOPS operations. The FAA also invited comments, if any, to its newly released 207-minute proposal. Unless the FAA issued a revision to its position based on the public comments, the 207-minute policy would be effective from March 21, 2000.

The FAA also declared its intent to task the Aviation Rulemaking Advisory Committee (ARAC) to recommend safety standards and procedures for extended-range operations, regardless of the number of engines.

The law allows the US Government to form and use the ARAC as necessary. Typically, the ARAC forms a working group composed of experts with an interest in the assigned task. Any individual with an interest and expertise on the subject can apply to join the working group. Even though the ARAC meetings are open to the public, the working group meetings are open only to those members of the public who are selected to participate.

In the Federal Register, referring to the 207-minute policy, the FAA said:

> This policy is effective on March 21, 2000. ...
>
> The FAA does not believe, though, that approval of a limited 207-minute North Pacific ETOPS operation must await further ETOPS rulemaking. The FAA recognizes the potential safety benefit that is provided with an extension to 180-minute ETOPS as it applies to operations in the North Pacific. ...
>
> Another reason the FAA is confident in proceeding with the 207-minute approval is the basic manner in which the 777 was type certificated. It is the only airplane that was designed from the start for ETOPS operation on its first day of service. This required Boeing to address all possible failure modes of past airplanes and engines and demonstrate the 777 was designed to preclude those failures. This extensive safety analysis has produced an airplane that exceeds the dispatch reliability of any previous airplane, which is a measure of the reliability of the airplane design and air carrier maintenance programs.

> The FAA believes the operational history of the airplane has proven the validity of this approach and the uniqueness of the 777 for consideration of 207-minute ETOPS operations....
>
> Air carriers approved to use the special 207-minute authorization must amend their MEL and receive FAA approval of the amendment, prior to exercising the special authorization. Application for the special authorization will only be considered from air carriers that currently hold 180-minute ETOPS operational approval. The authorization will only apply and be valid for use in the North Pacific area of operation....

Although it was a policy that would apply to all twins, Boeing was pleased to see the FAA officially acknowledge the superiority of the 777 design and the effectiveness of the Early ETOPS process for the airplane. Boeing could not have expected any better outcome than this. Boeing was ecstatic, as were the US airlines gearing to jump to the 207-minute ETOPS. ALPA was pleased that the FAA accepted the additional safety demands placed on the manufacturer and the airlines for the 207-minute approval.

Despite the FAA's public acclamation for the 777 Early ETOPS process, AECMA told the media, "... [AECMA] cannot support the view that only aircraft whose original ETOPS approval used the Early-ETOPS methodology as a substitute for real service experience should be eligible for a future increase of their maximum diversion time beyond 180-minutes."[27]

Three days before the comment deadline, on March 3, 2000, Airbus submitted a 12-page comment, mostly reiterating some of its earlier comments. The APA argued that there was no demonstrable need for change and requested that the FAA postpone implementation of the new 207-minute policy. AECMA called it a deviation from the ICAO published standards. Most of the other commenters were supportive of the FAA's decision.

This time also, Boeing submitted a set of comments, which were essentially the rebuttal to Airbus, the APA, and AECMA. In the March 6, 2000, submittal to the FAA Docket, Boeing proudly cited records of ETOPS success and said, "Boeing has had an opportunity to review some of the comments already received by the FAA during the comment period for this Docket. In our view, many of these comments repeat comments previously submitted and disposed of by the FAA for Docket number 29547. In addition, some of the current docket comments are not germane to 207-minute in the North Pacific, while others contain inaccuracies about Boeing airplanes or other factual errors and misrepresentations. Therefore, Boeing submits the attached enclosure to this letter for the purposes of clarification and accuracy. Boeing supports the 207-minute Extended Range Operations with Two-Engine Aircraft (ETOPS) Operation Approval Criteria and strongly urges the FAA to adopt the policy effective March 21, 2000."[28]

Boeing's observations, fully backed by supporting facts, neutralized the adverse comments.

The 207-minute ETOPS policy became effective on March 21, 2000.

* * *

Boeing had been anxiously waiting to submit its application to the FAA Certification Branch for the 207-minute approval for the 777 airframe-engine combinations. The FAA issued the 207-minute approval for the 777 on April 26, 2000. This opened the door for the airlines to pursue their Operational Approvals.

United Airlines received its approval for the 207-minute on May 2, followed by Continental Airlines on June 15 and American Airlines on November 2. It did not take long before the Asian countries in the Pacific Rim allowed a similar level of approval for their operators.

It was pure coincidence that Boeing launched the two very-long-range airplanes just over a month after the FAA declared its intent to allow 207-minute ETOPS. On February 29, 2000, Boeing launched the 300-seater ultra-long-range 777-200LR and the 380-seater long-range 777-300ER to compete with the 300- to 400-seater ultra-long and long-range A340-500 and -600, which Airbus had launched in 1997. The A340-500 and the 777-200LR flew longer ranges than the A340-600 and the 777-300ER. Within a couple months of the launch, the 777 orders were catching up to the total A340-500/600 orders.

The media quoted aviation analysts who attributed the strong sales of the newly launched 777-200LR and the 777-300ER, worth many billions of dollars, to the advent of the 207-minute ETOPS.

Reportedly, Airbus approached the European Commission to intervene. We were told that Airbus argued that the 207-minute operation was unsafe and endangered the lives of European travelers flying on US airlines over the North Pacific. We learnt that on May 31, 2000, the European Commission circulated a position paper on the FAA approval of 207 minutes ETOPS operation for the Boeing 777 airplane. But in the end, the European Commission did not intervene.

Northwest Airlines was the only US airline to operate the A330s on the transpacific routes. Like its competitors operating the 777s in the North Pacific, it also sought the 207-minute ETOPS flexibility. But the ETOPS rules required the airplane to qualify for the 207-minute before the airline could be granted the approval. Airbus approached the FAA Certification Branch for the 207-minute approval for the A330. However, I understand that the airplane was not able to meet the minimum airplane system regulatory requirement to qualify for the 207-minute ETOPS. Apparently, the "poison pill" that Airbus promoted at the ATA ETOPS Subcommittee to stop the 767s and the 757s backfired on Airbus by also stopping the A330s. Neither Airbus nor the FAA released any public statement regarding the inability of the A330 to qualify for the 207-minute. Even at the end of February 2010, the 777s were the only airplanes that could meet the FAA's stringent 207-minute ETOPS requirements.

* * *

The FAA kept its promise. On June 14, 2000, it announced in the Federal Register[29] that it had tasked an ARAC to provide advice and recommendations to the FAA. It assigned the ARAC ten tasks:

1. Review the existing policy and requirements found in Advisory Circular (AC) 120–42A, applicable ETOPS special conditions, and policy memorandums and notices, for certification and operational regulations and guidance material for ETOPS approvals up to 180 minutes.
2. Develop comprehensive ETOPS airworthiness standards for 14 CFR parts 25, 33, 121, and 135, as appropriate, to codify the existing policies and practices.

3. Develop ETOPS requirements for operations and excess of 180 minutes up to whatever extent that may be justified. Develop those requirements such that incremental approvals up to a maximum may be approved.
4. Develop standardized requirements for extended range operations for all airplanes, regardless of the number of engines, including all turbojet and turbopropeller commercial twin-engine airplanes (business jets), excluding reciprocating engine powered commercial airplanes. This effort should establish criteria for diversion times up to 180 minutes that is consistent with existing ETOPS policy and procedures. It should also develop criteria for diversion times beyond 180 minutes that is consistent with the ETOPS criteria developed by the working group.
5. Develop additional guidance and/or advisory material as the ARAC finds appropriate.
6. Harmonize such standardized requirements across national boundaries and regulatory bodies.
7. Any proposal to increase the safety requirements for existing ETOPS approvals up to 207 minutes must contain data defining the unsafe conditions that would warrant the safety requirements.
8. The working group will provide briefings to the Transport Airplane and Engine Issues group.
9. The recommendations should consider the comments received as a result of the April 27, 1999 and January 21, 2000 Federal Register notices.
10. Within one year of publication of the ARAC task in the Federal Register, submit recommendations to the FAA in the form of a proposed rule.

The JAA also launched a similar activity in Europe. Sometimes it appeared as if the regulators from the two sides of the Atlantic were competing to see who would prevail in the end.

Possibly fearing the FAA's global leadership on ETOPS, Airbus and some of the European countries prompted the ICAO to play a leadership role in setting new ETOPS global standards. ICAO Member States are required to follow the ICAO standards unless the States have a valid reason to file differences with the ICAO.

The German and the French ambassadors were successful in resurrecting the ICAO Operations Panel, which had been dormant since 1992. In 2000, one of the tasks on the agenda for the panel was to examine ETOPS.

* * *

Encouraged by the 207-minute ETOPS authority, US airlines started to expand the twin's services in the transpacific. The Asian airlines were not far behind.

In the mid-1990s, Boeing expected the 777 to change the Pacific market for ever, just like the 767 had done for the transatlantic market. In 2009, the 777 displaced the 747, the queen of the skies over the Pacific.

The 207-minute authority helped the 777 dominate the Pacific. An airplane that Airbus had declared unsuitable for operations in the "extreme" areas over the Pacific ended up dominating the region.

6

THE FINAL VERDICT

Changing the ground rules—the new rulemaking

When the FAA announced the tasking to the ARAC, it solicited public participation. Around 50 participants responded to the FAA request. They represented various manufacturers of airframes and engines, US and international airlines, US and non-US pilot unions, US and international regulators, various industry associations, and public interest groups. Boeing submitted its list of participants and designated me as the leader of the Boeing team.

Since 1997, Airbus had been advocating an all-inclusive LROPS concept in the media and with the airlines. An article in *Flight Newsletter*[1] captured the intent of LROPS thusly: "Airbus is particularly concerned about current services that can take airliners into 'extreme' locations—defined as areas such as the Arctic and Antarctic, and the northern Siberia, South Pacific, and Himalayan regions—and wants a new regulatory concept that would recognize environmental factors."

Quoting the Airbus product integrity vice president, the *Flight Newsletter* added, "Criteria based only on diversion time penalize operations in 'benign' areas and fail to address safety aspects related to extreme environment and very long flights. ... Existing long- and extended-range criteria and current aircraft design will not be sufficient to ensure the safety of occupants."

In the comprehensive LROPS CD-ROM that Airbus had distributed around the world, LROPS was defined as longer flights of up to 20 hours and with up to 8-hour cruising time from diversionary airports. Airbus stated that LROPS should apply to all airplanes regardless of the number of engines. Moreover, according to Airbus, the LROPS philosophy would control design, maintenance, and operational parameters so that diversions were "not needed at all."

Some in the industry were not sure if Airbus was proposing these new so-called "LROPS" standards because there was a genuine safety shortcoming or if it was just a way for Airbus to stop the 777 at 180-minute ETOPS to protect the A340 and the A380. After all, Airbus had publicly declared its intent to constrain twins such as the 777 from operating on the long-range routes.

Even though the LROPS CD contained a great deal of information, internally, Boeing concluded that the primary purpose of the CD was to create uncertainty and ambiguity. The intent was to make the airlines rethink their positions on the use of twins in some parts of the world. Some of us felt that it was an effective marketing tool.

However, only time would tell if the Airbus proposals would withstand the scrutiny of the technical experts in the ARAC. Now it would be up to Airbus to convince the ARAC, the JAA, and the ICAO to change the national and international regulations.

Airbus was fully aware that justifying the constraints on twins with sound technical arguments would not be as easy as preparing a marketing brochure or blasting the twins in a full-page paid advertisement in a magazine.

Boeing had thoroughly scrubbed the LROPS CD. It was prepared to challenge Airbus claims.

Airbus was under no illusion that Boeing would do everything it could to discredit the LROPS proposal. It knew it had an uphill task, but Airbus was not to be easily intimidated.

* * *

In the LROPS CD, Airbus questioned the feasibility of en route alternate airports on long-range routes. It went into excruciating detail to show that en route alternates, on routes that required greater than 180-minute ETOPS, were marginal and not acceptable. Airbus cited Siberian and North Pacific weather conditions in winter, the potential for volcanic activity in the Kamchatka regions in the far eastern regions of Russia, bird activity in mid-Pacific airports, or lack of suitable accommodation for passengers at remote airports around the world as factors that would render many en route alternates unsuitable for ETOPS.

Many of the airports cited were in the Siberian regions. Because Boeing had actual data from its airport surveys, Boeing questioned the data in the LROPS CD. For example, the Airbus CD claimed there was no rescue and fire fighting (RFF) equipment at Shemya, an airport in the North Pacific. We challenged Airbus by showing the actual pictures of the RFF facilities at this airport. The airport survey reports included data that refuted many of the Airbus claims of deficiencies.

* * *

Airbus also proposed incorporating design features on the A340 and the A380 such that they would not require a diversion. Therefore, they could skip all of what it called the "marginal airports" in the mid- and North Pacific and the Siberian regions. Many airline representatives were apprehensive of a manufacturer's promise to design an airplane that would not require a diversion.

Even though US regulations did not require a quad to land at the nearest suitable airport, certain flight conditions would require even a quad to land at an en route alternate because of a fuel situation. One of these flight conditions was decompression. The regulations required commercial airplanes operating above a certain altitude to carry sufficient oxygen to clear obstacles en route and descend to a safe altitude after a decompression or depressurization.

During engine design, the fuel consumption for the airplanes is optimized for typical cruise altitudes. Operating at lower altitudes for any reason requires more fuel and could result in the inability of the airplane to reach the planned destination and thus to divert. The LROPS CD showed that Airbus had a solution for its quads—the A340 and the A380.

Airbus proposed installing an onboard oxygen generation system (OBOGS) for LROPS. This system separated oxygen and nitrogen from pressurized air by means of a molecular sieve, using a specialized technique called "rapid pressure swing adsorption." OBOGS had been used in military airplanes but had not been tried on passenger airplanes with a few hundred passengers on board. Airbus proposed that with OBOGS the depressurized aircraft would be able to maintain a higher altitude and thereby reduce fuel consumption and avoid any diversion. Airbus said the aircraft would never be required to descend to "uneconomic flight levels" following depressurization.

The media questioned the effect on the body of an average passenger flying at these unpressurized altitudes. To save fuel, Airbus had proposed operating around 18,000 feet (5,500 m) with **OBOGS**. Breathing oxygen would keep the passengers alive, but the change in pressure could wreak havoc on a person's body.

According to medical experts, the passengers would suffer from conditions such as barotraumas, decompression sickness, and hypoxia. The pressure changes would create changes in the size of trapped gas inside the body, causing severe pain and possible internal damage. The passenger would feel thousands of pinpricks as the body's fat tissues released the dissolved nitrogen. Some passengers could face extreme joint pain or choking due to vapor lock from air bubbles. The partial pressure of oxygen in the blood could result in a decrease in color vision/tunnel vision, drowsiness, impaired judgment, or loss of motor coordination. The age and pulmonary status of an individual would make a big difference in how a person would react to flying unpressurized for any considerable time.

One of the medical doctors who had researched aviation medicine suggested the passengers would get some relief by "releasing gas any way they could with reckless abandon."

The media questioned if the airlines would be prepared to expose the passengers to such risks to save a few pounds of fuel or to avoid planning for an alternate en route.

Air Transport World said, "Airbus is pushing a 'no diversion' capability of up to 8 hr. with an onboard oxygen generating system for its A340 and A380. This, Airbus says, 'would remove the need for diversion to the nearest airport and the need to demonstrate recovery plans in Polar Regions.' However, some medical experts wonder about how well elderly or overweight passengers might cope with up to 8 hr. in a depressurized environment above 15,000 ft. ... Physiological needs of passengers under 100% oxygen for 8 hr. above 15,000 ft. is an additional issue that needs to be addressed."[2]

* * *

While justifying the **LROPS** concept, Airbus surprised the industry by challenging the basic tenet of ETOPS itself. Airbus questioned the ICAO safety risk model from the early 1980s, which was the linchpin of ETOPS approval.

On all airplanes, when an engine fails, the remaining engine(s) can be operated at a higher thrust level than the level used during cruise. This higher level of thrust is called Maximum Continuous Thrust (MCT). As the name implies, MCT can be used continuously during the entire duration of the remaining flight. Being a higher thrust level, it puts additional stress on the engine and as a result increases the probability of engine failure. Based on data analyzed up to the 1980s, the ICAO had conservatively assumed that operating at MCT doubled the average risk.

Airbus astounded the industry by saying the risk was 86 to 1—43 times greater than what had been considered a conservative number in all the risk models.

The issue Airbus raised, if valid, would stop all ETOPS, including those with less than 180-minute. This would not only stop the 777s but all ETOPS twins, including the A330s. But Airbus had a way out to preserve the existing operations up to 180 minutes.

Airbus proposed that based on satisfactory in-service experience since 1985, operations below 180-minute ETOPS would be allowed to continue. However, in light of the Airbus findings, the data would not support any extension of ETOPS beyond 180-minute.

The big problem with the Airbus assertion was that we in the industry had not seen any data to support this claim. The industry eagerly waited to see the data that Airbus said it had.

Pratt & Whitney, GE and its partner Snecma, and Rolls-Royce are the only engine options available for all the Boeing and Airbus airplanes. None of these jet engines on any Boeing twin or a quad showed such a trend. It was difficult for Boeing to assume that for some reason a jet engine would behave drastically different when mounted on an Airbus airframe.

Citing the proprietary status, Airbus did not release the data even when requested by the airlines. There was no way Boeing was going to let Airbus make the same assertion to the ARAC while hiding behind the proprietary curtain. If it wanted to influence the ARAC, it would have to find a way to get around the so-called "proprietary" nature and convince the group with facts and data. Although the media preferred the sound bites, the technical groups generally liked to scrutinize the raw data.

Some in the industry thought creating a cloud around an issue was a common tactic if the issue could not be refuted outright with facts and data. It was possible that Airbus' assertion of proprietary data was just a smokescreen because Airbus really did not have the data to back up its claim.

By making such an outrageous claim, it was possible that Airbus was attempting to create some psychological discomfort among some of the ARAC members. After all, just like Boeing, Airbus was a respectable manufacturer, and people gave it the benefit of the doubt. If Airbus could get enough members to waver, it could stall the issue and stop twins from going beyond 207 minutes.

Boeing was not going to let the situation go that far. If Airbus made this claim of 86 to 1 to the ARAC and refused to share the data, Boeing could always request the ARAC Working Group to task the three engine manufacturers to comb their entire database and submit the findings. After all, they had all the data on the engines that Boeing and Airbus had.

* * *

To encourage free and frank discussion on technical issues, the ARAC restricted members of the Working Group from publicly divulging the proceedings of the meetings. Often, the members brought data from their organizations, which, if made public, could be misused by detractors. Sharing facts and data helped deliberations and led to a rational and fact-based conclusion.

Most of the participants were seasoned veterans of the aviation industry. That ARAC Working Group contained a tremendous wealth of aviation knowledge.

Airbus lost some credibility when the ARAC found that Airbus had been misusing the data presented to the Working Group. It had used the "restricted" data provided by an airline at the Working Group in its sales campaigns. It was embarrassing even for Boeing to see Airbus, a reputable manufacturer, chastised so badly at the Working Group meeting in Palm Coast, Florida.

This embarrassing episode resulted in a formal apology from Airbus. On January 26, 2001, Alain Garcia, Airbus senior vice president of engineering, apologized to the FAA and the chairman of the ARAC, for going against an ARAC ground rule. Garcia promised to remove the data in question from all presentations, and made a commitment never to use such data henceforth for any other purposes other than permitted by the ARAC.

These were not the best of times for Airbus. It was about to get another shock!

* * *

With the demise of the Soviet Union, Russia was opening more of its airspace for international flights. In 1993, Russia met with US and industry representatives to explore opening direct routes over the North Pole, which would significantly cut the flying time between cities in North America and Asia. For example, the airlines would be able to fly directly between New York and Beijing without having to stop in Anchorage for refueling. The route was open for trial flights in July 1998.

After nearly 650 trial flights, on February 1, 2001, four polar routes were open between North America and Asia that went right over or near the North Pole.

Airbus strongly advocated that the Siberian airports were not suitable as diversion airports. Because the ETOPS twins required diversion airports, it argued that twins should not be permitted on the north polar routes. Airbus said, "… weather conditions may be such that landing is not possible. This is particularly true on trans-polar and trans-Pacific routes."[3] It advocated the use of quads on these routes because these airplanes could continue to their destination even after the failure of an engine.

We perceived this as another Airbus attempt to exclude 777 operations from the polar routes. Even though Boeing disagreed with the Airbus position, the regulators could not ignore the safety concerns raised by a reputable manufacturer.

On March 5, 2001, the FAA issued a "Polar Policy" that permitted twins to operate on these polar routes but had to comply with a set of requirements. It was a big disappointment for Airbus. As if to add insult to injury, the FAA also concluded that the same requirements were equally applicable to all airplanes operating on these routes, including the quads.

* * *

The FAA's polar policy was a vindication of the Boeing position.

Boeing was eager to share with airlines around the world its belief that the FAA's polar policy supported the viability of the 777 over the polar routes. Within a couple of months after the FAA's release of the policy, in May 2001, Boeing invited all the airlines around the world to a symposium.

At the symposium in Phuket, a resort in Thailand, Boeing discussed the challenges of operating on the polar routes, the FAA requirements and the support that Boeing provided to address those challenges and the regulatory requirements. Boeing had a ready-made support package for the airlines that were planning to start polar operations.

Under the leadership of Capt. Jim Starley, senior director of flight operations, Continental Airlines had pioneered 777 polar operations. Boeing was delighted to have Capt. Starley present the airline's perspective of polar operations. Capt. Starley presented all the steps that Continental went through in preparing for polar operations and the experience of actual 777 operations.

United Airlines had been operating 747s on the polar route at the time and was planning to start 777 operations on the route. Gene Cameron, chief of flight dispatch, presented United Airlines' perspective.

Having the airlines share their actual operating experience on the polar routes made the symposium very productive and worthwhile for many airlines.

Most of the major airlines around the world were at the symposium. Almost every airline in the Pacific corridor that was even vaguely contemplating polar operations was there. The symposium not only dispelled the Airbus myth that twins could not be operated on the polar routes, but it also supplied the airlines with a systematic checklist for operating on the polar routes.

Capt. Jim Starley and Gene Cameron have participated in many Boeing ETOPS symposiums. The insights and the airline perspectives they brought to this symposium and to many others have greatly enhanced the safety of airline operations around the world.

$$* * *$$

The ARAC had nominated Tim Gallagher as the chairman of the ARAC ETOPS Working Group. Tim had held various management positions at United Airlines. He flew the Airbus A320s.

At its first meeting, the Working Group decided to form two subgroups. One subgroup would focus on the Type Design Approval—develop criteria to allow the ETOPS approval of airframe-engine combinations. The other group would focus on operational issues. This group would also tackle policy issues such as ETOPS beyond 180 minutes. There were about 10 to 12 people in the Type Design group and as many as 40 in the Operations group.

Selecting the chairmen for the subgroups was tricky. Because I had a meeting in Europe, I had to leave the first meeting early and did not participate in the actual discussion or the selection process. Nevertheless, I found later that the airlines did not want the pilot unions to chair the Operations subgroup. Likewise, the pilot unions did not want the airlines to head the Operations subgroup. Apparently because I had worked closely with the airlines and the pilot unions during the 207-minute ETOPS, I became the preferred choice to chair the Operations side. I understand selecting the chairman for the Type Design side was much easier. Because they could not have a manufacturer lead the Type Design group, they selected a member from the pilot union to chair the group.

Leadership is about setting the tone. Tim Gallagher did something that I believe was responsible for the success of the ARAC ETOPS Working Group. Tim wanted the members to focus on "what can I live with" rather than "what I want." I think this changed the entire mindset. It brought in the attitude of compromise. Whenever some members objected, they really had to explain why they could not live with the issue, which would be more difficult than saying they did not want it. Further, to foster consensus within the group, we were called "coordinators" rather than "subgroup chairs."

Although the FAA had tasked the ARAC to complete its work in 12 months, the combination of 9/11and the Working Group's desire to come to a consensus—"I can live with it"—delayed completion. The Working Group finalized its report on October 26, 2002, and submitted it to the ARAC Air Carrier Operations Issues Group on December 16, 2002.

The ARAC Air Carrier Operations Issues Group meeting is public. It was held at FAA headquarters in Washington, D.C. All the interested parties were there. I represented Boeing, and there were three Airbus representatives.

The ARAC Air Carrier Operations Issues Group accepted the report of the ARAC ETOPS Working Group without dissent. The report was submitted to the FAA and became a public document. The FAA posted the report immediately on its public Web site.

On January 28, 2003, Nicholas A. Sabatini, the FAA's associate administrator for regulation and certification, wrote to the chairman of the ARAC Air Carrier Operations Issues Group, "... the working group did an excellent and thorough job in meeting the tasks assigned them. The minutes of the December 16 Air Carrier Operations Issues group meeting reflect the wide range of consensus that was achieved throughout industry and with certain public interests in developing these recommendations. The next task is within the FAA – to gain priority for the project so that resources may be dedicated to publishing an NPRM [Notice of Proposed Rulemaking]. I understand that my staff is working diligently toward achieving that task. I appreciate the dedication of the working group to the tasks assigned and the leadership of Tim Gallagher, who persevered in completing the tasks."

The report proposed allowing twins to go beyond 180-minute ETOPS to the design limit. It stipulated requirements the manufacturers would have to meet to allow ETOPS beyond 180 minutes. If a manufacturer could comply with the stringent requirements, it could even certify a twin to 300-minute or longer ETOPS. For the first time, even the tris and quads would have to meet similar stringent requirements if these airplanes were to be operated on routes that were more than 180 minutes from the nearest en route alternate.

Obviously, Airbus did not prevail. The ARAC report included seven different risk models, including the one proposed by Boeing. But it did not include the Airbus risk model that claimed that the risk of engine failure while operating at MCT level was 43 times greater than the most conservative ratio determined by the ICAO in the early 1980s. The ARAC report stated that the three engine manufacturers—GE, Pratt and Rolls— confirmed that the risk level had not changed. Based on the analyses of the data with the three engine manufacturers, the ARAC confirmed that the ratio of 2 to 1 was still a conservative value.

Without divulging the proceedings of the ARAC ETOPS Working Group, it is obvious from the ARAC report published by the FAA that the three engine manufacturers had to dig into their database and examine the validity of the Airbus claim.

The 86 to 1 ratio was the linchpin of the Airbus risk model. Without the 86 to 1 ratio, the Airbus risk model collapsed like a house of cards. Along with the house of cards, the Airbus plan to cordon off the areas of the world it called "extreme" from the 777 operations quickly fizzled.

It might be a mere coincidence but in 2001, Airbus dropped the 86 to 1 ratio from its LROPS CD.

* * *

The 86 to 1 ratio saga prompted many in the industry to wonder why Airbus had not been more careful with facts and data. In contrast, Boeing was meticulous about the integrity of the data. Our credibility depended on it. Besides, data was all we had to make our case. We had no emotional cords to pull to justify increased flexibility on ETOPS.

I had two full-time people on my staff, Al Benaltabe and Daryl Heinzerling, who did a superb job of keeping track of ETOPS data and analyzing it. Having the extensive database and the ability to analyze the data from different angles greatly helped Boeing during the ARAC deliberations.

Alan Mulally, Boeing Commercial Airplanes president, had the habit of saying, "Data will set us free." ETOPS proved him right. Boeing relied on the data to get its ETOPS message across.

Convincing people with data took time. It was an arduous process. It was much easier to pull the emotional cords. All one needed were a few dramatic pictures. To communicate the dangers of flying a twin over the polar routes, Airbus used picture of an airplane that had crashed in a blizzard, and pictures of polar bears with blood-stained faces on a leisurely stroll after a feast.

Although the media was more receptive to the emotional arguments, the technical groups such as the ARAC Working Group usually preferred to examine the facts and data.

* * *

Airbus was not going to let the deliberations in ARAC dampen its public relations drive. It started a new twins versus quads campaign.

At the 2002 Farnborough Airshow, Airbus had a colossal billboard at the edge of the runway that read: "A340 – 4 engines 4 long haul." The Airshow coincided with the delivery of Virgin Airline's first 380-seater long-range A340-600. Sir Richard Branson, the founder of the Virgin Group and a charismatic entrepreneur with global name recognition, joined Airbus in playing the two-versus-four-engine card. Sir Richard said he had considered the Boeing 380-seater long-range 777-300ER, but that surveys showed that passengers, given a choice, wanted to fly across the Atlantic in a four-engine airplane—not one with only two engines.

Airbus followed with an advertisement in the print media. Under the picture of an A340 the caption read, "The Airbus A340. 4 engines 4 long haul." This was followed by smaller text that read, "The Airbus A340 is the only modern 4-engined, long-haul aircraft in service today. So unlike its twin-engined competitors, it's free from ETOPS restrictions and can fly the most direct routes. No matter how far from civilization. As the A340 flies for up to 18 hours non-stop, it takes passengers a lot farther, yet makes long haul seem a great deal shorter."

Even though Rolls-Royce was the only engine supplier for the A340-600 and it fully supported Airbus efforts to promote the airplane, it did not want to be perceived as openly supporting the two-versus-four debate. After all, Rolls-Royce was one of the three engine suppliers for the 777, and its engines powered other Boeing twins. Following Virgin's A340-600 delivery ceremony, the head of Rolls-Royce released a statement supporting all airplanes regardless of the number of engines. It was possibly an attempt to appease Boeing. After all, the heads of Airbus and Rolls-Royce were standing next to Sir Richard at the Farnborough Airshow when he criticized the 777—the twin.

Some industry insiders believed that Airbus was winning the two-versus-four battle in the media.

* * *

However, a December 2002 posting of the ARAC report on the FAA Web site prompted many in the industry to start re-evaluating their thinking.

After all, it was a body of international experts who proposed allowing twins to go to the design limits. If anything, for the first time, it recommended that tris and quads had to step up to the ETOPS standards for twins on certain routes. Absence of any dissenting opinion in the ARAC Air Carrier Operations Issues Group's public meeting, even though Airbus was in attendance, further added to the credibility of the ARAC work.

Airbus had minor victories. In the 207-minute ETOPS docket, it had proposed that satellite communication (SATCOM), passenger recovery in polar operations, and wind accountability on system limits be required for ETOPS operations beyond 180 minutes. The ARAC report included these provisions.

The Seattle Times wrote, "One of the few perceived weaknesses of the Boeing 777 relative to its Airbus competition could be eliminated if the federal government adopts a proposal made yesterday to extend rules governing long-haul operations of twin-engine jets to three- and four-engine aircraft. Such a policy shift by the Federal Aviation Administration (FAA) would force the four-engine Airbus A340 and the Boeing 747 to meet the same safety requirements as the twin-engine 777. Such a leveling of the regulatory playing field could help Boeing extend the 777's already considerable sales lead over the A340, particularly in the hotly contested Asian market."

Quoting a well-known aviation industry consultant, the newspaper added, "The exemplary safety record of the 777 has assuaged most airline executives' concerns about using a twin-engine jet on their longest routes. But a leveling of the regulatory playing field would still give Boeing a lift. 'We've gone well over a decade with ETOPS generally taken for granted,' [an aviation industry consultant] said, 'but I'm sure there are vestigial doubts in certain airline executives' minds. Any lingering doubts you can remove enhance the 777's sales prospects.'"[4]

* * *

Even though the media and many industry observers associated Boeing with promoting twins at the expense of quads and Airbus with promoting quads at the expense of twins, actually Boeing was hesitant to place any requirement that would penalize the quads.

Certain industry groups, whose support was vital to allow flexibility on twins, had no interest in supporting ETOPS authority beyond the 207-minute unless the total risk from engine failures on twins was further decreased, and the industry agreed to levy ETOPS-type requirements on tris and quads. They had latched on to the Airbus LROPS proposal to levy additional requirements on tris and quads.

We desperately wanted the authority beyond 207-minute but levying ETOPS-type safety requirements on quads had many ramifications for Boeing. After all, we still built the world-famous four-engine 747s, which made money for the company. Similar to cutting off one's nose to spite one's face, Boeing could not afford to agree to levy requirements on quads just because they penalized the Airbus A340 and A380.

We decided to elevate the issue to the Boeing ETOPS Executive Committee.

The committee included vice presidents from various Boeing divisions. The committee had to weigh the prospect of allowing twins to go beyond 207-minute ETOPS, which would benefit the 777s, against levying additional requirements on quads, which could adversely affect the venerable 747s. The committee eventually agreed to support ETOPS beyond 207 minutes even though it might adversely affect 747s.

Besides benefitting the 777s, Boeing agreed to the ETOPS-type requirements on the quads for another strategic reason.

Thanks to the Airbus publicity machine, Boeing had just gone through a two-year ordeal in the media over the 207-minute ETOPS. Boeing knew that the proposal to expand the ETOPS capability of twins beyond 207 minutes would be met with fierce opposition from Airbus. The discord between the two aviation titans would create media frenzy.

By agreeing to consider the quads, Boeing would divert the focus and split the issues.

For one thing, the world would know that some of the ETOPS-type safety enhancements were equally applicable to the quads. Airbus would find itself in a difficult position. It would have to choose between attacking the ETOPS authority of the twins beyond 207 minutes versus protecting its quads—the A340 and the new jewel in the crown, the

A380—from being levied new requirements. Of course, Airbus could try to attack on both fronts, but that would dilute the message.

* * *

The ARAC ETOPS Working Group typically met for two to three days almost every month. Besides the formal monthly meetings, there were smaller subgroup meetings dedicated to working on some specialized issue. The subgroup would then present its findings to the Working Group.

For example, we created a maintenance subgroup with members from the US and non-US airlines, other industry members and the regulators to focus on airplane maintenance issues, and we asked John Kelly, who was a maintenance manager at Continental then and in 2009 became its Managing Director of Maintenance Control, to lead the subgroup. John and his fellow maintenance experts did an excellent job of developing the ETOPS maintenance requirements and guidance material.

The meetings were held at various locations within the United States, Europe, and Canada and were hosted by the members of the Working Group. The ARAC, in its report, estimated that the Working Group spent about 20,000 labor-hours over the two-year period of its deliberations at a cost of several million dollars.

The Working Group members were subject matter experts and always behaved with professional decorum. The grueling meetings and intense discussions did not dampen the camaraderie at dinnertime. We always had group dinners. Most of us have very fond memories of the ARAC ETOPS Working Group dinners.

Since 1990, I had been participating in the ETOPS discussion groups and committees around the world and had the pleasure of working with representatives from different organizations and interest groups. But I had never worked with anyone from the Air Crash Victims Families Association (ACVFA), the US chapter of International Air Crash Victims Families Group, until I joined the ARAC ETOPS Working group.

Hans Ephraimson-Abt, represented the ACVFA. Despite having some initial reservations on ETOPS, Hans became one of the staunchest supporters of what ARAC was trying to accomplish. He was a great advocate for the protection of passengers. A few of us even developed a very close personal relationship with him. As the coordinator of the ETOPS Working Group on the operational side, my job was to corral a bunch of "big cats," at times 40 of them. It was rather stressful at times. Hans, who was a fatherly figure, always tried to boost my morale by reminding me of the great contribution I was making to aviation. I am grateful for his encouragement and moral support.

* * *

Allowing greater than 207-minute ETOPS would increase the flexibility of the 777, which would increase the value of the airplane. Aviation experts estimated that the ARAC recommendation, if adopted by the FAA, would increase the value of a 777 by $1million. Obviously, this could hurt the A340 sale.

Flight International reported, "Airbus vice-president John Leahy says the FAA's move is 'a serious mistake.' … He adds that allowing the operation of twinjets on 4h [240-minute] over-water sectors with an engine failed is unacceptable."[5]

Several airlines in Southeast Asia were bombarded with an Airbus four-page memorandum titled "ARAC publishes draft ETOPS Proposal," which extolled the virtues of its four-engine airplane over the twins. It essentially repeated the LROPS CD. The memorandum was on Airbus letterhead but had no dates or names of Airbus officials. The memorandum was critical of the ARAC report. It said the ARAC proposal was influenced by the economic pressure to decrease the cost of ETOPS flights and increase the ETOPS upper limit.

In the memorandum, Airbus insinuated that the ARAC proposal compromised the level of operational safety. Possibly, fearing that other authorities besides the FAA might use the ARAC report to develop their own rule, Airbus asked the operators to alert their national aviation authority and discourage it from adopting rules based on the ARAC draft. Airbus asked the operators to contact the JAA and Airbus for data that they could use to support their national rulemaking.

It did not take too long for a copy of the memorandum to land on the FAA administrator's desk. According to the rumor in aviation circles, the head of Airbus in North America was asked to explain. Supposedly, Allan McArtor, chairman, Airbus North America, in a letter on March 17, 2003, apologized to the administrator for the memorandum. Apparently, he characterized it as an unauthorized release of an internal memorandum.

The memorandum also had made its way to the aviation media. Some of them contacted us and the ARAC chairman and, apparently, Airbus and the FAA. But in the end, the media did not pursue the story.

* * *

The task of the ARAC ETOPS Working Group was to examine technical issues and make recommendations. It had neither the authority nor the expertise to analyze the economic impact of its recommendations.

The FAA, by law, is required to balance safety requirements with the economic impact to the industry. The FAA economists have the challenging task of estimating the potential impact to the industry of the regulation especially if it is not in response to a fatal accident.

For a proactive regulation such as ETOPS, the economic impact is an estimate based on many factors, and often it is open to debate. The detractors normally concentrate on picking the economic analysis apart. This prompts the FAA economists to be gun-shy and to take a long time to complete their work.

Based on the economic impact to the industry, the FAA determined this proposed regulation to be "significant." This finding had a legal significance. Being declared "significant" meant that the rule had to be agreed on by the DOT and the Office of Management and Budget (OMB), a branch of the White House.

As some would say, the wheels of bureaucracy move at a glacial pace. The FAA eventually completed its study and decided to consider proposing a rule and issuing it for public comments. It forwarded its proposed rules to the DOT for its concurrence.

A small group of industry members who had diligently worked to draft the proposals in the ARAC ETOPS Working Group were getting a little impatient and wanted some visibility of the process. The group, which was led by Hans and included his fellow members from the ACVFA, ALPA, ATA, and Boeing met with the FAA and the DOT on September 15, 2003 and requested them to expedite the review process.

On November 14, 2003, nearly a year after the ARAC submitted its recommendation, the FAA published its NPRM in the Federal Register. The FAA had accepted more than 99% of the ARAC recommendation. The FAA solicited comments on its proposal. It allowed a 90-day comment period, which was later extended by 30 days to March 15, 2004.

It was a major rulemaking effort on the part of the FAA. The FAA received comments from around the world. The operators of twins welcomed the FAA proposal, but the tri and quad operators had reservations about the proposed rule. Many tri and quad operators, who had been operating these airplanes for decades, were concerned with the possible additional cost of the new rules.

From 1998 through 2000, when the US airlines, ALPA, and Boeing sought the 207-minute ETOPS, Airbus launched the media campaign that depicted the 207-minute as a risky operation. Boeing was caught up in the media frenzy for a couple of years. However, when the FAA NPRM proposed allowing twins to operate to 240 minutes and beyond, amazingly there was no uproar in the media.

As Boeing had anticipated, with the ETOPS requirements on certain types of operations for the tris and quads, the media focus shifted from twins to tris and quads.

Boeing also correctly predicted the actions by Airbus.

Rather than launch a campaign to prevent twins from operating above the 207-minute ETOPS, Airbus chose to stop ETOPS-type requirements from being levied on quads such as the A340 and the A380. As expected, Airbus did not try to attack on both fronts either, that is, prevent the ETOPS authority beyond 207 minutes for twins and the ETOPS requirements on quads.

With no organized opposition to the twins, permitting twins to operate ETOPS to the design limit, which might even be 330 minutes, became a non-issue. The Boeing strategy worked.

Almost all the discussion and media coverage in 2004 was on the application of ETOPS rules on tris and quads. The implication was that ETOPS on twins was no longer an issue, and, if anything, the tris and quads had to step up to the same standards as ETOPS twins.

Operators—who operated the Boeing 747, the Airbus A340, or who had ordered the Airbus A380—were greatly concerned, and their comments about the NPRM reflected it. There was a fair amount of similarity in the comments.

* * *

Most of the US airlines had been phasing out the tris and quads in favor of twins. On the passenger side, only United Airlines and Northwest operated quads, the Boeing 747. However, on the cargo operations side, FedEx and UPS had quads in their fleet and had plans to add newer quads, the A380s.

FedEx in its submittal to the FAA Docket on the new NPRM said, "The new Airbus A380 is also heavily impacted by the NPRM. This 4 engine state-of-the-art aircraft is specifically designed to haul heavy loads (passengers and freight) over extremely long distances. Because of its size, the number of suitable enroute alternate airports may prove to be problematic. If the A380 is not able to operate on routes because enroute alternate airports are unavailable, operators will be forced to conduct less direct (less efficient) routes, or not operate the aircraft at all. Given the mission and design of the A380, this is a ridiculous outcome. FedEx strongly believes that the A380 should not be subject to ETOPS regulations, and that it can be safely operated on any long distance route in the world. The costs of not being able to do so are huge, and not considered by the FAA."[6]

Besides being a consultant to Airbus, Tony Broderick consulted for FedEx and a few others. As one of the Airbus representatives, Broderick participated in almost all the ARAC ETOPS Working Group meetings. Broderick, with his FAA senior leadership background, played a key role for Airbus in trying to thwart the application of ETOPS requirements on quads.

Broderick and a few other leaders of aviation even engaged in open debate in the media. *Aviation Daily* had a column called "Departures" in which people could express their opinions on current aviation issues. Broderick wrote in the *Aviation Daily* column:

> FAA has proposed new regulations for ETOPS flying that would, for the first time, apply to 3- and 4-engine aircraft, and operators of business jets. ... FAA estimated costs for the 3- and 4-engine aircraft and business aircraft operators are not only wrong, but indicate net benefits when there are only costs. These FAA cost estimates are characterized as "incredible and ludicrous" by one commenter. ... A safety rationale for proposing expensive new regulatory requirements for 3- and 4-engine passenger and

(separately) freighter operations, and business jet operations, must be provided, or the proposals dropped.[7]

Incidentally, the words "incredible and ludicrous" appeared in
the comments submitted by FedEx, an operator that had never operated ETOPS. According to one of my contacts, Broderick, because of
his ETOPS expertise, had prepared most of the Docket comments for
FedEx. Therefore, when Broderick referred to "one commenter," it is
possible that he might have been referring to himself!

Boeing did not want to prolong any of these discussions in the
media. Boeing was content with the FAA's proposal in the NPRM. The
ARAC had done thorough work, and Boeing was pleased that the FAA
accepted virtually the entire ARAC recommendation.

However, Broderick's comments rattled a few nerves. A few weeks
later, Duane E. Woerth, president of ALPA, replied to Broderick in the
same column. Under the heading "ETOPS NPRM Is Not 'Over The
Top'," he wrote:

> A recent Departures column on FAA's proposed
> Extended-range Twin-Engine Operation (ETOPS) rule
> (DAILY, March 29) suggested that the agency had "gone
> over the top" by extending these regulations to cover
> three- and four-engine operations without providing
> adequate safety justification.
>
> Although we at ALPA are not surprised that some ele-
> ments of the industry would oppose some of the specifics
> for reasons of cost, we are dismayed that the processes
> used to develop the NPRM have been wrongly character-
> ized and now are being subverted.
>
> First, it is crucial to note that the focus on, and sub-
> sequent proposal of, these long-range rules did not origi-
> nate with the FAA, but were in response to the desires
> of many in the worldwide aviation community. In March
> 2000, the FAA issued a policy letter extending twin-en-
> gine ETOPS authority to 207-minutes. Many groups on
> both sides of the issue expressed the view then that the
> time had come to put ETOPS policies into the FARs and

that a review of such procedures should produce a uniform regulatory standard for all long-range operations.

This was the position of a number of diverse groups, including ALPA. Airbus's comments to the docket were typical: "We [Airbus] explicitly recognize that some of the issues we raise in our comments are applicable to any long-range operation regardless of the number of engines, and we urge that the modernization [that] we suggest of ETOPS regulations take all types of extended-range operations into account, not just twin-engine operations."

Such views led to the establishment of an Aviation Rule-making Advisory Committee (ARAC) ETOPS Working Group, consisting of more than 50 members from all elements of the industry, including ALPA. When the ARAC proposal was submitted to FAA in December 2003, there were no dissenting opinions submitted. It was this proposal that formed the basis for the Notice of Proposed Rulemaking (NPRM) now being finalized by the FAA.

ALPA finds it alarming that there now are voices and arguments being raised in opposition from groups that were, at a minimum, fully aware of the ARAC deliberations, and others who were, in fact, members of the ARAC Working Group. Each had every opportunity to interject its ideas and concerns during the lengthy deliberations and as a result had the ability to affect the results.

If anything in this process has gone "over the top," it is the claim that the combined work of ARAC and FAA fails to provide justification for the proposed rules that would bring all ETOPS operations under a comprehensive set of FARs.

Opponents of the NPRM have not concealed the fact that their concerns are based on cost. It is true that the costs of these new requirements are not easily quantified. However, we must not revert to the tombstone mentality, whereby proposals for safety improvements often were dismissed on the rationale that "it costs too much and nobody has died from it." Throughout its evolution, the ETOPS process has attempted to be proactive in its risk management in order to prevent accidents. That is the goal of processes such as ARAC, where the industry is able to provide technical input on issues that demand our attention.

The measure of a "safe" operation is not the absence of accidents, but the freedom from undue risk in the operation. The FAA's proposals define and manage the ETOPS risks. As operational frequencies increase throughout aviation and in long-haul operations, we cannot afford to rely on "business as usual" approaches. We also cannot afford to have the ARAC/NPRM process subverted by last-minute naysayers who lie back when the real work is being done and then try to do an end run around the considerable efforts and the conclusions of the vast majority of the participants.[8]

It was interesting that Capt. Woerth chose to use the words "tombstone mentality."

Broderick had retired from the position of FAA's associate administrator for regulations and certification a month after the May 11, 1996, Value Jet DC-9 accident that killed 110 people on board. The inspector general of the US DOT, Mary F. Schiavo, criticized the FAA for enacting safety regulations only after an accident, after counting the number of dead bodies. She had accused the FAA of fostering a "tombstone mentality."

* * *

Until the release of the FAA's NPRM, Airbus focused on attacking 777operations on long-range routes in the Pacific, polar, and other areas of the world that it considered "extreme." After the NPRM, the tables were turned.

Airbus had a real problem at hand. Under the LROPS, Airbus had proposed additional requirements on tris and quads. It was the price that Airbus was prepared to pay to limit the 777 to 180-minute ETOPS.

Now Airbus could be stuck with the additional requirements on the quads even though it would not be able to limit the 777.

Despite having proposed the LROPS requirements, Airbus decided to protect the A340 and the A380 from being levied ETOPS-type requirements. All of a sudden, attacking twins became a lower priority.

Airbus even scaled back the production and distribution of the LROPS CD. On April 30, 2004, Allan McArtor, chairman, Airbus North America, while speaking at the Aviation Safety Alliance Newsmakers breakfast, questioned the FAA's proposed rulemaking and predicted that the FAA would withdraw the NPRM.

Many in the industry wondered if McArtor had inside knowledge or if he was making a veiled threat to use Airbus' political influence to force the FAA to withdraw the proposal. After all, McArtor himself was a former FAA administrator.

Airbus also had some natural allies in the United States: the airlines that were planning to introduce the Airbus A380s in their fleets. If the submittal to the Docket was any indication, FedEx was concerned with the impact of the new rules on the A380 operations. Some of the charter operators who used tris and quads and business airplane operators, who were also concerned with the possible impact on their operations, were sympathetic to Airbus.

Reportedly, the FedEx founder, President and Chief Executive Officer Fred Smith, had close personal ties to President George W. Bush, the 43rd president of the United States. Smith was in the same Delta Kappa Epsilon fraternity as President Bush at Yale University. Both of them also belonged to the university's elitist secret society, the Skull and Bones. Shortly after the 2000 presidential election, it was even speculated that President Bush might appoint Smith to his cabinet. Many in the industry wondered if the rule, which could adversely affect Smith's A380s, would ever see the light of day.

It was a major rulemaking effort supported by the major airlines in the United States; a major airplane manufacturer, The Boeing Company; and the biggest pilot union, ALPA. It was a proposal submitted by the ARAC that would greatly enhance the safety of all aviation. Now the question was—would the White House quash the rule because of its adverse impact on the business operations of the president's close friend, who was going to use an airplane built by Airbus?

* * *

In August 2004, the FAA announced that it would release the final rule by April 29, 2005. But there was no guarantee that it would actually happen. Reportedly, some factions within the FAA were sympathetic to the views espoused by Airbus and others.

Even if the FAA were to agree, because it was classified as a "significant rule," both the DOT and the OMB had to concur with it. The probability of it being derailed at any stage was great.

Boeing felt that the effort by Airbus and others to overturn the rule was having an impact. The rule activity often stalled or moved slower than Boeing anticipated. Obviously, it was only natural for Boeing, Airbus, and the various industry groups to be involved in presenting their case to influence the decision-makers.

Possibly, to McArtor's great disappointment, the FAA did not withdraw the proposal. In January 2006, the FAA forwarded its final proposal to the DOT for its concurrence. The action shifted from FAA headquarters to the DOT.

Despite the delay in the release of the final rule, the fact that the FAA was engaged in rulemaking had a profound impact on the industry. The FAA's newly proposed ETOPS rule in the NPRM alleviated any concern the airlines had with operating twins on long ranges. The airlines had started to evaluate the 777s purely on their technical merits.

* * *

ETOPS was an "enhancer." It enhanced the value of the 777s. Because the 777 complied with ETOPS, it became a better airplane. Boeing had spent a great deal of money and effort to ensure that the 777s would be service ready and reliable to start ETOPS at entry. Almost from the outset, the airplane was able to maintain a dispatch reliability of around 99%, something the airlines loved. Based on the record of performance, efficiency, and safety in actual airline operations over the preceding year, the 777 was even declared the winner of the prestigious Collier Award in 1995 as the top aeronautical achievement of the year.

The relentless focus on reliability and service readiness also resulted in lowering the eventual maintenance cost for the airlines. The 777 operators were seeing exceptionally low maintenance cost. The 777 engines needed to go in for an overhaul after 12,000 to 15,000 engine hours. This was 20% to 30% better than the engines on the 747s. The airlines found that even then, the work required was not comparable to what they would find for the 747 engines. Another focus was on major checks, commonly known as "D checks"—checks normally done every six to seven years. Airlines would typically change around 30 or so seat tracks on most of the airplanes, but on the 777 typically they would find that only one seat track needed to be changed. This had a great impact on the airline's financial bottom line.

By 2005 and 2006, major airlines were openly complimenting the 777s.

In 2006, *The Wall Street Journal*[9] wrote, "Tim Clark, President of Emirates, said that its new 777-300ERs have had fewer problems than its new A340-500s. The 777 has 'exceeded all its planned performance criteria' for fuel consumption and range, Mr. Clark said. 'That's why there's a resurgence of interest' in the 777... Air Canada Chairman Robert Milton said in April (2005) that the carrier chose to replace its A340s with 777s because, they 'have considerable economic efficiencies' compared with the Airbus models. He said that 'had a very dramatic impact on the decision.'... Air France, another major Airbus customer but also a big 777 buyer, is one of few carriers that has flown both A340s and 777s on the same routes. Chief Financial Officer Philippe Calavia said a first-generation A340-300 from the 1990s burns about 15% to 20% more fuel per seat than a 777 of the same vintage. 'It's more costly to maintain four engines than two,' he said, adding that Air France expects 'to further increase the proportion of 777s in our fleet.'"

Airbus was quickly losing ground. In mid-2005, Air Canada signaled a momentous shift in the global airplane market. It ordered 96 Boeing 777s and 787s, including options, to replace all the Airbus A330s and A340s in its fleet.

In 2005, Emirates—the launch customer for the airplane—was threatening to delay the delivery of 20 Airbus 380-plus-seater long-range A340-600HGWs. Even though the 380-seater long-range 777-300ER competed with the A340-600 family, according to published reports the Airbus product was supposedly heavier and less fuel efficient. Airlines preferred the 777-300ERs to the A340-600s.

The Wall Street Journal added, "Noel Forgeard, the former chief executive of Airbus and now co-CEO of its parent company, European

Aeronautic Defence & Space Co. ... said ... that the 777's success against the A340 is 'a point of real concern for us.'"[10]

However, the media reported, "Airbus executives say they will not be 'panicked' into a rash decision to reinvigorate the A340-500/600 family and believe they can compensate for the higher operating costs of the four-engined aircraft over the rival Boeing 777 twinjet by offering cash back deals to potential customers rather than investing in a costly redesign. While Airbus Chief Operating Officer-Customers John Leahy concedes that the A340-600's four-engined configuration means it has a 'single-digit fuel burn penalty' over the 777-300ER, he says this can be 'traded off' through financial compensation to operators."[11]

Despite having said, "For a slight increase in speed, they [Boeing] will have higher fuel consumption (on the Sonic Cruiser) ... and a higher impact on the environment," Leahy was no longer concerned with the environmental impact from higher fuel consumption on the A340s.[12]

* * *

By early 2006, the Boeing 777 virtually dominated the Airbus A340. Airbus was not doing so well when it had to market its A340s purely on technical merits against the 777s.

However, Leahy was reluctant to come to terms with reality.

Even after launching the long-range twin A350XWB to compete with the 777s and the 787s, at the 2006 Farnborough Airshow, "Leahy insisted there was a 'strong market' for ... four-engine planes for polar routes or airlines unwilling to invest in training and qualification needed to fly long distances on two engines within limits on the time needed to divert to the nearest airport in emergencies, known as ETOPS."[13]

In spite of Leahy's assertion, by August of 2006, even the poster child for Airbus A340's "4 engines 4 long haul"—Sir Richard Branson's Virgin Atlantic Airways— had started to take off the decals it had on its A340s extolling the virtues of four engines.

Some in the industry also recognized the ETOPS program as a commitment to safety enhancement in aviation. ETOPS brought about new requirements in the design of airframes and engines, which enhanced the capabilities and the reliability of the airplane. It introduced a safety culture in an airline in which measures were taken at every step of the airline maintenance program to minimize undue risk.

Every mechanical event had to be thoroughly analyzed so that a program could be established to minimize the frequency of such events. It introduced aggressive health monitoring of engines, so that "sick" engines could be pulled off on the tarmac before the airplane got in the air. Airlines had flight operations programs that planned for eventualities during diversions.

In the year 2006, 2.3 billion people flew in commercial airliners, or, on average, about 6.3 million people around the world were in the air every day of the year. Of this amount, more than 92% flew on twins, which meant that every day, on average, 5.7 million out of 6.3 million people flew safely on twins—nearly 240,000 people in a twin every hour of the day, every day of the year.

* * *

The new rules the FAA was proposing extended some of the ETOPS twin safety concepts and proactive measures to enhance the safety of operations to all airplanes.

The FAA was not alone in proposing regulations in this arena. The European JAA ETOPS/LROPS Working Group had been working in parallel with the FAA since 2000, and the ICAO had a group, called the ER Sub-Group, that had been working on it since 2001. Boeing participated in both these forums. For several years, I was the chairman of the ICAO ER Sub-Group.

The JAA had a unique arrangement. Even though the JAA ETOPS/LROPS Working Group took direction from the regulations director, the recommendation of the Working Group had to be approved by the Operations Sectorial Team (OST).

The OST consisted of the heads of the Flight Operations side of the European Regulatory Authorities who were members of the JAA. In 2007, the JAA had 42 members; it included 15 more countries than the 27 EU member states. Besides the regulators, members from selected European industries were invited to participate as "interested parties." The OST had allocated one seat for the United States, which was already taken by the organization representing the business airplane manufacturers. Throughout 1990, Boeing attempted to get a seat for the Aerospace Industries Association of America, Inc. (AIA), which is the Boeing parent industry organization. In the late 1990s, a Briton, who was the JAA operations director, chaired the OST. He created all kinds of excuses on why they could not add one extra "interested party" to the OST.

In 2001, the British operations director left the JAA for a more lucrative assignment, and a Frenchman, George Rebender, an Airbus employee who had extensive regulatory and flight operational background, replaced him. Even though he came from Airbus, Rebender warmly welcomed AIA. He believed the OST would greatly benefit by having Airbus and Boeing at the same table. From 2001 until the dissolution of the JAA OST at the end of 2007, I represented the AIA on the OST. In 2008, all the functions normally carried out by the JAA OST were transferred to the European Aviation Safety Agency (EASA) when the agency was granted legal competence to handle operations and flight training.

Having a seat on the OST allowed Boeing to make suggestions on many operational issues, including ETOPS. On several occasions, the JAA ETOPS/LROPS Working Group did not allow open discussion on certain issues. For any recommendations from the JAA ETOPS/LROPS Working Group that were not thoroughly discussed and that Boeing was not comfortable with, I had the opportunity to make our case on the OST. This helped Boeing on several occasions.

The JAA ETOPS recommendations on twins were similar to the FAA recommendations. In Europe, the JAA and EASA decided to hold the tri and quad ETOPS rulemaking in abeyance.

* * *

By 2006, Boeing was nearing a critical phase in the 787 program when significant further delay in the FAA's rulemaking could adversely affect the airplane program. For the 777 program, the FAA had issued a Special Condition that stipulated requirements that Boeing would have to comply with for the 777 to qualify for ETOPS certification at entry into service. Anticipating a timely release of the new rules, Boeing did not aggressively pursue an ETOPS Special Condition on the 787. Boeing needed the new rules fairly soon if it were to meet the commitments it had made to its customers.

Eventually, on August 29, 2006, the DOT completed its evaluation of the FAA's proposal for the new ETOPS rule and forwarded it to the OMB for concurrence. Normally, the DOT and the OMB would take 90 days to complete their assessments, but the delay tactic of the detractors was taking its toll. The battleground shifted from the DOT to the OMB.

We were nearing the finish line.

On September 7, Boeing briefed the OMB on the urgency for the new ETOPS rules to support the 787 program. We also conveyed our willingness to abide by the new rules as proposed by the FAA in the NPRM. Boeing made its case for the prompt release of the rule and elaborated on the impact the delay was having on the 787.

Records released by the OMB showed that on October 18, 2006, a group consisting of FedEx, UPS, Cargo Airlines Association, and Atlas Air paid a visit to the OMB to object to the new rules. Instead of declaring as a consultant for Airbus, Tony Broderick presented himself as a consultant for FedEx, even though another FedEx employee was also in attendance. It was possibly a prudent move on the part of Airbus. Otherwise, it could have provided some fodder for the media.

A week later, on October 25, at a National Air Carriers Association (NACA) Maintenance Conference in Washington, which also included many FAA employees, the president of NACA told the audience that NACA and others had needed to go around the FAA to the OMB to oppose the ETOPS rule. We received a third-hand report that the NACA president told the audience that they had been successful, that the rule had been sent back to the FAA, and that he fully expected the FAA to take out all requirements for the tris and quads and Part 135 airplanes. The FAA regulation on Part 135 dealt with commuter and on-demand operations.

I was not able to get hold of the NACA president to confirm the third-hand report and find out if someone at the OMB had given that assurance or if it was just wishful thinking on the part of the NACA and others. Regardless, the news sent a shock wave through Boeing.

Even though Boeing strongly supported the FAA proposal, the likely exclusion of tris and quads or Part 135 from ETOPS rules did not overly concern us. Our immediate concern was the potential delay in rule release if the rule was sent back to the FAA and the impact it could have on the 787 program.

The OMB did not send the rule back to the FAA.

A high-level meeting was set between the OMB and the FAA. The FAA must have considered the rule important enough for the FAA, because the associate administrator for aviation safety, Nick Sabatini, personally attended the meeting with the OMB.

Just before the end of 2006, after the FAA agreed to make some last-minute alterations to the new rules, the OMB concurred. The ETOPS rule would apply to tris and quads and Part 135 operations. But the tris and quads on cargo operations would be exempt from the ETOPS rule, even though the rule applied to twins on cargo operations. Therefore, the FedEx A380 Freighter would not have to comply with ETOPS.

It was not clear if the FedEx founder, President and Chief Executive Officer Fred Smith, had influenced the White House. Many wondered about the reason for excluding such a small segment of aviation from the ETOPS safety rules.

However, by then the Airbus mismanagement of the A380 program had started to take its toll. On November 8, 2006, FedEx had canceled its orders for the A380 Freighter and switched to the 777 Freighter. In March 2007, UPS also canceled its A380 Freighters after Airbus decided to postpone the A380 Freighter program indefinitely.

The Boeing 747-8 Freighter may end up being the beneficiary of this little quirk in the rule!

* * *

The FAA announced the release of the final rule on January 8, 2007. It was published in the US Federal Register on January 16 and became effective as of February 15, 2007. It was a watershed moment in aviation.

While announcing the new ETOPS rule, FAA Administrator Marion Blakey said, "This is an extremely important new rule that will open up safe flights all around the world."

With the announcement of the new rule, in one motion, the FAA cleared any reservations people had regarding the operations of ETOPS twins on long-range routes. If anything, it also declared that the tris and quads had to step up to the level of safety of the ETOPS twins while operating on these long-range routes.

Regarding the new regulations for airplanes with more than two engines, the FAA said, "A lack of regulatory oversight in areas of equipment requirements and fuel planning for a maximum diversion creates a very real safety risk." To address the safety risk, the FAA announced, "This final rule also extends most requirements previously applicable only to Part 121 [FAA Regulations on Airplane Operations] two-engine airplanes to a limited number of Part 121 passenger-carrying three- and four engine airplane operations."[14]

* * *

ETOPS on twins were extended beyond 207 minutes to the limits of the airplane system capabilities. The new ETOPS rule permitted twins unrestricted point-to-point operations around the world on the optimal routing.

The FAA's new rules set 180 minutes as the threshold for tris and quads. Hence, the manufacturers and operators would have to comply with the new ETOPS requirements for passenger operations beyond the 180-minute diversion time.

It required the tris and quads manufactured after February 17, 2015, to meet the FAA's ETOPS certification standards if the manufacturer expected the airplanes to operate on ETOPS. Tri and quad operators were exempt from any ETOPS maintenance requirements. However, these operators were required to consider fuel for depressurization when operating on the ETOPS routes.

Rather than wait until 2015, Boeing decided to certify its 747-8 Intercontinental to ETOPS standards immediately. Unless Airbus does not intend to sell any of its A380s in the United States, it will have to certify the A380 also to the higher ETOPS standards by 2015. It may decide to voluntarily certify it earlier if there is a market perception that the 747-8 is a safer product than the A380 because of the compliance with higher ETOPS safety standards.

* * *

By diligently working together with the various factions of the industry, Boeing realized its strategic vision. However, the road had not always been easy. We went through many impasses; the long arduous discussions were demanding and, often, we felt we had run out of all options. With facts and data, diplomatic skills, persistence, and tremendous patience, we kept on pursuing our vision, and in the end we prevailed.

Airbus lost out in almost every major ETOPS initiative. It was out-maneuvered. It tried but failed to stop the 777 Early ETOPS approval;

applicability of Accelerated ETOPS Operational Approval method on the 777; extension of ETOPS from 180 to 207 minutes, which benefited the 777s; and use of the 777 on the polar routes.

Airbus pioneered big twins in the 1970s. With great leadership and management skills, it brought the fractious Europeans together to successfully challenge the best of the best in aviation. Airbus had many successes on the regulatory front. However, when it came to ETOPS, it looked like Airbus could do nothing right while Boeing could do nothing wrong.

The new ETOPS rule from the FAA was the last and most severe blow to the efforts by Airbus to marginalize the 777.

* * *

As the world's leading regulator, the FAA makes decisions that can greatly influence the thinking of the aviation regulators around the world. Several countries including China have already updated their regulations, and many others are in the process of doing so.

Australia was the first one after the United States to update its ETOPS rules. The rules are similar except that Australia requires all tris and quads in operation under the Australian operational specifications to be type design certified by 2015. The FAA exempts the tris and quads that are no longer in production from this requirement. As a result, unless Boeing spends millions of dollars to certify the 747-400, an airplane that is no longer in production, Qantas will not be able to continue operating the 747-400 beyond 2015.

Shortly after the release of the US rules, some of the Airbus people had told me that the US rule to exempt the tris and quads that were no longer in production gave Boeing an unfair advantage because Boeing had more tris and quads currently in operations around the world. I do not know if Australia was swayed by this apparent perception of unfair advantage.

However, one thing is certain: If Airbus wants Qantas to continue operating the A380 beyond 2015, it will have to type design certify the airplane for ETOPS. Australia does not issue its own type certification but rather accepts the airplane type certification issued by the State of Design. Thus, Airbus will have to obtain A380 ETOPS Type Design certification from EASA, which may provide an impetus for the

Europeans to finalize ETOPS rule for three- and four-engine airplanes before 2015.

* * *

Since 1990, my counterpart at Airbus had been Andre Quet, deputy vice president. A brilliant fellow, he had a quick wit and was very knowledgeable on aviation matters. Andre led the Airbus team.

Because ETOPS was at the core of the 777/A340 battle, I found myself confronting Airbus at every step in almost all the meetings. I have to admit that, in the committees and work groups I participated, most of the people who represented Airbus were very capable and proficient in their field of expertise. Airbus was a very worthy competitor.

By disparaging twins and challenging Boeing at every step, Airbus may have forced the industry to levy standards that are more stringent, which hopefully will help make ETOPS even safer.

* * *

At the June 2007 International Aviation Safety Conference in Prague, Czech Republic, nearly five months after the release of the new rules, it was evident that Airbus was shifting gears. At the conference, Airbus had new leaders who were more interested in certifying the A350XWB to 350-minute ETOPS rather than disparaging twins on long-range operations.

It appears as if Airbus is trying to forget the past and morph itself into a big advocate of ETOPS. Despite Leahy's comment to *Flight International* in 2003 that the "operation of twinjets on 4h [240-minute] over-water sectors with an engine failed is unacceptable,"[15] Airbus became the first airplane manufacturer in the world to obtain 240-minute ETOPS authority for one of its twins. While announcing the EASA approval of the 240-minute ETOPS for the A330, on November 12, 2009, Airbus issued a press release that said the new authority will permit "... direct routings to reduce CO_2 emissions, shorten flight times, and open new routes."[16]

Because the A330 could not even qualify for the FAA's 207-minute requirement, it remains to be seen if the FAA will accept the EASA's findings and grant 240-minute ETOPS for the A330. The FAA's approval would open the possibility for Delta Airlines to seek a higher level of authority than the 180-minute it currently has on its A330s, the airplanes it inherited from the merger with Northwest Airlines. The higher level of authority would allow Delta to compete on an equal footing with the 777 operators in the North Pacific.

* * *

With the release of the new ETOPS rule and the launch of the A350XWB, the "4 engines 4 long haul" has fallen by the wayside. The A340 lost out to the 777. The Airbus pincer strategy to suffocate the 747 between the A340 and the A380, a strategic action to cripple Boeing to such a degree that Europe could permanently wrest from the United States its traditional global dominance of commercial aviation, collapsed.

7

A NEW DAWN

Launch of the 787 and the A350XWB

In December 2002, Boeing announced its plan to build a new long-range twin, which was later called the 787. By mere coincidence, it was the same month that the ARAC submitted its ETOPS recommendations to the FAA. By the time the FAA released its new rules on ETOPS in 2007, the Boeing 787, aptly named the Dreamliner, had become the most successful new airplane launch in the history of commercial aviation. ETOPS twins dominated the long-range market.

Designed to carry 210 to 330 passengers, depending on the model, the 787 has a maximum range of up to 8,500 nm (15,750 km). It is designed for optimal cruise at Mach 0.85, or at 85% the speed of sound.

Its promise of 20% better fuel efficiency, a 30% savings in maintenance costs, lower noise footprints, improved environmental performance, and better system capabilities has made the airplane a "must have" for the airlines. The 787 is pushing the boundaries of technology. Boeing dubbed the 787 the "game changer."

Boeing expects to gain such efficiencies by increased use of composites, better aerodynamics, and improved system architecture. The share of composites in the 787 will be 50% compared to 12% on the 777. Boeing hopes the use of composites will lower the maintenance costs and increase the fuel efficiency of the 787.

During major checks, unlike in other airplanes with floor beams made of aluminum alloy, it was very rare for airlines to replace sections of the 777 passenger floor beams, which were made of composites. Traditionally, the passenger floor beams have been notorious for fatigue cracking and corrosion. Another area in the 777 that had composites was the tail section. Even though the 777 composite tail was 25% larger than the aluminum tail of the 767, the 777 required 35% fewer scheduled maintenance labor-hours due to reduced risk of corrosion and fatigue of composites compared with metal.

The composite material is stronger than traditional aluminum, resistant to corrosion, and lighter than traditional aluminum airframe structures. But depending on the grade, it can be several times more expensive than aluminum. Boeing anticipates that the use of composites will lessen the total weight of the 787, thus allowing the gain in fuel efficiency.

Besides the 50% composites, the 787 will have 20% aluminum, 15% titanium, 10% steel, and 5% other material.

The operating environment, the loads, and the type of loads dictate which material is optimal for a certain design. In some areas, metal may be preferable to composites, but environmental considerations—risk of corrosion—may indicate that aluminum would be a poor choice. In such instances, titanium may be the optimal choice because it can withstand comparable loads even better than aluminum. Titanium has minimal fatigue concerns and is highly resistant to corrosion. Hence, it would be an excellent choice from a maintenance perspective also. However, all materials have their pluses and minuses. Besides being more expensive than aluminum, titanium is a hard material to work with and creates its own challenges in manufacturing.

* * *

"Composite" is a generic term. It can mean anything that combines two or more organic or inorganic materials. Most composites used on the 787 are carbon fiber reinforced by an epoxy resin. Because these are essentially sandwiched layers of carbon fiber and epoxy, delamination and bubbling in the materials can potentially undermine their integrity.

Carbon fiber used on airplane structures is difficult to make. Only a few companies in Japan, the United States, and Europe are capable of making it. Because carbon fiber has a crucial role in missile production, the technology will not likely be widely shared. Boeing is working with the world's largest producer of carbon fiber, Toray Industries, a Japanese company that also has manufacturing operations in the state of Washington, the home base for Boeing Commercial Airplanes. Because of the limited number of suppliers, airframe manufacturers tend to enter into a long-term contractual agreement with the composite manufacturers. Toray will supply the composites to Boeing past 2020.

However, even composites have their own challenges. They are dielectric—unlike the aluminum skin, they cannot dissipate lightning charges. Boeing has developed a proprietary lightning protection system on the 787. According to media reports, the lightning strikes are dissipated with a phosphor bronze wire mesh interwoven into the composite fabric. The lightning concern also required redesign of fasteners used in the composite structures. Fearing the gaps between fasteners and composites might cause arcing, Boeing redesigned fasteners with tighter seals.

Working with its supplier partners, Boeing developed the technology to manufacture the round, hollow sections of the fuselage in one piece, known as barrels. Huge ovens called autoclaves bake the complete barrels. Using composite barrels in the 787 fuselage greatly reduces the number of fasteners required and the associated labor. For example, according to the published reports, each barrel section will save nearly 1,500 aluminum sheets and 40,000 to 50,000 fasteners. The upper and lower surface panels and the spars of the wings also will be made of composites.

* * *

Just like the 777, the 787 was digitally designed. Reportedly, the 787 took more than 800,000 hours of computing time on Cray supercomputers.

However, this time Boeing fundamentally changed how it designed and manufactured airplanes. Boeing did the high-level design and established the major parameters but allowed the suppliers to complete the detailed design. This prompted some in the aviation community to say that the 787 changed Boeing from an Original Equipment Manufacturer (OEM) to an Original Equipment Assembler.

Suppliers around the world designed and manufactured the major pieces of the airplane. The globalized 787 business model was meant to save money—not through cheap labor, but through sharing the upfront investment in the launch of a brand-new airplane. As risk-sharing partners, suppliers took on more risk than usual in signing up to supply the Boeing 787. Unlike the top-down OEM-supplier relationship in the 777 program, the 787 suppliers worked more like partners with Boeing.

As expected, a partner's ability to invest, reducing Boeing's upfront costs, was also a big consideration when deciding which companies would participate in the 787 program. Suppliers had to invest heavily in such things as manufacturing tools and factory space. Many invested billions of dollars.

Often the work was proportionate to the share of the risk. As the 787 supplier-partners who carried big pieces of the burden, they were entitled to manufacture huge sections of the 787.

Three Japanese industrial giants—Mitsubishi Heavy Industries, Kawasaki Heavy Industries, and Fuji Heavy Industries—co-designed and built 35% of the 787.

Reportedly, the 787 program pushed outsourcing to new levels—about 70% of the airplane. On previous airplane programs, Boeing and Airbus both averaged about 50%.

Because the outsourcing has gone from 50% to 70% does not necessarily imply a trend. Both Boeing and Airbus constantly monitor the quality of work and efficiencies gained. If they conclude that the outsourcing has not produced the desired efficiencies, they will quickly pull the work back.

With the outsourcing component on the 787 development, Boeing expects stability in its core employment. In previous airplane programs, normally Boeing geared up for the new airplane development program but, if there was nothing to keep the engineers employed after the development program ended, the engineers would be laid off.

By going global, Boeing could tap into engineering and technical capabilities around the world. In addition, some of the suppliers were able to tap into their local or national subsidies, which helped lower the price of the airplane.

Believing the 787 greatly benefited from the subsidy to the Japanese risk-sharing partners, the media reported that Airbus even contemplated dragging Japan into the US-Europe World Trade Organization (WTO) subsidy battle. But possibly fearing a potential loss of future Airbus airplane sales to the airlines in Japan, Airbus backed off at the last minute.

* * *

Despite globalizing the 787 design, Boeing was not oblivious to the fact that today's supplier-partners might be tomorrow's competitors. Just because it wanted to share the risks on the 787 did not mean it was going to share its core technologies or give away its "crown jewels.

To protect one of its crown jewels, Boeing designed the airplane wing itself. It provided only the shape to the wing manufacturer. However, this does not mean that Boeing might unknowingly have shared other technologies that it may come to regret later.

In September 2005, the 787 program with some of the world's most capable top-tier supplier-partners finalized the airplane's configuration. Boeing was connected virtually with its partner sites around the world in the detailed design of the airplane.

The new partner relationship altered how Boeing did its design work compared to its previous airplane programs. On the previous programs, the supplier would literally follow the detailed specification as prescribed in Boeing's specification control document to design and manufacture a system. On the 787, Boeing wrote only the high-level requirements. The supplier working in partnership with Boeing did the detail design. Boeing did not micromanage the design as long as it met the overall high-level requirements.

Undoubtedly, designing the airplane around the world digitally in hundreds of sites created its own challenges. All the engineers had to be able to speak exactly the same digital language. There was no room for even a small variation.

Having been impressed with Dassault's CATIA during the all-digital design of the 777, Boeing decided to use Dassault's Product Life-cycle Management (PLM) platform for the 787. It decided not to mix and match different vendors' platforms, but use all three components—CATIA V5, Delmia, and Enovia—of Dassault's V5 PLM application suite.

The 787 was designed on CATIA V5. Delmia created the virtual manufacturing package. It showed how those parts or components designed on CATIA would be manufactured on the factory floor. Enovia maintained all the 787 design and engineering information.

Boeing required all suppliers to use the same PLM suite; no substitutions were allowed. It also strictly controlled the software version and the revision cycle. Boeing also maintained a central control on all computer applications used in the design and engineering process to do everything from test the stress tolerance of composite materials to achieve optimal aerodynamics. It allowed the thousands of engineers around the world to communicate in exactly the same digital language.

Reportedly, with about $20,000 per desktop for each engineer, Boeing and its partners invested hundreds of millions on the hardware alone to ensure the common digital platform.

In 2006, Boeing also conducted a digital "virtual rollout" of the Dreamliner, a virtual rendition of the airplane. Boeing expected to lower the development cost by eliminating costly physical mockups and by working out kinks in manufacturing before going into production.

The digital platform allowed Boeing to have a single source of digital data from inception to design, manufacturing, and providing support to the airlines after the airplane is delivered.

In the history of Boeing Commercial Airplanes, the 787 is only the second Boeing airplane launched by a non-US airline, Japan's All Nippon Airways. The 737 was the first one—Germany's Lufthansa launched it on February 15, 1965.

* * *

The ability of the composite structures to handle material stress better has allowed Boeing to build bigger windows and operate at a lower cabin altitude than the current generation of airplanes. Because the composites do not create the same concern for corrosion as the aluminum structures, the airplane can operate with higher levels of humidity in the cabin.

Boeing has designed electro-chromatic dimmable windows rather than mechanical window shades. High-intensity discharge and light-emitting diode lighting will replace the incandescent bulbs in the cabin. Boeing expects the 787 lighting system to last 10 to 20 times longer than the current systems.

Consistent with all Boeing airplanes, the 787 has a wheel-and-column flight control arrangement. Unlike Airbus, Boeing has always believed that such an arrangement provides the feedback and awareness that pilots need to make and execute decisions during critical periods. The wheel-and-column controllers are cross-linked between pilots to avoid confusion. They are back-driven to give the pilots better visual and tactile understanding of what either the autoflight system or the other pilot is doing.

Boeing says the flight deck of the 787 has the industry's largest pilot display screens and comes with all the latest features such as dual head-up displays and dual electronic flight bags. A head-up display is a clear screen mounted at eye level. It displays the flight information so that pilots can see what is going on with the airplane even while looking outside the cockpit. The electronic flight bag is an integrated hardware and software package that calculates airplane performance data, displays charts, improves taxi positional awareness, allows electronic access to documents, and provides video surveillance of flight deck entry.

The 787 has built-in sensors in the airplane nose to automatically dampen the flight during turbulence and create a smoother ride. The software will quickly respond to up-and-down wind gusts.

The airplane has moved away from pneumatic to more electrical power. The only remaining bleed-air systems on the 787 are the anti-ice system for the engine inlets and the pressurization of hydraulic reservoirs. Bleed air is the hot air extracted or bled from the engines. Electric brakes have replaced hydraulic-powered brakes.

These changes will also ease airplane maintenance. Airline mechanics will no longer have to contend with leaking brakes or problems with the bleed air in the air-conditioning ducts.

Similar to the 777, the 787 is relying on CATIA to ensure that mechanics can perform various procedures effectively and efficiently, which will result in a more maintainable airplane. As with the 777, Boeing plans to validate the 787 maintenance procedures before the airplane enters airline service. The 787 will also incorporate health-monitoring systems that will allow the airplane to self-monitor and report maintenance requirements to ground-based computer systems. The airplane system information will help maintenance and engineering crews quickly isolate failed components. When the airplane arrives at the gate, maintenance crews can be ready with the parts and information to quickly make any necessary repair and reduce the airplane's return-to-service times.

Besides lowering the daily maintenance costs for the 787, Boeing recommends a much longer interval between major maintenance visits.

In December 2008, the FAA approved the maintenance plan of the 787, which required fewer maintenance tasks, thus minimizing the out-of-service time and allowing longer intervals between the scheduled checks. Compared to the 767, which requires a routine base maintenance check every 18 months or a major structural check every 6 years, the 787 will require the base maintenance check every 3 years and the major structural check only once every 12 years.

Boeing hopes the FAA-approved maintenance plan will contribute to the goal for the 787 to be 30% less expensive to maintain than today's comparably sized aircraft.

With the 787, Boeing is not only focusing on enhancing the reliability, lessening the maintenance requirements, and enhancing the maintainability but also decreasing the actual repair time when a repair is necessary. Besides schedule reliability, airplane availability is equally important in airline operations. Airlines can minimize disruptions if the length of time an airplane must be out of service for required maintenance can be lowered.

* * *

Boeing is also touting the environmentally friendly credentials of the 787. Because of the improved fuel efficiency, the airplane will have lower carbon dioxide and nitrogen oxide emissions. To lower the noise footprint, the 787 uses acoustically treated engine inlets. The back of the engine will have serrated edges, called the variable geometry chevrons.

The 787s offer a choice of Rolls-Royce Trent 1000 or General Electric GEnx engines. Unlike most of the airplanes operating around the world today, the 787 has a common engine interface, which makes it easier to swap the engines from the GE to the Rolls-Royce or vice versa. When the Chinese airlines that had ordered the airplanes with the GEnx engines decided to delay the delivery, the common engine interface allowed Boeing to switch to the Rolls-Royce engines and place the airplanes with All Nippon Airways.

The engines and the airplane parts are manufactured around the world, which makes the logistics of transporting all of them to the final assembly site challenging. Boeing modified the 747s to carry the airplane sections from around the world. The modified 747, aptly called the Dreamlifter, can carry the 787 wings in its belly.

Besides the hiccups in the early stages of the 787 program, the airplane sections coming from different parts of the world will be fully prestuffed ready for the final assembly. For example, the fuselage assemblies will have the wiring, hydraulic lines, and system connections. The final assembly of the airplane, initially expected to take six days, will take only three days after the system matures.

The 787 will comply with the new ETOPS rules. Boeing plans to design and certify the longer range versions of the airplane to 330-minute ETOPS capability. This level of ETOPS authority will permit airlines around the world to operate point to point between any two cities in the world, using optimal routing. Many airlines in the world may not need more than 180-minute or 240-minute ETOPS authority, but it is reassuring for the airlines to know that the manufacturer will design, test, and certify the airplane systems and the engines to operate up to 330-minute ETOPS diversion time.

* * *

The risk-sharing arrangement with the suppliers and the globalization of the design and manufacture of the 787 might have lowered the upfront cost by billions of dollars and lessened the overall risk of the airplane program for Boeing, but it complicated the management process.

On October 10, 2007, Boeing delayed the delivery of the first 787 by six months, attributing it to shortages of fasteners and difficulties in the supply chain. Boeing also disclosed that not all the supplier-partners were as "top-notch" as Boeing had anticipated. All Nippon Airways, the 787 launch customer, would receive its first airplane in November or December instead of May 2008.

On January 16, 2008, Boeing announced another delay of nearly three months. The first delivery to All Nippon would slide to the beginning of 2009.

However, the Boeing announcements were premature. It still lacked a realistic assessment of its challenges. In addition to the problems with the supply chain and the parts shortages, the 787 required engineering and manufacturing changes as well. In March 2008, Boeing announced that design changes were necessary to further strengthen the composite center box. As a result, on April 9, 2008, Boeing announced another delay, causing a loss of confidence in the financial market. Boeing announced that the first flight of the 787 would move into the fourth quarter of 2008, and the first delivery would slide to the third quarter of 2009.

However, things did not go as planned!

The Boeing machinists' labor contract was up for renewal in 2008. The machinists assembled the airplanes on the factory floor. With a backlog of more than 3,700 airplane orders to keep the factory humming for at least the next five years and the pressure to deliver the 787 as soon as possible, the machinists' labor union found itself in a strong negotiating position. It rejected the Boeing offer and went out on strike for 57 days. On November 2, 2008, once Boeing further sweetened the deal, the machinists returned to work.

To add insult to injury, on November 4, 2008, Boeing announced that it had learned a few weeks earlier that it had installed nearly 8,000 faulty fasteners on the 787. Replacing the faulty fasteners required a person to crawl through the nearly finished airplanes and undo much interior installation work that had already been completed.

The labor strike and the quality problems with the faulty fasteners took a toll on the 787 schedule. On December 11, 2008, Boeing announced that the first flight of the 787 would move into the second quarter of 2009 and the first delivery would slide to the first quarter of 2010—two years behind the original schedule.

Having acknowledged the problems with the supply chain and quality control, Boeing also announced a management shakeup. Commenting on the management changes, the president of Boeing Commercial Airplanes said, "The steps we are taking today will sharpen our management focus and bring our organizational structure to bear to improve execution in our supply chain, as well as on our development programs."[1]

However, on June 23, 2009, the composite wing failed during static testing; it revealed weak points where the wings joined the fuselage. The program was going to incur further delays. Boeing announced that it would release the new dates after fully assessing the problem and the necessary fix. Boeing did not disclose the load the static wing was under when it failed.[2] During the manufacture of the composite structure Boeing also discovered microscopic wrinkles in the skin plies in two locations near the fuselage door. Even though the problem was fixed with a simple patch, it required the Alenia fuselage plant to temporarily stop work. The problem was traced to a new tooling machine at the Italian factory.

Having recognized continuing problems with one of its major suppliers, on July 30, 2009 Boeing spent $1 billion to bring the Vought Aircraft Industries 787 work on aft fuselage sections back in house. Vought's South Carolina factory is next door to Global Aeronautica, a 787 fuselage integration center founded by Vought and Finmeccanica's Alenia Aeronautica. In 2008, Boeing had bought out Vought's share in Global Aeronautica.

On August 31, after announcing that the first flight of the 787 would take place before the end of 2009 and the first delivery would occur toward the end of 2010, Boeing Commercial Airplanes President and CEO 63-year-old Scott Carson announced his retirement from the company as of the end of the year. Jim Albaugh, who had been managing the defense side of the Boeing business, replaced Carson.

Boeing took a $1.56 billion loss for the third quarter of 2009, driven by $2.5 billion in new costs associated with design and production problems on the 787and $1 billion in additional costs on the 747-8.

Analysts had their own opinions on the reasons for Boeing's never-ending problems. Some even blamed it on the merger with McDonnell Douglas. "Boeing's slide can be traced to the company's ill-fated $13 billion purchase of McDonnell Douglas Corp. Under chairman John McDonnell and chief executive Harry Stonecipher, McDonnell Douglas starved its design and engineering operations and became little more than a sales organization ... McDonnell and Stonecipher, both of whom joined Boeing's board, successfully argued for improving profit margins on existing lines instead of introducing new commercial jets. ... But by 2003, Alan Mulally, who headed Boeing's commercial-airplane division, was convinced that Boeing needed a fresh plane. ... Mulally was told that the plane's projected development costs would have to be 50 percent or more below the 777's. To meet this demand, Mulally ... would farm out the design, engineering, and manufacturing of the 787—virtually everything except final assembly—to suppliers that would shoulder more than $9 billion of the project's $13 billion cost ..."[3]

Instead of blaming it on the merger, "Boeing Co. Chairman and Chief Executive Jim McNerney said the company had overreached in attempting to build a new plane with pioneering composite technology while simultaneously pushing major design and construction responsibility out to partners."[4] At a conference call with the reporters, McNerney said, "We need to bring more of the engineering, especially at the systems level, back into Boeing."[5]

On October 28, 2009, Boeing announced that it would open a second 787 production line in South Carolina near the Vought plant. "By locating some production and an estimated 3,800 jobs across the country, CEO W. James McNerney Jr. is signaling the lengths he's willing to go to loosen the union's chokehold on the company. The last thing he wants, insiders say, is for Boeing to become yet another U.S. manufacturer hamstrung by costly labor and recalcitrant unions when competition from China and India looms."[6]

On December 22, 2009, Boeing announced that it also bought the remaining shares of Finmeccanica's Alenia Aeronautica in Global Aeronautica and consolidated its 787 manufacturing in the state.[7] The South Carolina plant will assemble and test the 787-9; the assembly line for the 787-8 will remain in Everett, north of Seattle.

Everett is where the first Boeing 747 rolled out on September 30, 1968. Guinness World Records recognizes its main assembly building as the largest building in the world by volume. Over the years, Boeing has built more than 3,000 widebody airplanes at this site. The airplanes built in Everett have flown a total distance that is equivalent to going around the globe 3.3 million times. By May 2007, just the 777s built in Everett had flown more than 1 million ETOPS flights.

Analysts believe that the move to South Carolina opens the door for Boeing to locate the new airplanes to replace the 777 and 737 family in a non-unionized South Carolina.

* * *

The news of the delays was a great disappointment. After all, Boeing's previous all-new airplane, the 777, was delivered on time to United Airlines. The holdups affected Boeing credibility with customers and investors.

The 787 was ridiculed as the "7-LATE-7," and Dreamliner was replaced by the "Nightmare Liner." The more sobering thought is that much of Boeing's troubles had been self-inflicted.

However, the 787 delay had no real tangible impact on the competition. Boeing still enjoyed a lead over Airbus, whose comparable wide-body airplane, the A350XWB, had only half the orders of the 787 and who will not be able to have a competing airplane until 2013 at the earliest.

Some airlines canceled orders for the 787. Disappointed by the Boeing performance, airlines even publicly threatened to become exclusive Airbus customers. For example, Qatar Airways, which had 60 787s and 24 777s on order, including options, said, "Qatar Airways is also considering pulling its order of 777 aircraft, which the airline had planned to bring forward. 'Then Boeing will be left with a load of parked planes,' he said. Al Baker [CEO of Qatar Airways] said he will have to 'seriously think' before doing any further business with Boeing. ... 'It may be that we become an exclusive Airbus customer,' he said."[8]

However, analysts believe that some airlines only threaten to cancel in order to extract maximum compensation for the delay. The global economic slowdown that gained prominence during the last quarter of 2008 and continued to plague the industry in 2009 had altered airlines' immediate need for additional capacity. Despite the rhetoric to claim maximum penalties from Boeing for the 787 delay, many airlines probably considered the 787 delay a blessing.

However, "McNerney sees some silver lining in the 787's delays and is confident in the Dreamliner's future ... The technology that Boeing is using on the Dreamliner will be used on aircraft for decades ... 'We've figured out how to build airplanes for the next 75 years,' McNerney said. Boeing is using a spun composite barrel for its 787. Airbus plans to use composite panels instead. McNerney isn't sure Airbus' strategy will pay off."[9]

Despite the bad news, analysts predict, "When ... the 787 is being produced at 120 a year, [it] has the potential to be the most profitable aircraft Boeing has ever had."[10]

* * *

The overwhelming market success of the 787 in early 2000 forced Airbus to launch a product that could compete with the 787. Disparaging long-range twins on ETOPS was not working for Airbus. By early 2000, the airlines knew better.

The only way Airbus could achieve efficiencies comparable to the 787 was by abandoning its "4 engines 4 long haul" strategy. A quad could not match the operating efficiency or the emission level of a comparable twin. The Airbus attempt to limit the twins to medium-range operations through regulations failed. Airbus had run out of options. It decided to have its own long-range ETOPS twin similar to the 787.

When Boeing called the 787 a "game changer," obviously it did not anticipate that the 787 would change the Airbus game.

Airbus launched three versions of the long-range twin—the A350XWB—that would compete with the 787 and some high-capacity versions of the 777s. The A350-900 is expected to compete against the 787-9 and the Boeing 777-200ER, while the 350-seater A350-1000 will challenge the popular 777-300ER. The A350-800, which is a shrunken version of the A350-900, with 270 passengers in three classes will compete primarily against the 787-8.

The A350XWB is expected to have design features and capabilities comparable to the 787. It plans to have all the bells and whistles of the 787, including a lower cabin altitude, bigger windows, and electronic window shades. Even the material composition is similar to the 787. On the A350XWB, Airbus "foresees the use of 53% carbon-fiber reinforced plastic, 14% titanium, 6% steel, 19% aluminum and aluminum-lithium, and 8% other materials."[11]

Although Airbus is adopting the "risk-sharing partners" concept from the 787 program, it is also learning from Boeing fumbles. "Enders [President and Chief Executive of Airbus] said Airbus had also been looking at the problems experienced by Boeing, including the huge supply chain problems the Americans had faced with outside suppliers in its extended enterprise. It seemed Boeing had been too lenient with its suppliers and risk-sharing partners."[12]

Boeing appears to share Enders' assessment. Boeing admitted that it erred on the side of giving the partners more free rein than in retrospect it should have, and it intends to monitor the suppliers closely. [13] "Trust but verify," may become the new slogan for Boeing and Airbus. In future, Boeing also plans to do more engineering designs in-house before handing them off to its partners.

Airlines have successfully convinced Airbus to go with composites such as those for the 787. But it may have to contend with comparatively low-tech composite panels rather than the Boeing proprietary spun composite single barrel. Industry experts believe that it would have taken Airbus two to five years and a sizable investment to acquire a technology to manufacture a spun composite single barrel.[14]

Airbus plans to certify the A350XWB, for the namesake, to a 350-minute ETOPS diversion time capability.

When Boeing eventually gets over the challenges and delivers its first 787 to All Nippon Airways, it will set new standards for building modern airplanes. Having learned from the Boeing mistakes, Airbus will probably have an easier time with the A350XWB. However, it is not certain if the A350XWB, which has a different composite structure than the 787, will deliver the same maintenance cost savings. But it is certain that the A350XWB will be a strong competitor to the 787.

* * *

Had it not been for the overwhelming success of Early ETOPS on the 777, neither Boeing nor Airbus would have embarked on long-range twins such as the 787 and the A350XWB. Unlike in the 777 program, neither Boeing nor Airbus has to contend any longer with the uncertainty of promulgation of new standards to permit ETOPS at entry. With the new ETOPS rules in place, now it is just a matter of execution.

Only time will tell if the 787 or the A350XWB will dominate the market. But one thing is certain: ETOPS twins such as the 787 and the A350XWB will control the medium-range and long-range markets in the future.

8

REVERSAL OF FORTUNES

The fumbles, misfortunes, and management meltdown

During the past 20 years, Boeing and Airbus have gone through the cycles of boom and bust. Furthermore, most of the busts have been self-inflicted. Flush with cash, during the boom cycles they appear to expand the business to be the global one-stop shopping center for aviation. But when they hit the bottom, they quickly divest, often at a financial loss, and focus on their core business.

In the mid-1990s, Boeing was riding high. Despite all the risks, the 777 was a success. Boeing made good on its promises. Early ETOPS permitted United to launch the 777 on the transatlantic route from the first day of revenue operations. Boeing merged with McDonnell Douglas. It purchased many aviation- related businesses. Then, the bottom fell out.

Boeing suspended production of airplanes for a few weeks. Boeing had no product to counter the new A340 derivatives. Moreover, Boeing was in no position to bring the new derivatives of the 777 to compete with the newer derivatives of the A340s until the middle of 2004.

The Sonic Cruiser, which was started in 1999 and officially launched on March 29, 2001, was a disaster. The market was not receptive to the 250-passenger airplane that would fly close to the speed of sound and burn an additional 15% to 20% fuel. Eventually, Boeing was forced to abandon the Sonic Cruiser.

Boeing tried to divert the airlines from the A380 by promising to launch the 747X program. Unfortunately, there were no takers.

9/11 severely disrupted the US airlines. They canceled or postponed many airplane orders. Boeing felt the pain.

As if Boeing did not have enough problems, "Sears fiasco" and "Harry's affair" badly tarnished Boeing's stellar reputation. Boeing had lost its moral compass.

* * *

While Boeing was fumbling, these were wonderful years for Airbus. It had boosted the 19% market share in 1995 to 50% in a few years. By 2001, it had overtaken Boeing on the number of total orders. In 2002, it brought to market two brand-new derivatives of the A340, the 300- to 400-seater ultra-long and long-range A340-500 and -600.

On December 19, 2000, based on orders for 55 airplanes from six launch customers, the Supervisory Board of the newly restructured Airbus voted to launch the A380, an airplane much larger than the 747.

Leahy declared that soon there would be two types of airlines—those with the A380 and those without. It had an eerie similarity to the 1960s theme—there would be two types of airlines: those with the Concorde and those without.

The A340s were popular in the market. Some industry experts had even started to write Boeing's obituary.

Airbus was propelled to new heights. The media paid homage to the new rising leaders. The January 8, 2001, issue of *BusinessWeek* recognized Airbus Chief Executive Noel Forgeard as one of "The Top 25 Managers" from around the world. None of the Boeing executives made the grade. In 2003, Airbus became the world's largest producer of passenger airplanes.

In 2004, CNN interviewed Forgeard and credited him for steering the A380 program toward success. When asked what sort of characteristics Forgeard looked for in the management team on the A380, he stressed having "people with strong character who never surrender, who always go further and who inspire spirit and faith in their colleagues."[1]

Time magazine recognized Noel Forgeard as one of the world's leading "Builders & Titans." The magazine had picked the top 100 leaders from around the world. Forgeard was one of the 100. Again, no one from Boeing made the grade. Writing the piece for *Time* magazine, Sir Richard Branson complimented Forgeard for taking Airbus to a higher plane.[2]

However, the tide was about to turn!

* * *

While Airbus emphasized size with the A380, Boeing concentrated on the middle point-to-point market. Even though the Sonic Cruiser was an airplane for the middle of the market, it was not what the airlines wanted. Failure of the Sonic Cruiser was a wakeup call for Boeing. It had failed to do its homework. Airlines preferred efficiency to speed.

Boeing had learned its lesson. It quickly abandoned the Sonic Cruiser and, in December 2002, announced the 7E7, which would be more efficient than comparable products in the market. "E" stood for "efficiency." The Boeing board of directors granted authority to offer the airplane for sale in December 2003.

When Boeing announced the 7E7, Airbus did not take its US rival seriously. Airbus dismissed claims about the 7E7 economics and called it far-fetched. John Leahy ridiculed the Boeing twin as a "Chinese copy" of the A330. It was critical of the 7E7 composite fuselage and wings, and openly shared those criticisms with the airlines. Leahy proposed refitting the old A330 with new fuel-efficient engines to compete with the 7E7. It would retain the A330 fuselage, which was a 1972-vintage fuselage common with other Airbus models.

In April 2004, Boeing launched the 7E7 with an order for 50 airplanes from All Nippon Airways. In December 2004, following the Boeing traditional naming system, it was called the 787. Based on public input, it was called the Dreamliner.

Regardless of the popularity of the 787, Airbus stuck to its proposed revamping of its A330. It ignored comments from its best customers about the inadequacies of the A330 revamp proposal.

Undoubtedly, Airbus was convinced of its ability to read the market. After all, in about five years, it had gone from a small player with a tiny market share to be the new market leader. Airbus exuded a well-deserved confidence.

Airbus detractors might have characterized it as management hubris.

Airbus stuck to its position even when, in April 2005, Air Canada, a major operator of Airbus airplanes, decided to replace its entire Airbus fleet with the Boeing 787 and the 777. The order was for 96 airplanes, including options. By the middle of 2006, when many airlines, including some of the major Airbus airplane operators such as Northwest and Qantas, opted for the 787, Airbus recognized the futility of its A330 revamp proposal. But it was a little late; by then, Airbus was in the middle of a major crisis.

* * *

On June 1, 2005, Airbus announced a six-month delay of the A380 program to sort out a wiring problem. The media also reported that the airplane was nearly six tons heavier than anticipated. The A380 wings failed in the certification tests. They could not withstand the required ultimate load.

Airbus found that the wiring problem was more severe than anticipated. On June 13, 2006, it announced a second six-month slide. The stock market took the news badly. EADS stock dropped precipitously.

Shortly thereafter, the media reported that several executives of EADS and Airbus, and their family members, had cashed in their stock options or stocks just before the news of the second delay of the A380 was made public. There was a whiff of insider trading.

The media reported that even Forgeard had exercised his stock options and that his children had cashed in thousands of EADS shares. Forgeard was reported to have made a profit of €2.5million.

Actually, Forgeard's take was puny compared to Arnaund Lagardère's, the co-chairman of EADS and the head of the Lagardère Group, who was reported to have sold €2 billion worth of shares.

The French Government had brought in the Lagardère Group when the formation of EADS required the government to privatize Aerospatiale, which was a leading partner of Airbus under the old GIE structure. The deal was intended to keep the shares within the French sphere of influence. Lagardère merged its defense-aerospace business, Matra Hautes Technologies (MHT), with Aérospatiale. Under the deal, Lagardère got one third of the merged firm Aerospatiale-Matra and controlled management of the bigger company.

The media accused the French Government of selling off a state enterprise at a bargain-basement price. Lagardère's worth in the new company was supposedly twice the value of MHT. Forgeard, who was known as one of "the Lagardère boys," led MHT before he became the head of Airbus in 1998.

Lagardère became one of the main EADS shareholders when Aerospatiale-Matra joined with DaimlerChrysler Aerospace of Germany, BAE of the United Kingdom, and CASA of Spain to form EADS.

A few weeks before the news release of the A380 delay, the Lagardère Group sold half its 15% stake in EADS for €2 billion. Coincidentally, for the benefit of France, a French state-owned bank, CDC, signed up for nearly one third of the shares that Lagardère was selling. The media reported that after the EADS stock slide, the French bank was sitting on a loss of €200 million. The media commented that this sale to CDC and the earlier privatization meant that, for the sake of "French-ness," French taxpayers twice had gotten the worst of a deal with Lagardère.[3]

Like Lagardère, DaimlerChrysler also had sold 7.5% of its shares. But DaimlerChrysler did not receive the same level of media attention for its sale as that of Lagardère. Maybe the media scrutiny was prompted by Lagardère's perceived close ties with the French bureaucracy.

Notwithstanding the talk of cross-border unity among the Western Europeans, lingering nationalistic sentiments prevailed. The A380 delay made it obvious that Airbus was terribly balkanized. The German and the French factories clung to their traditional operating methods and harbored cross-border jealousies.

EADS even had two CEOs, French and German. In June 2005, Forgeard was promoted to the French slot and shared the EADS CEO responsibilities with Tom Enders, a German. Reportedly, Forgeard did not like sharing the responsibilities and advocated for one CEO. At the same time, he canvassed to make sure a German would not get his old job as the head of Airbus.

Airbus was always a part of the European conglomerate and now was a part of EADS, but somehow the French always perceived it as a French entity. A German running Airbus was possibly too much to bear for the French psyche and the Gallic pride!

The media reported that Forgeard's over-obsession with being the only CEO of EADS and, in the meantime, stopping a German from heading Airbus, had strained relations between the French and the Germans. While the A380 was in the midst of development, EADS was fully embroiled in a French-German tussle over management structure.

The Germans were suspicious that the French political machinery was trying to dominate both EADS and Airbus.

Despite having the president of France, Jacques Chirac, as a mentor, Forgeard could not muster the German support to be the sole CEO of EADS. Reality had taken over. The in-fighting had started to take its toll.

The June 1 announcement of the six-month delay of the A380 was a wakeup call. The impasse could not continue any longer. On June 25, 2005, EADS announced that the current arrangement would continue. Noel Forgeard would share the position with the German. As a consolation prize, Forgeard received supervisory responsibility over Airbus, which would be managed by a German, Gustav Humbert.

* * *

According to the media, constant political meddling was the price Airbus had to pay for the European governments' financial backing. Reportedly, the politicians used Airbus as the government's employment program; work was rationed around 16 factories in four countries.

Instead of business efficacy, political considerations dictated the allocation of work. According to industry experts, the Airbus Finkenwerder factory—a vast complex on the waterfront near the port of Hamburg—would have been a more logical site for the A380 final assembly line than the landlocked Toulouse. Shipping the massive A380 parts to Toulouse required custom-built river barges. More than 100 miles of highway had to be widened and straightened for the flatbed trucks.

Finkenwerder was allotted to build sections of the A380 fuselage and the wiring for the cabin power supply, lighting, and electronic systems such as video-on-demand for passengers.

Unlike Boeing, who had very stringent software control on the 787 program, reportedly, Airbus management had overlooked the potential pitfalls of factories clinging to their traditional operating methods.

Finkenwerder was using Dassault's CATIA Version 4, and the engineers at Toulouse were using Version 5. Although these were two versions of the same program, apparently they were not fully compatible. According to the published reports, because these two versions did not handle the three-dimensional drawings in the same way, it was possible for data to be corrupted if information was transferred between the two versions. Normally the software vendors did a decent job of backward compatibility. Reportedly, Dassault failed to implement a smooth interoperability with the earlier version, and Airbus paid the price.

According to the media reports, when the large packs of preconfigured wires that powered the cabin power supply, lighting, and electronic systems began arriving from Finkenwerder to the assembly plant in Toulouse, they did not fit properly from the rear section into the front section of the fuselage. Workers tried to pull the bundles apart and feed the wiring through the fuselage by hand, but with hundreds of miles of wire and more than 40,000 connectors on each airplane, Airbus had a horrendous challenge ahead. Apparently, Airbus had failed to notice the shortcoming earlier during the three-dimensional digital mockup of the A380.

French workers blamed the Germans for the fiasco.

* * *

While Airbus' fortunes were plummeting, Boeing's were rising. Boeing was on its way to a full recovery.

The 787 was becoming a best seller. Even though Boeing considered the 747/A380 market to be comparatively small, it was patiently waiting for the right engine and the advances in technology to build a new-generation 747 to challenge the A380.

In November 2005, Boeing launched the 747-8 with the GEnx engines from the 787 program. The last version of the 747 was the 747-400. Rather than calling the new-generation 747 a -500, Boeing opted to call it 747-8. The dash 8 was subtle marketing to convey to the airlines that it would incorporate many of the advanced technology from the 787 program. Boeing promises that the 747-8 will have 17 percent lower fuel costs and 16 percent lower overall operating costs than the 747 -400.

* * *

Airbus had started to unravel on its own. Despite his attempts to dissociate from the A380 problems because of only supervisory but no direct operational control of the program for the previous 12 months, Forgeard became the poster child for the A380 problems. His stock dealings did not help either. On July 2, 2006, both Forgeard and Humbert resigned.

On October 4, 2006, Airbus announced a third delay of the A380 program. The first delivery to Singapore Airlines was delayed by 18 months, and the others were delayed by an average of 2 years.

Airbus had a new CEO every few months. In two years, between 2005 and 2007, Airbus had five CEOs.

On October 9, 2006, the new co-CEO of EADS, Louis Gallois, who had replaced Forgeard, stepped in to run Airbus. In February of 2007, he embarked on an eight-point cost-cutting program, called Power 8. For "strategic reorientation," Airbus decided to revert to its core competencies.

In addition to plans to sell many plants in the United Kingdom, France, and Germany to raise capital, under Power 8, Airbus intended to eliminate 10,000 jobs across Europe in the next four years. Airbus was doing what Boeing had done a few years before. Besides eliminating thousands of jobs, Boeing had sold off its Wichita Division, which built major parts for almost all Boeing airplanes.

At the time Gallois was talking about cutting jobs across Europe, EADS disclosed that, according to his contract, Forgeard would receive a total of €8.56 million in severance payments.

Severance payments are quite common in the United States. It is not out of the ordinary for failed executives to grab at least $20 million or $30 million on the way out. But such practices were not widely prevalent in Europe. Even the French politicians were not amused by the news of €8.56 million. Enders disclosed to the media that the French Government had convinced EADS to include such language in the severance contract.

Forgeard, once regarded by *Time* and *BusinessWeek* as one of the world's top managers, fell from grace. He blamed the fiasco on the German manager's "false sense of pride" at Finkenwerder.

Forgeard was also blamed for the A400M military transport fiasco, which was four years late and €5 billion over budget.[4] "Enders regards the fixed-price contract negotiated by one of his predecessors, Noel Forgeard, as a disaster rooted in naivety, excessive enthusiasm and arrogance."[5] For his brusqueness, many in Toulouse have nicknamed the former paratrooper Enders "Major Tom."

Allegations of insider trading haunted Forgeard, Lagardère, and several EADS executives. The French stock market regulator—the Autorite des Marches Financiers (AMF), the French State Prosecutor's office, and the German authorities launched independent investigations into the allegations.[6]

In April 2008, the media reported that AMF had filed charges against EADS and Lagardère, and approximately 15 EADS and Airbus executives for insider trading.[7] In July 2009, the independent examiner appointed by the AMF recommended a fine of €5.45 million against Forgeard and €3.6 million against Leahy. While clearing Lagardère and Daimler, it recommended a fine of €700,000 against EADS for alleged market information delays.[8] However, on December 17, 2009, the AMF Sanctions Committee cleared all the executives and EADS of any charges.[9]

For many, perceptions are the reality. Sometimes the court of public opinion is quick to render its judgment. Regardless of the legal outcomes, allegations of insider trading might have already tainted Forgeard and the multi-billion-dollar Lagardère enterprises.

It is debatable if Airbus made the right decision to launch the A380, but there is no argument that EADS management worsened the situation and compromised billions of dollars of potential profit.

Incidentally, the A380 was not the only problem child. The Airbus problem went beyond the A380.

* * *

In the 380-seater long-range market, the success of the 777-300ER destroyed the A340-600 and the A340-600HGW. The media reported that several A340-600 operators were trading accusations with Airbus regarding the front section of the airplane being too heavy, resulting in a loss of five tons of cargo.[10]

The A340-600 with a payload range of 380 passengers and 7,500 nm (13,900 km) challenged the earlier versions of the 747. Boeing had no option but to build the 777-300ER to counter the A340-600. The 777-300ER had a slightly better capability. To match the 777-300ER, Airbus felt it was necessary to launch a heavier gross weight version of the A340-600—the A340-600HGW.

However, the A340-600HGW was a disappointment. In 2006, citing performance concerns, Emirates, which was one of the launch customers for the A340-600HGW, canceled its entire order for 20 airplanes. The cancellation effectively killed any future prospects for the airplane.

In an effort to satisfy the Emirates performance concerns with the A340-600HGW, Airbus announced that it would consider launching an "enhanced" version called the A340-600E, which would match the operating economics of the 777-300ER. But in reality, Airbus did not seriously pursue the A340-600E.

* * *

Airbus also had problems with the A330 revamp. It was a slow airplane and would not have the efficiencies that Boeing was predicting for its 787.

The founder and chief executive of the Los Angeles–based International Lease Finance Corporation Steven Udvar-Hazy—a person who lives and breathes the aviation industry—is one of the most influential aviation leaders. "Perhaps the most telling evidence of Hazy's influence is the very public role he played in forcing Airbus to go back to the drawing board and spend US\$8 billion to US\$10 billion to redesign its new A350 twin-aisle mid-size jet after he found the design lacking. … Before a stunned crowd at an industry gathering … Hazy lowered the boom on the A350 and almost overnight, killed the design. … Hazy complained that the proposed A350 was just a 'warmed up' version of an existing plane, and that its wing design made it too slow."[11]

Prescient as he was, even Leahy, the super-salesman, must have missed the signs or refused to acknowledge the reality. Neither Boeing nor Airbus enjoys being chastised publicly by one of its most valued customers.

By the time Airbus came to recognize the futility of its A330 revamp proposal, its engineering resources were too occupied on the A380 program for it to mount an aggressive campaign against the 787. Moreover, Airbus was already in the middle of a major crisis; Forgeard's position in EADS was untenable, and people who owned EADS stock were livid.

Eventually, at the July 2006 Farnborough Airshow, Airbus formally abandoned the A330 revamp. It announced an all-new A350, and called it the A350 Extra-Wide-Body (A350XWB). The airplane would be comparable to the 787. Airbus claimed its cabin would be five inches wider. In December 2006, Airbus formally launched the A350XWB.

Airbus was going to use composite panels on metal frames for the fuselage. Airlines were still dissatisfied. Airbus and some of its best customers argued openly in public on whether the A350XWB fuselage design was "frozen" or "thawing." In mid-September 2007, Airbus announced another version of the redesigned fuselage. It would have composite panels on composite frames instead of the metal frames. Because Airbus had no immediate access to the technology to manufacture a single-barrel composite structure similar to the 787, analysts believed this would be the best that Airbus could offer.

Notwithstanding Leahy's assertions of optimal design, the A350 went through several iterations. Nevertheless, at each juncture, Leahy claimed that the design was superior to the 787. He also frequently assured the market that the newer version was "better" than the previous one, which, according to Leahy, was already "very good."

Leahy no longer called the 787 a Chinese copy of the A330. If anything, the A350XWB became the Airbus copy of the 787.

Boeing chose GE and Rolls-Royce engines for the 787; however, Airbus chose the Rolls-Royce Trent as the only engine for the A350XWB. Because the long-range version of the A350XWB would compete with the 777-300ER, for which GE was the exclusive engine supplier, it made no business sense for GE to offer an engine to power the longer range version of the A350XWB.

Airbus planned to pursue a more global supply chain similar to what Boeing had adopted on the 787 program. Although Airbus was attempting to reduce the cost and improve the financial performance, some analysts thought Airbus had an uphill battle. In spite of Gallois' comments that Airbus would not sacrifice price to get orders, industry experts believed that Airbus had no alternative but to discount the price of the A350XWB heavily to capture some share of the market from the 787.[12]

With rising fuel prices in 2007, the A340 lost its market appeal. The 777 had marginalized the A340. The residual value plummeted. The increased focus on the environment also took its toll.

Even Sir Richard Branson of Virgin Airlines, once a great advocate of "4 engines 4 long haul," vowed to avoid purchasing fuel-thirsty four-engine airplanes in the future. The headlines read, "Virgin's Branson to shun thirsty 4-engined planes," in an article in which Virgin Group's boss Sir Richard publicly said that he "would aim to avoid buying fuel-thirsty four-engined aeroplanes in future to curb fuel costs and the environmental impact of his fast-growing airlines."[13]

It appeared the only way Airbus could sell an A340 was to make the price so attractive that a price- conscious customer could not refuse. "'With the 777, Boeing has a better product that uses less fuel,' the head of India's low-cost Kingfisher airline, Vijay Mallya, told AFP [Agence France Presse] in February[2006]. 'Nevertheless, we are contemplating buying the A340 all the same, if we can come to an agreement on the price.'"[14]

Airlines such as Finnair, which had ordered the A340, switched to the twins—the A330s. Even the French Government elected to buy an A330 instead of an A340 for the president of France to use.[15] The A330 sales were picking up.

Although Airbus, in an effort to challenge the supremacy of the 747, advanced the A340 family and confined the A330 to short to medium range market, in the end it may be the A330 that saves Airbus until the A350XWB starts flying.

* * *

Because the A380 was not yet a "must-have airplane," the airlines were not willing to pay top dollar. Reportedly, the airlines demanded, and often received, the same steep discount on the A380 that the launch customer, Singapore Airlines, received.

In the duopoly, possibly Airbus had no option but to buy the market share through heavy discounting. "Airbus' aggressive attempts to close the gap on arch rival Boeing Co. (BA) by discounting airplane prices run the risk of harming its profitability going forward, analysts said. The move to drum up sales of its wide-bodied airplanes and the new A350 XWB in particular with reduced prices may counteract the company's ongoing efforts to boost its financial performance under a major restructuring program [Power 8], according to industry experts ... Airbus is discounting prices to buy and build its depleted market share. 'The discounts are just storing up future profitability problems ...'"[16]

Even Gallois acknowledged that there were "unfavorably priced aircraft" in the Airbus backlog.[17] "Gallois said there was a 'severe' price war when Boeing started selling the 787, but that Airbus [in 2009] has 'returned to a level of pricing that's more reasonable.'"[18]

* * *

The A380 delays had cost Airbus dearly. The airlines extracted every concession they could for the delays.

Keeping the weight down is always a major challenge for all manufacturers. The A380 was reportedly six tons overweight, which resulted in performance penalties. After any delay in an airplane program, it is not unusual for the airlines to threaten to cancel all the existing orders if they are not able to reach an amicable settlement on the compensation for the delays. In accordance with the contractual agreements, both Boeing and Airbus try to placate the customers with further concessions.

Often the misfortunes of the manufacturers pay handsomely for some of the airlines.

"Despite any frustration over the delays, some analysts said A380 customers have good reason to stick with their orders, because the cost of those planes drops with every concession and fine Airbus is forced to pay. 'By the time the airlines get through extracting all the penalties and concessions out of Airbus for all of the delays ... they're going to have the cheapest damn widebody in the world. They'd be crazy to let that deal get away from them.'"[19]

Airbus stopped predicting the break-even point for the A380. In addition, some of the analysts believed any forecast of the break-even point would be meaningless because of the steep discounts.[20] Some analysts believed Airbus would have to sell more than 500 airplanes to break even.

* * *

Just as misery loves company, because of poor program management, unrealistic planning, and increased outsourcing combined with inadequate monitoring of the supply chain, Boeing also stumbled with the 787. Having committed to dramatic leaps in technological advances, new material, and more global manufacturing, it failed on execution. "The program [787] seemed to be spiraling downward, rivaling the A380 for sheer programmatic dysfunction."[21] Boeing incurred penalty payments for the delay.

"The 787 is Boeing's most successful new aircraft. ... But analysts are asking difficult questions about how profitable the whole programme could be if penalty payments are added to other cost concerns. 'The large number of 787s sold at low prices, combined with rising recurring costs, are steadily eating away at programme margins and long-term programme profitability,'..."[22]

However, "These 787 problems have basically been a windfall for Airbus. They have resulted in badly needed revenue [with the A330] and the breathing room needed to create a competitive response [with the A350XWB]. Since the 787 delays were first announced, Airbus has enjoyed record A330 demand ... Many of these have gone to leasing customers ... It is likely that some of Boeing's penalty payments related to 787 delays are going directly to A330 leases, indirectly benefiting Airbus ... The most direct benefit to Airbus of the 787 delay has been time to get the A350 response right."[23]

The resulting extra costs from the 787 delay have depleted the Boeing cash reserve and could compromise the timely launch of the 787-10 or an improved version of the 777 to compete with the A350-1000. Reportedly, the 787 also is overweight, which could result in additional penalties. Boeing is also under pressure to bring the weight down quickly to stop the financial hemorrhaging.

The 787 was not the only problem child. Boeing had problems with the 747-8 also.

Compared to the 747-400, the 747-8 has newer engines, new aerodynamically efficient wing and updated flight-control avionics. Boeing underestimated the engineering efforts that would be required to work on the 747 blueprints from the 1960s. According to the media reports, the increased costs have made it difficult for the passenger-version of the 747-8 to compete against the heavily discounted A380s.

However, with virtually no competition in the high-capacity-long-haul air cargo market, the 747-8 cargo version may have the market to itself.

* * *

The airlines take maximum advantage of the intense rivalry between Boeing and Airbus. But the competition within the airlines also is brutal. The profit margins in airline operations are thin. Airlines also cannot afford not to have the most efficient airplane in their fleet.

Some leading airlines have ordered the latest offering from both Boeing and Airbus—the 787 and the A350XWB. Analysts believe some of these airlines may be hedging their bets and may ultimately dispose of the airplane they deem unsuitable. Nevertheless, the manufacturers cannot afford to be too aggressive in imposing penalties for the last-minute cancellation because of the stature of these leading airlines in the marketplace. Airbus had to swallow its pride when Emirates canceled its order for 20 A340-600HGWs.

Boeing and Airbus make some of the most technologically advanced airplanes. Being fierce competitors, they often push the technological boundaries on the new airplanes to get an edge over each other. It is not unusual for an airplane manufacturer to stumble occasionally. But unfortunately, the impact of the "stumble" can be far-reaching.

Even though the manufacturers compensate the airlines for airplane delays, the delays also can create a challenge for the airlines. Because the airlines base their fleet planning, lease arrangements, and long-term financial planning on the manufacturers' promised delivery dates, any delay in the airplane delivery can reverberate through the entire chain and can even affect the flight schedules.

A few strategic blunders can badly tarnish the manufacturers' reputation and hurt the financial bottom line. In the cyclical aviation business, neither Boeing nor Airbus can take its market dominance for granted.

9

THE FUTURE

We live in the future we create

Fortunes can change overnight in the aviation industry. It is nothing new.

Only three years after founding the company, Bill Boeing nearly closed the business in 1919. Boeing had to drastically cut the payroll just to keep afloat in 1934, after World War II and in the late '60s and early '70s. Just after 9/11, the Commercial Airplanes side of Boeing nearly halved its payroll. Boeing has gone through many booms and busts over the last 90 years.

Boeing dominated the commercial airplane market for nearly four decades. In 1995, Airbus controlled only 19% of the market. But, it overtook Boeing in 2001 and led every year until Boeing's comeback in 2006.

"Experts" had started to write off Boeing.

Academics proclaimed, "Boeing was once a great company ... Boeing has exhibited a lack of strategic vision that has pushed the company backwards in the competition with Airbus."[1]

In 2004, even veteran journalist John Newhouse[2] was ready to proclaim Airbus the winner in his book, *Ascendancy of Airbus and Decline of Boeing*. Newhouse wrote, "... [Boeing's] driving principle—making money on every deal—excluded a sharp focus on gaining or protecting market share. By contrast, Airbus, which seemed then to be doing everything right, was all about market share. In the five years preceding 9/11, it had erased Boeing's dominance and pulled even in aircraft sales."

Speaking about Jean Pierson, the head of Airbus from 1985 to 1998, and T. A. Wilson, a legendary figure who retired as Boeing chairman on

January 1, 1988, Newhouse added, "And just as Pierson's arrival marked the start of Airbus's ascent, Wilson's departure marked the start of Boeing's decline."[3]

To Newhouse's surprise, when Boeing bounced back and claimed its mantle in 2006, he had to rewrite the final chapters and rename the book *Boeing versus Airbus* just before publishing it in 2007.

Experts have their opinions, but no one can truly predict if Boeing or Airbus will dominate the market in the next 10 or 20 years. There are too many variables. The history of airplane manufacturing is full of trials and tribulations.

No single factor makes an airplane successful in the marketplace, but one major factor can destroy an airplane program. One international event such as 9/11, an incorrect assessment of the market, or one critical management oversight can make or break a program and can cost a company billions of dollars. If history is any guide, sometimes all it takes is one major misstep to set back the manufacturer for decades.

Boeing forfeited its leadership in commercial aviation for nearly a quarter of a century because of its refusal to sell the Model 247 to TWA in 1933. 9/11 badly hurt Boeing. Inadequate management oversight hurt both the A380 and the 787 programs, costing the two companies billions of dollars. In the process, it damaged their reputation and sent the stocks tumbling.

* * *

Some in the industry question if Airbus ignored the market trend for fuel-efficient twins when it launched the A340-500 and -600 in 1997. By 1991, US airlines had shifted to big twins. Twins had overtaken the tris and quads in the North Atlantic. Airplanes such as the 767s were displacing the 747s, the DC-10s, the MD-11s, and the L1011s. By 1997, the big twins such as the 767s and the 777s had made major inroads in most of the key markets around the world.

After all, when Airbus launched the A340-500 and -600, it must have expected Boeing to counter with comparable 300- to 400-seater long-range and ultra-long-range versions of the 777. Boeing was not going to let Airbus monopolize that share of the market. Besides, because the Boeing airplanes were twins, they would be more fuel efficient and have a lower operating cost than the A340-500 and -600.

Moreover, Boeing already had the GE90 family of engines readily available to power the 777s to compete with the A340-500 and -600. Boeing countered the new Airbus family of airplanes with the 777-300ER and the 777-200LR.

While launching the A340-500 and -600 in 1997, it is not clear if Airbus misjudged the market because it was fixated on pushing the Boeing jumbo jet 747 from its pedestal. Alternatively, it could have concluded that any deficiency in operating cost could be compensated for in the airplane pricing. After all, because of the so-called "loan guarantees," Airbus had a substantial advantage in airplane pricing.

However, Airbus detractors believe that, by developing the A340 family, Airbus wasted billions of European tax dollars. They believe that Airbus would have done better if, in 1997, it had spent the money in launching a longer range version of the A330 with even more fuel-efficient engines. It would have been a revamped A330—essentially the A350, which Leahy proposed in 2004.

Only after being overwhelmed by the success of the 787, Airbus recognized its error in judgment. The A340 became a disappointment. By 2004, airlines had no interest in the revamped A330 either. They pushed Airbus into a completely new design, the A350XWB.

* * *

Airbus attacked ETOPS at entry into service on the 777. But surprisingly, the ETOPS at entry into service essentially marginalized the A340 family. By concentrating on disparaging ETOPS at entry, Airbus possibly overlooked the benefits of designing in the reliability

The future of Boeing rode on the success of the 777. The ETOPS approval at entry into an airline's revenue operation was of vital importance. Having to comply with ETOPS at entry, Boeing paid more attention to design, test, and support requirements, which made the 777 a very reliable airplane. Boeing designed in and tested the reliability.

Even the best airline maintenance cannot improve the inherent reliability of the airplane. To the best of my knowledge, the A340 and the A330 did not have the same rigor in design as the ETOPS-ready 777; reliability was not the major driver in the A330/340 design.

The A330/340 family of airplanes could not compete with the 777 family in terms of reliability in airline operations. Incorporating the inputs from the airline flight crew and the mechanics into the design of the 777 early on established the 777 as a user-friendly airplane.

* * *

Failure of management oversight resulted in Airbus losing billions on its A380 program. Boeing was no better; its management also failed to meet the program commitments on the 787. The delay of the 787 due to inadequate oversight of the supplier chain, parts shortages, and engineering and manufacturing changes is expected to cost Boeing billions of dollars.

Eventually, Airbus got its arms around the problem. On October 15, 2007, with great fanfare, it delivered the first A380 to Singapore Airlines. It was a major milestone in the history of aviation.

Airbus advertised the A380 as the airplane that would solve the airport congestion problem.

Airbus believed that the only way for the airlines to be able to accommodate the increasing traffic from the congested airports with a limited number of available takeoff and landing slots would be by increasing the size of the airplane. The A380 was the answer. Airbus often cited the example of London's Heathrow International Airport, whose two runways were already operating at 98.5% of permitted capacity.

Reportedly, the limit at Heathrow is around 480,000 airplane movements per year. It is one of the most popular destinations and transit points. The slots at Heathrow are so precious that, reportedly, airlines are prepared to pay around $60 million for a takeoff and landing slot. Some of the airlines operating out of Heathrow are worth more for their slots than for the airline business itself.

It made sense for Heathrow to encourage airlines to use bigger airplanes rather than increase the frequency.

Because the A380 wingspan is nearly 50 feet (15 m) wider than that of the 747-400, the terminal gates in most of the airports around the world have to be resized to ensure that the A380 wings do not block adjacent gates. Airports have to provide multiple jetway bridges for simultaneous boarding on both decks, service vehicles capable of reaching the upper deck, and tractors capable of handling the maximum ramp weight of the A380. Airports may have to pave the taxiway shoulders to reduce the likelihood of foreign object damage caused by the outboard engines.

The British Airport Authority spent nearly a billion dollars upgrading Heathrow's facilities to handle the A380. But it is not clear how effective the A380 will be in solving Heathrow's congestion problem.

The promise of higher passenger numbers has prompted airports to invest in building special stands and jetways. In addition to Heathrow, many airports around the world have spent billions of dollars widening their runways and taxiways and building extra loading gates to accommodate the added capacity of the A380.

As of February 2010, the airlines that have declared their intent to use the A380 with a higher seating capacity appeared to concentrate on ferrying the "guest workers" from South and Southeast Asia to the Middle East, or on moving the pilgrims on the Hajj flights. Thus far, the Reunion-based Air Austral is the only airline that plans to operate the A380 at a higher seating capacity, around 840 passengers between Paris and the tiny island in the Indian Ocean.[4]

Airlines in the Middle East plan to turn the Middle Eastern cities into transit hubs. As of February 2010, Emirates accounted for nearly one third of all the A380's firm orders. As Airbus starts delivering the A380s in bigger numbers, Emirates and other airlines may use the A380s with higher seating capacities to transport passengers from the United States and Europe to Asia, and in the process ease the congestion at the airports in the West.

However, thus far most airlines appear to advertise the A380 as a "luxury product." Notwithstanding the Airbus recommendation of 525 passengers in three class configurations, Singapore Airlines fitted its first A380 with 471 seats configured in three classes with 12 luxury suites on the main deck, 60 business-class seats on the upper deck, and 399 economy-class seats on both decks. On the Singapore–Sydney route, Singapore Airlines charged a 20% to 25% premium for all the luxury in first class and a 15% to 20% premium in business class. Some of the A380 operators planned to charge a small premium on the economy seats also. But as the numbers of A380s increase in airline operations, the market forces will determine the level of premium, if any.

When British Airways became the first international airline with seats that converted to flat beds in first class in 1996 and business class in 2000, it set off seat wars. Today, most of the reputable airlines offer competing products. Although most of the people who travel in first class pay their own fares or are high corporate officials to whom money may be no object, most of the people who travel in business class normally work for a company. It is not clear if the companies will be willing to pay a premium for their employees to travel on the A380. Besides, the business travelers often prefer airlines that offer more frequency on the route than the size of the airplane.

When Boeing introduced the 747 in the 1970s, it dramatically lowered the price of travel. It made air travel affordable to the masses. Psychedelic bags with stickers joined the matching Gucci bags. It appears that some of the airlines are trying to get more of the Gucci crowd back with the A380.

Singapore Airlines, which likes its passengers to conjure up what it calls "the romance of travel," has installed first-class seats that can be converted into beds in which two people can sleep together. Some believe that Singapore Airlines should advertise them as "the last refuge from the prying eyes of the private investigators!" Others think that Singapore Airlines should take a page from Las Vegas' motto and proclaim, "What happens in first class stays in first class!"

According to the 2006/2007 market forecasts for passenger airplanes in the 747 and the A380 category, Boeing anticipates 960 airplanes and Airbus sees a need for 1,660 airplanes through 2025. Whether these forecasts will materialize is open to discussion. Surprisingly, both agree on needing nearly 400 freighters.

* * *

Although some of the trunk routes would benefit from added capacity, in general, there is an ongoing debate among the airlines on adding capacity versus increasing frequency. While the airlines that have ordered the A380s see value in adding capacity, others see more benefit in increasing frequency than capacity.

Chief Executive Officer of Cathay Pacific told the media, "'All our financial modeling shows that we are better off offering more frequency with a very efficient aircraft like the 777 than simply adding more capacity to an existing frequency, which is what we would be doing if we introduced the A380.'"[5]

Flight International quoted, All Nippon Airways as saying, "'We prefer frequency rather than capacity.'"[6]

Furthermore, not every major airport in the world may be ready to accept A380s. Unlike Heathrow, which spent over $1 billion, A380 has worsened the congestion at airports that have not been substantially upgraded. Even after spending $100 million on the airport upgrade, "Every time Qantas lands one of its giant Airbus A380s at LAX [Los Angeles], parts of the nation's fourth-busiest airport come to a halt. Service roads, taxiways and runways must be closed to airfield trucks, cars and other commercial aircraft."[7]

However, the impact on the airport is not limited to the ground. According to published reports, the A380 generated more wake turbulence during the approach and takeoff phases than existing aircraft types. Hence, the ICAO required increased spacing between the A380 and the airplane behind it during these phases of flight. This could effectively curtail the number of airplanes an airport can handle during busy times. In light of the spacing concerns due to the vortex separation combined with the airline's use of the airplane as a luxury product, it is difficult to see how the A380 will help solve the air traffic congestion issues around the airports.

The global economic turmoil that started in 2008 and the resulting global travel slump took its toll on the A380 also. Emirates has decided to replace the A380 with the 777-300ER on the Dubai–New York flight until the market recovers. Some of the A380 customers even tried to cancel the orders for the airplane. "Thai Airways International (THAI) has no other options but to keep its order for six Airbus 380 megajets it wanted to cancel as doing so would lead to huge adverse consequences. … as it had come to believe the world's largest commercial aircraft would not be economical to operate."[8]

Thai Airways delayed the delivery of the airplane to December 2012. On October 30, 2009, Air France became the first European airline to take delivery of its first A380; however, both British Airways and Lufthansa have delayed delivery. As of the end of October 2009, 13 of the A380's 16 buyers had delayed deliveries.[9]

Despite an earlier plan to deliver 24 A380s in 2009,[10] Airbus had actually delivered only 10 airplanes in 2009.[11] "There is still uncertainty over when Airbus will reach its optimum production level of four A380s per month or 45 aircraft per year."[12]

"EADS Chief Executive Louis Gallois recently said that building the plane 'is still a challenge.' Manufacturing one A380 requires the same manpower as nine of its single-aisle A320 jetliners, he said."[13] Even two years after the delivery of the first A380, Airbus was still manually completing the work on electrical wiring and harness systems of the aircraft. In August 2009 "Gallois said Airbus is examining remedies for the A380. 'The learning curve is still too steep for the moment,' he said. 'We're spending too much money for each plane and we must see how this learning curve brings us to an average price per plane that we can rely on.'"[14]

Although Airbus could not afford to surrender the long-range-jumbo-jet market segment to Boeing and its 747, some analysts have called the A380 the "worst product-launch decision since New Coke."[15] Only time will tell if the A380, whose service entry was a major milestone in the history of aviation, will be the most dazzling jewel in the Airbus crown or the greatest white elephant in the history of commercial aviation and a colossal failure—just an $18 billion millstone pulling Airbus down.

* * *

Airlines encourage the fierce competition between Boeing and Airbus, which helps them play one against the other and get the best deal. The media has reported that even with the great demand for the 787, the pricing situation has not improved. Airlines cajoled and threatened Airbus until it created the A350XWB with composites.

At the end of each year, the industry proclaims Boeing or Airbus the winner based on the number of airplanes sold. Because none of the airlines pay the catalog price for the airplanes, judging the success purely based on the comparative sales numbers can be misleading. The number of orders gives the manufacturers the bragging rights, but it does not necessarily guarantee healthy profits.

* * *

Although the future of the current A380 is not certain, some of the airlines such as Emirates are already pushing Airbus to spend anywhere up to $5 billion to further stretch the airplane to provide a maximum certified passenger capacity of 900 or more (A380-900). Some prefer newer technology engines on the A380, engines that could power the A350XWB family of airplanes.

"Airbus should work with General Electric to develop a new large turbofan for the A350 XWB that is also capable of powering future A380 growth variants, says International Lease Finance boss Steven Udvar-Hazy. ... because the current engines on the A380 are not the latest technology.'"[16]

Boeing and Airbus leapfrog each other. Just as Boeing developed the 777 to compete against both the A330 and the A340, Airbus launched the A350XWB family to challenge not only the 787 family but also the Boeing 380-seater long-range 777-300ER—the airplane that greatly contributed to annihilating whatever was left of the A340 family.

Some of the airlines are telling Boeing that the popular 777-300ER is in trouble with the A350-1000, and they want Boeing to launch a 787-10 that would be 20% more efficient than the 777-300ER.

In response to the challenge, Boeing floated the proposal to upgrade the 777-300ER to a -300ERX, which would improve fuel burn by 10%.[17] Unless Boeing can offer an upgraded 777 that has better operating economics compared to the A350-1000, and at a considerably lower price, the market may force Boeing into launching the 787-10 sooner than Boeing would prefer.

The intricate dance ritual between the airlines and the manufacturers is a part of the multi-billion-dollar commercial airplane industry. The stakes are high. History shows that ignoring the market can be costly. At the same time, going after the wrong product can be devastating.

* * *

With the proliferation of point-to-point operations and some of the operator's preference for increased frequency rather than additional capacity, analysts believe the future of Boeing and Airbus will depend on the success of the 787 and the A350XWB.

Boeing created global alliances to fund and develop the 787. Airbus has similar plans for the A350XWB program. Even though Boeing has gone through some early problems with the new initiative, the concept of global collaboration is unavoidable.

Boeing and Airbus will refine their process of global alliances based on the lessons learned from the 787 supplier problems and the resulting program slide. Nevertheless, despite objection from labor unions and local governments, a refined version of the global alliance will very likely be the template for both Boeing and Airbus for all future airplane programs.

Besides sharing the risks associated with the launch of a new airplane, the global alliances allow companies to tap into the best engineering brains and the state-of-the-art technologies around the world. The looming retirement of baby-boomers, and the decreasing number of engineering graduates from the universities in the US, may further increase the potential for such alliances for Boeing.

Sometimes, Boeing and Airbus have no option but to spread the work around the world. Countries that order airplanes in large numbers demand offset arrangements that generate employment in their countries. China convinced Airbus to collaborate with Chinese companies to assemble the A320s in China.

Having the major parts of Boeing airplanes built in Japan, indirectly helps foster Japanese airlines' loyalty toward the Boeing airplanes. For years, Airbus has been trying to win over the airlines by farming out increasingly more manufacturing work to Japan.

For Airbus, the global alliances also act as a natural hedge against currency fluctuations. The rise of the euro against the dollar has the potential to hurt Airbus because airplanes are normally sold in dollars.

In response to the European political outcry against Power 8, EADS has frequently said a change of 10 cents in the euro's value against the dollar makes a difference of €1 billion in EADS' operating profit.

To minimize the vagaries of euro/dollar exchange rates, Airbus has expanded manufacturing in the dollar zone. Besides assembling A320s in China, it is setting up a parts factory in Tunisia. It plans to expand in India to tap the engineering talents.

In the fierce cutthroat business, Boeing and Airbus have no option but to realize efficiencies in any way they can. According to the president and chief executive of Airbus Tom Enders, "… we … need the courage to press ahead with the expansion of Airbus beyond the borders of Europe. We have to leave national sentiment behind us. Airbus will only remain competitive in the long term if it develops resources and markets globally and becomes a genuinely international company, with development and production also in the US, China, India and elsewhere."[18]

However, the plan by Airbus to seek global alliances may disappoint the European leaders, who would like to use Airbus as the "jobs program." The interference by the French and the German governments is prompting Daimler and Lagardère, the two prominent private shareholders of EADS, to start divesting. Some analysts believe that unless the governments stop meddling in EADS and let it run as a global business enterprise, Daimler and Lagardère may completely divest from EADS and focus on their core automotive sector or publishing industries, respectively.

To prevent Daimler and Lagardère shares from falling into foreign hands that could take over EADS, the Europeans are considering protection mechanisms such as the "golden share," which would give the French and the German governments the power to veto any foreign takeover attempts. Alternatively, the French and the German governments may create "sovereign wealth funds," similar to the ones created by the oil-rich countries in the Middle East and buy all the Daimler and Lagardère shares.

* * *

Boeing and Airbus are two formidable aerospace giants with some of the world's sharpest minds working on leading edge technologies. The fierce competition to leapfrog each other is creating airplanes that are more efficient and user friendly. They dominate the global market for the 100-plus-seater airplanes. But this does not mean that Boeing and Airbus will always be the global leaders.

Countries often attach prestige and national pride to the airplane industry. It is synonymous with the intellectual prowess of a nation. New entrants have already started to challenge the Boeing and Airbus duopoly. The Russians, the Chinese, and the Canadians have launched twins to encroach into the 737 and A320 market. Brazil's Embraer may not be far behind.

The highly popular 737s and A320s dominate the short-range 100 to 200-seater market. Boeing and Airbus, each, enjoy an order backlog of over 2000 for these airplanes.

Russia, an airplane manufacturing powerhouse in the Soviet days, has created Unified Aircraft Corporation, combining its main aircraft designers and manufacturers. It hopes to have the 150-212 seaters MS21 by 2016. The twin is expected to be 15% more fuel efficient than B737 and A320.

China has set up its own Commercial Aircraft Corporation of China, which expects to bring out its first large passenger jet C919 with a seating capacity of 190 in 2016. It will have CFMI's "Leap-X" engines, which are expected to have 16% lower fuel consumption compared to the engines on the 737s and the A320s.[19]

Canada's Bombardier claims that its new 100- to 149-seat narrow-body C-Series aircraft with a Pratt & Whitney "PurePower" geared-fan engine, slated to enter service by 2013, will have at least 15% lower fuel burn than the competing Boeing and Airbus models.

Boeing and Airbus may decide to respond to the competition with more fuel-efficient engines on the 737s and the A320s, and wait to launch completely new airplanes in the early 2020.

Alternatively, with the freeing of resources from the 787 and the 747-8 programs, Boeing may decide to up the ante by launching a successor to the 737 family sooner using the latest technologies from the 787. It could be an efficient airplane that would be a generation ahead of the competition, which would put additional pressure on Airbus.

Because of the lingering challenges with the A380, A350XWB program commitments and the resources devoted to the A400M, Airbus may find it hard pressed to immediately respond to the Boeing's challenge. Boeing could have the market to itself for a few years.

But on the other hand, Boeing may find that its engineering resources will be fully committed in developing a challenger to the A350-1000, and upgrading the 767 tanker with the 787's new digital flight deck.

Although, it is unlikely that Boeing and Airbus will lose their domination in the commercial airplane market anytime soon but the duopoly will continue to be under great threat from the emerging challenges looming across the horizon. The decisions Boeing and Airbus make in the next few years will shape their coming decade.

* * *

Advances in materials technology, new scientific breakthroughs, development of alternative fuels, radically different methods of propulsion, enhanced air traffic systems, security challenges, environmental issues, and noise and emission concerns will play a role in shaping aviation in the next 20 years. But there is no longer any doubt that ETOPS became one of the great successes in aviation and ETOPS-ready twins will dominate commercial aviation.

The A380 and the 747-8 are niche players; Airbus and Boeing may succeed in selling a few hundred of these airplanes. It is highly unlikely that either Airbus or Boeing will ever launch a totally new three- or four-turbofan-engine airplane in the future.

The future of Boeing and Airbus will depend on their ability to produce incredibly reliable and fuel-efficient twins that are environmentally friendly.

We create our own future with the decisions we make every day. The pincer strategy and the subsequent launch of the 777 set in motion a chain of events that changed the direction of aviation forever and made history. As did all-metal airframes in the 1920s and jet engines in the 1950s, ETOPS has changed the future direction of aviation.

Acknowledgement

I am grateful to a great friend and Boeing colleague, Jay Spenser, for encouraging me to write this book. As an aviation historian and author of many books, including *The Airplane: How Ideas Gave Us Wings* (New York: HarperCollins, 2008) and co-author (with Joe Sutter) of *747: Creating the World's first Jumbo Jet and Other Adventures from a Life in Aviation* (New York: HarperCollins, 2006), Jay felt that this story should be told.

However, writing a book when I was once deeply involved in many campaigns to confront Airbus directly created its own challenges. On one hand, I had to ensure I did not accidently release any information proprietary to Boeing and, on the other hand, I had to make sure I presented the Airbus perspective fairly and accurately. By making maximum use of supporting material that is publicly available, I hope I have addressed these challenges.

My heartfelt thanks to Clive Irving, author of *Wide-Body: The Triumph of the 747* (New York: William Morrow and Company, 1993), and currently managing editor of *Conde-Nast*, for his advice and guidance.

I had the great honor and privilege to work with many men and women in the aviation industry, who helped change ETOPS and the direction of aviation forever. I am grateful to Boeing for giving me the opportunity to be in the forefront of ETOPS evolution for more than two decades. I am indebted to many of my Boeing and industry colleagues for their guidance, advice, and support. Having recently retired after 37 years in aviation, I will greatly miss their camaraderie.

Even though this book is an insider's account, it in no way reflects Boeing's position; it is only my personal perspective. I hope I have represented all sides—Boeing, Airbus, and various industry positions—fairly and accurately. I would like to hear if I have not fully succeeded in this endeavor so that I can correct that in future editions. Jude Baughn did excellent work correcting my grammar, and offered many invaluable suggestions; my sincere thanks to her.

This book is my humble attempt to capture the events as I perceived them. I had great fun writing it; hope you enjoy reading it.

Mohan
etopsB777@yahoo.com

Notes

Chapter 1: The History

[1] Norris McWhirter, ed, *Guinness Book of World Records* (New York: Bantam Books, 1980) p. 315

[2] Dominic O'Connell, "Airbus A380 gets to work: The Airbus A380 is two years late and way over budget, but it's still a cause for concern for Boeing," *Sunday Times (London)*, March 23, 2008

[3] Opinion: "A hot-air plane," Times of India, May 13, 2007

[4] Robert J. Sterling, *Legend and Legacy: The Story of Boeing and Its People* (New York: St. Martin's Press, 1992) p. 469

[5] O. Casey Corr, "European Consortiums not taken seriously as a Potential Threat to Boeing's Dominance – Airbus Arrives," *The Seattle Times*, June 21, 1992

[6] Clive Irving, *Wide-Body: The Triumph of the 747* (New York: William Morrow and Company, 1993) p. 344

[7] Aubrey Cohen, "More debate on whether Air Force should consider WTO ruling," *Blog: Seattle Post-Intelligencer*, November 12, 2009

[8] Barry James, "Airbus Superjumbo Faces Trade Storm," *International Herald Tribune*, December 20, 2000

[9] Bradley S. Klapper, "WTO to Offer Glimpse of U.S.-EU Dispute," *Associated Press Newswires*, March 19, 2007

[10] Jean Pierson's speech to the The Wings Club, New York City on June 17, 1992, p.3-4

[11] www.airbus.com , total orders, March 6, 2010

[12] "U.S. Says Airbus Aircraft Are Not Commercially Viable," *Aviation Daily*, September 10, 1990

[13] Stephen Womack, "Deal with EC over Civil Airliner Industry Subsidies Remains Elusive," *The Engineer*, March 19, 1992

[14] Bradley S. Klapper, "WTO to Offer Glimpse of U.S.-EU Dispute," *Associated Press Newswires*, March 19, 2007

[15] Mark Landler, "At Air Show, Echoes of Boeing's New Assertiveness in Duel With Airbus," *New York Times*, July 23, 2004

[16] John Newhouse, *Boeing versus Airbus* (New York: Alfred A. Knopf, 2007) p. 222

[17] Dominic Gates, "Boeing, Airbus disagree on impact of WTO subsidy ruling," *Seattle Times*, March 24, 2010

[18] Jeremy Lemer, "Mandelson fuels clash with US over Airbus aid," *Financial Times*, August 15, 2009

[19] Andrea Rothman and Brian Parkin, "Airbus A350 Loan in Germany Projects at Least 1,500 Deliveries," *Bloomberg*, September17, 2009

[20] Donna Borak, "Air Force issues first phase of refueling tanker contract," *The Associated Press*, January 30, 2007

[21] Amy Butler and David Fulghum, "USAF Says Tanker RFP 'Levels the Playing Field," *Aviation Week & Space Technology*, February 05, 2007

[22] Donna Borak , "Air Force Issues First Phase of Refueling Tanker Contract," *The Associated Press*, January 30, 2007

[23] Sara A. Carter and Sean Lengell, "Air Force contract under fire," *Washington Times*, March 6, 2008

[24] Dana Hedgpeth, "Pentagon: Tanker Bids Differed by $3 Billion," *Washington Post*, September 18, 2008,

[25] Eric Rosenberg, "Boeing backers blame McCain for losing deal," *Seattle Post-Intelligencer*, March 7, 2008

[26] Emelie Rutherford, "Boeing Backers Assess McCain Role In Latest Tanker Row,' *Defense Daily*, November 19, 2009

[27] Ibid

[28] Statements printed in *Seattle Post-Intelligencer*; Eric Rosenberg , "Air Force tanker deal splits Congress: Support based on value of deal to states," *Seattle Post-Intelligencer*, March 4, 2008

[29] Les Blumenthal, "Europe lobbies Bush on tankers, Contract not his decision, he tells leaders," *Tacoma News-Tribune*, July 17, 2008

[30] Ibid.

[31] Matthew Lynn, *Birds of Prey, Boeing vs. Airbus: A Battle for the Skies* (New York: Four Walls Eight Windows, 1997) pp. 158, 171

[32] Jean Pierson's speech to The Wings Club, New York City on June 17, 1992, p.2

[33] Barry James, "Airbus Superjumbo Faces Trade Storm," *International Herald Tribune*, December 20, 2000

[34] "Bureaucrat Who Wants to Make Four Go into One," *Financial times*, August 10, 1998

[35] John Tagliabue, "Airbus to Be An Independent Corporation," *The New York Times*, January 14, 1997

[36] Matthew Lynn, *Birds of Prey, Boeing vs. Airbus: A Battle for the Skies* (New York: Four Walls Eight Windows, 1997) pp. 121-123

[37] Ibid., pp. 167-168

[38] John Newhouse, *Boeing versus Airbus* (New York: Alfred A. Knopf, 2007) p. 4

[39] Matthew Lynn, *Birds of Prey, Boeing vs. Airbus: A Battle for the Skies* (New York: Four Walls Eight Windows, 1997) p.123

[40] Guy Norris & Mark Wagner, Airbus: A340 and A330 (St. Paul, MN: MBI Publishing, 2001) pp. 32-33

[41] John Newhouse, *Boeing versus Airbus* (New York: Alfred A. Knopf, 2007) p. 4

[42] Charles Goldsmith and Frederic M. Biddle, "Airbus Chief Shifts Focus to Profitability — Price War With Boeing Hits a Turning Point," *The Wall Street Journal Europe*, September 8,1998

[43] Ibid

[44] Stephen Aris, *Close to the Sun: How Airbus Challenged America's Domination of the Skies* (London: Aurum Press, 2002) p. 197-198

[45] Ibid

[46] John Newhouse, Boeing versus Airbus (New York: Alfred A. Knopf, 2007) p. 37

[47] "Aer Lingus Chooses Airbus over Boeing," Associated Press, June 7, 2007

[48] John Newhouse, *Boeing versus Airbus* (New York: Alfred A. Knopf, 2007) pp.188-189

[49] "India industry: Airbus demands re-bid on Air-India Deal," *Economist Intelligence Unit – Views Wire*, May 11, 2005

[50] "How Airbus Soared Past Its American Rival," *The Sunday Times (London)*, April 16, 1995

[51] U.S. Airways A320- sales negotiation, October 1997

[52] "How Airbus Soared Past Its American Rival," *The Sunday Times (London)*, April 16, 1995

[53] Matthew Lynn, *Birds of Prey, Boeing vs. Airbus: A Battle for the Skies* (New York: Four Walls Eight Windows, 1997) p. 5-6

[54] "Airbus's Secret Past - Aircraft and Bribery," *The Economist*, June 14, 2003

[55] "Action against bribery requires political will," *Financial Times*, April 10, 2007

[56] John Ward Anderson, "In Tangles of Airbus Project, a Reflection of Europe's Struggles," *Washington Post*, April 27, 2007

[57] "Airbus CEO accuses European Governments of Interfering," *AFX International Focus*, March 2, 2007

[58] "Airbus tries to spread its wings," *The Guardian (UK)*, January15, 2009

[59] Kevin Done and Gerrit Wiesmann, "EADS ends its rivalries to become 'normal' company," *Financial Times*, March 24, 2008

Chapter 2: Airbus Strategy

[1] Robert J. Sterling, *Legend And Legacy: The Story of Boeing and Its People* (New York: St. Martin's Press, 1992) p.403

[2] Airbus Industrie, "ETOPS: Twins through time" published in 1992

[3] Julian Moxon, "Family matters. (Airbus Industrie)," *Flight International*, May 15, 1991

[4] Ibid

[5] Matthew Lynn, *Birds of Prey, Boeing vs. Airbus: A Battle for the Skies* (New York: Four Walls Eight Windows, 1997) pp. 207-208

[6] Stephen Aris, Close to the Sun: How Airbus Challenged America's Domination of the Skies (London: Aurum Press, 2002) p. 142

[7] Arthur Reed and Douglas W. Nelms, "Covering the Market Place (Airbus A330 and A340 Aircraft): Interview with Airbus VP-Marketing David Jennings," *Air Transport World*, July 1, 1992

Chapter 3: Boeing Response

[1] Robert J. Sterling, *Legend and Legacy: The Story of Boeing and Its People* (New York: St. Martin's Press, 1992) p. 455

[2] Jeremy Main, "Betting On the 21st Century Jet (The Boeing 777 Aircraft)," *Fortune*, April 20, 1992

[3] "FAA's Broderick Expresses Doubt About 'Out Of The Box' ETOPS," *Air Safety Week*, July 9, 1993

[4] Jeremy Main, "Betting On the 21st Century Jet (The Boeing 777 Aircraft)," *Fortune*, April 20, 1992

[5] Caroline Daniel, "The Death of a Golden Goose: U.S. airlines and Unions Clash over Pay and Benefits," *Financial Times*, December 28, 2004

[6] Byron Acohido, "Boeing's Lobbying over 777 Blasted," *The Seattle Times,* April 21, 1991

[7] Byron Acohido, "Boeing Co. Pushing the 'Envelope'- Could Early ETOPS Erode 777's Margin of Safety?" *The Seattle Times,* April 21, 1991

[8] Bob Reich, Letter to the Editor: "Negative Slant- Setting the Record Straight on Boeing's New 777 Airliner," *The Seattle Times,* May 7, 1991

[9] "FAA's Broderick Expresses Doubt about 'Out of the Box' ETOPS," *Air Safety Week,* July 19, 1993

[10] Byron Acohido, "European Ruling a Blow for Boeing 777 – Fate of Orders left Hanging; Airbus Could Gain an Edge," *The Seattle Times,* August 4, 1993

[11] "The 777's good Notices," *Seattle Post-Intelligencer,* June 1, 1995

Chapter 4: The Collaboration

[1] Malcolm Gladwell, *Outliers: the story of success* (New York: Little, Brown, 2008)

Chapter 5: Battle of the Pacific

[1] Daniel Michaels, "Dogfight: In the Secret World Of Airplane Deals, One Battle Up Close — Boeing, Airbus Vied to Meet Cutthroat Terms of Iberia; Strong Carriers Call Shots — Dangling the `Used Car' Option," *The Wall Street Journal*, March 10, 2003

[2] Russell Hotten, "Boeing Beats Airbus to $4bn Malaysian Deal," The Independent (London), January 10, 1996

[3] Airbus publication: FAST/Number 17, June1995, p. 36

[4] "Airbus Industrie: Iberia increases A340 fleet by up to 11 aircraft," *M2 Presswire*, September 23, 1998

[5] "Airbus Industrie: Olympic Airways receives first A340s," *M2 Presswire*, February 2, 1999

[6] "Argentine Flag Carrier, Citing ETOPS, Orders Four-Engine Airbus Aircraft," *M2 Presswire*, April 20, 1999

[7] Airbus Press Release: "Air Tahiti Nui takes delivery of fifth Airbus A340-300," June 16, 2005

[8] Airbus Press Release: "South African Airways celebrates first A340-600," January 24, 2003

[9] Airbus Press Release: "Air Mauritius expands its fleet with new Airbus A340-300E aircraft," June 27, 2005

[10] Airbus Press Release: "Airbus wins first Asian customer for VIP A340-500," February 7, 2007

[11] Airbus, FAST Issue 28, a bi-annual publication (August, 2001), pp. 2-7

[12] James T. Mckenna, "Pilots Coalition Argues Against Easing ETOPS Rules" *Aviation Week & Space Technology*, November 30, 1998, p.50

[13] Paul Proctor, "Twins Edging Into Transpacific Routes," *Aviation Week & Space Technology*, February 22, 1999

[14] Article 126333, "Some Pilot Groups Aren't Ready to Endorse Longer ETOPS," *Aviation Daily*, March 3, 1999

[15] ALPA News Release (#99.17), March 4, 1999

[16] ATA Press release (#13 03-05-99), March 5, 1999

[17] U.S. Federal Register /vol. 64, no. 80/ Tuesday, April 27, 1999/ pp. 22667-22669

[18] Editorial - Can or should? – ETOPS, *Flight International*, March 10, 1999

[19] Docket: FAA-99-6717-12, dated June 1, 1999

[20] Docket; FAA-99-6717-21, dated June 7, 1999

[21] Docket: FAA-99-6717-32, dated July 8, 1999

[22] "A340 Residuals Obscured by Smoke Generated By Trade-In Deal," *Aircraft Value News*, July 19, 1999

[23] Remark made by Noel Forgeard, Chief Administrator of Airbus on Tuesday, Nov 10, 1998 to the French media.

[24] Stephen Aris, *Close to the Sun: How Airbus Challenged America's Domination of the Skies* (London: Aurum Press, 2002) pp. 54-55

[25] Daniel Michaels, "Did Airbus's Debated Ads Use Safety First?," *The Wall Street Journal*, November 22, 1999

[26] Docket No. FAA-99-6717: Federal Register/Vol. 65, No. 14/Friday, January 21, 2000, pp. 3520-3527

[27] "Europe Objects to FAA Grant Of 207-Minute ETOPS For 777," *Aviation Daily*, March 13, 2000

[28] Docket: FAA-99-6717-59, dated March 6, 2000

[29] Federal Register/Vol. 65, No. 115/Wednesday, June 14, 2000, pp. 37447-8

Chapter 6: The Final Verdict

[1] "Airbus Explore LROPS Alternatives to 207 ETOPS," *Flight Newsletter*, July 2, 2001

[2] Geoffrey Thomas, "Goodbye ETOPS, hello ETOPS: under FAA's proposed rule, extended twin operations are simplified to extended operations, but changes are more than skin deep." *Air Transport World*, January 2004, pp. 48-51

[3] http://WWW.AIRBUS.COM/, August 1998

[4] David Bowermaster, "FAA Proposes Policy Shift on Boeing, Airbus Passenger Jets," *The Seattle Times*, December 17, 2002

[5] Max KJ, "Airbus calls for LROPS unity," *Flight International*, January 21, 2003, p6

[6] FedEx submittal to Docket No. FAA-2002-6717, Notice 03-11, Extended Operations (ETOPS) of Multi-Engined Airplanes, March 12, 2004, p. 9

[7] Tony Broderick, "Departures Column: FAA ETOPS Proposal Needs More Work," *Aviation Daily*, March 29, 2004.

[8] Duane E. Woerth, President, ALPA, "Departures Column: ETOPS NPRM is Not Over the Top," *Aviation Daily*, April 22, 2004.

[9] Daniel Michaels, "Airbus Considering Cutting A340 Prices-Officials," *The Wall Street Journal*, January 16, 2006

[10] Ibid

[11] Kingsley-Jones, "Airbus to offer cash back on A340 as 777 stretches lead," *Flight International*, January 24, 2006

[12] Jason Nisse and Heather Tomlinson, "The Lowdown - It's beaten Boeing but Airbus can't take off," *Independent (London)*, June 17, 2001

[13] Tim Hepher, "Update 1-Interview-Airbus sales chief defiant over orders," *Reuters News*, July 19, 2006

[14] Federal Register/Vol. 72, No. 9/Tuesday, January 16,2007, p. 1809

[15] Max KJ, "Airbus calls for LROPS unity," *Flight International*, January 21, 2003, p6

[16] Airbus press release, "A330 is first airliner to be certified for ETOPS 'beyond 180 minutes,'" November 12, 2009

Chapter 7: A New Dawn

[1] J. Lynn Lunsford and Kerry E. Grace, "Boeing Shakes Up Management as Delays Plague Dreamliner," *The Wall Street Journal*, December 12, 2008

[2] Michael Mecham, Joseph Anselmo and Guy Norris, "A Wing and a Prayer: Boeing stares at major costs as 787 program remains in limbo," *Aviation Week & Space Technology*, July 27, 2009

[3] Jeffrey Rothfeder, "Bumpy Ride," *Conde Nast Portfolio*, May 1, 2009

[4] Ann Keeton and Peter Sanders, "Boeing Posts $1.56 Billion Loss," *The Wall Street Journal*, October 22, 2009

[5] John Gillie, "Blog: Boeing CEO admits outsourcing went too far," *Tacoma News-Tribune*, October 21, 2009

[6] Dean Foust and Justin Bachman, "Boeing's Flight from Union Labor: Wages will be lower at its plant in South Carolina. But the company may risk further delays of the Dreamliner," *BusinessWeek*, November 6, 2009

[7] Boeing News Release, "Boeing Acquires Alenia North America's Interest in Global Aeronautica," December 22, 2009

[8] Stefania Bianchi , "UPDATE: Qatar Air May Become Exclusive Airbus Customer –CEO," *Dow Jones*, June 17, 2009

[9] Michelle Dunlop, "What Boeing did right – and wrong on the 787," *Everett Herald*, June 21, 2009

[10] Dan Reed, "From Dreamliner to lost military deals, problems nag Boeing," *USA Today*, August 6, 2009

[11] Robert Wall, "No Carbon Copy," *Aviation Week & Space Technology*, January 14, 2008

[12] Robert Wall and Jens Flottau, "Cut to Fit: This time it's demand that is depressing A380 output," *Aviation Week & Space Technology*, May 11, 2009

[13] Jeffrey Rothfeder, "Bumpy Ride," *Conde Nast Portfolio*, May 1, 2009

[14] James Wallace, "Blog: Steve Udvar-Hazy on A350, 787 and more," *Seattle Post-Intelligencer*, August 10, 2007

Chapter 8: Reversal of Fortunes

[1] CNN's Becky Anderson interview with Airbus CEO Noel Forgeard; July 19, 2004

[2] 2005 edition of *The Time 100*

[3] "The making of a Jumbo Problem- Airbus," *The Economist*, November 11, 2006

[4] David Jolly, "EADS, Parent of Airbus, Reports Third-Quarter Loss," *New York Times*, November 16, 2009

[5] "Heavy going," *The Economist (UK)*, April 11, 2009

[6] Jens Flottau, "EADS' Investors Demand Resignation of Director," *Aviation Week & Space Technology*, October 29, 2007

[7] David Gauthier-Villars, "French Regulator Files Charges In Airbus Insider-Trading Case," *The Wall Street Journal Online*, April 01, 2008

[8] Scheherazade Daneshkhu and Kevin Done , "Fines call over EADS deals," *Financial Times*, July 29,2009

[9] David Gauthiers-Villars, "EADS, Others Cleared in Insider-Trading Case," *The Wall Street Journal*, December 18, 2009

[10] David Robertson, **"Carriers ponder compensation claims against Airbus for over-weight aircraft," *The Times (London)*, July 4, 2007

[11] "The real owner of all those planes," New Strait Times (Singapore), May 11, 2007, p.48-49; originally published in New York Times

[12] "Airbus may risk profit as it chases rival's lead," *The Wall Street Journal Asia*, June 20, 2007

[13] Pete Harrison, "Virgin's Branson to shun thirsty 4-engined planes," *Reuters News*, August 31, 2007

[14] DAB, "High oil prices hit four-engined Airbus," *Agence France Presse*, April 3, 2006

[15] Reuters, "France Upgrades Presidential Aircraft," New York Times, June 12, 2008

[16] Rod Stone, "Update: Discounting Seen Hitting Airbus Earns Going Forward," *Dow Jones International News*, June 19, 2007

[17] Max Kingsley-Jones, "Heavy weight bout for BA: As BA ponders whether to buy the Airbus A380 or Boeing 747-8 Intercontinental, its decision could have far-reaching consequences for other airlines," *Flight International*, June 12, 2007

[18] Andrea Rothman, "Airbus Keeps 2013 Goal for A350 to Enter Service, Gallois Says," *Bloomberg*, July 28, 2009

[19] Elizabeth M. Gillespie, "Airbus A380 Delay Could Aid Boeing Sells," *Associated Press Newswires*, October 3, 2006

[20] James Wallace, "Airbus all in on need for jumbo – but Boeing still doubtful," *Seattle Post-Intelligencer*, October 24, 2007

[21] Richard Aboulafia, "Airbus and Boeing: Beyond head-to-head," Aerospace America, May 2009

[22] Hal Weitzman, "Boeing admits Dreamliner rethink," *Financial Times,* March 20, 2008

[23] Richard Aboulafia, "Airbus and Boeing: Beyond head-to-head," Aerospace America, May 2009

Chapter 9: The Future

[1] Philip K. Lawrence and David W. Thornton, *Deep Stall: The Turbulent Story of Boeing Commercial Airplanes* (Hampshire, England: Ashgate, 2005)

[2] John Newhouse interview on CSPAN 2- Book TV, March 18, 2007

[3] John Newhouse, *Boeing versus Airbus* (New York: Alfred A. Knopf, 2007) pp. 199, 5

[4] Scott Rochfort, "Airline to turn A380 superjumbo into sardine can," *Sydney Morning Herald,* January 16, 2009

[5] Bill Rigby, "Interview: Cathay Pacific to wait on next-generation planes," *Reuters News,* October 30, 2007

[6] Brendan Sobie, "ANA to phase out 747-400s from long-haul fleet within three years," *Flight International,* April 10, 2007

[7] Dan Weikel, "Airbus A380 requires special handling at LAX: Operations have gone fairly well so far, but some fear that delays will mount as more of the aircraft arrive," *Los Angeles Times,* January 25, 2009

[8] Boonsong Kositchotethana, "THAI stuck with A380s:Cancellation penalties could reach $700m," Bangkok Post, July 11, 2009

[9] Cornelius Rahn and Steve Rothwell, "Update 2: Lufthansa Deals Blow to Airbus A380 With Order Delay,"*Bloomberg,* October 29, 2009

[10] James Wallace, "Blog: An A380 configured to carry 840 passengers: Want to be on a plane with more than 800 other passengers?" *Seattle Post-Intelligencer,* January 15, 2009

[11] Andrea Rothman, "Airbus Delivered 10 A380s in 2009, Trailing Forecast (Update1)," *Bloomberg,* December 30, 2009

[12] Robert Wall and Jens Flottau, "Cut to Fit: This time it's demand that is depressing A380 output," *Aviation Week & Space Technology,* May 11, 2009

[13] Daniel Michaels and Stefania Bianchi, "Emirates Pulls Airbus A380 From New York route: Redeployment to Toronto, Bangkok Is Blamed on Lack of Demand, but Change Marks Blow for Problem-Plagued Jet," *The Wall Street Journal,* March 19, 2009

[14] Andrea Rothman, "Airbus Keeps 2013 Goal for A350 to Enter Service, Gallois Says," *Bloomberg,* July 28, 2009

[15] Bill Saporito, "Postcard: Paris - Bringing the party back to the skies; Air France's transatlantic A380 service features comfy seats, six bars and an art gallery. But is the Airbus jumbo now a white elephant?" *Time,* December 7, 2009 ; quoting Aircraft Analyst Richard L. Aboulafia of Teal Group

[16] Laura Mueller, "A350 GE engine could power future A380 variants: Hazy," *Flightglobal.com*, February 25, 2008

[17] Geoffrey Thomas, "Qantas moves towards Boeing 777-300ER order," *The Australian*, August 29, 2008

[18] Tom Enders, "Airbus is once again in need of political courage," *Financial Times*, May 29, 2009

[19] Francois De Beaupuy and Rachel Layne, "Safran Wins $5 Billion China Aircraft Engine Order (Update2)," *Bloomberg*, December 21, 2009

Index

Made in the USA
Charleston, SC
01 June 2010